What is Black Art?

Dr Alice Correia is an art historian. Her research examines late twentieth-century British art, with a specific focus on artists of African, Caribbean, and South Asian heritage. She has worked at Tate Britain, Government Art Collection, and Touchstones Rochdale. She has held Fellowships at the Paul Mellon Centre for the Study of British Art and the UAL Decolonising Arts Institute. She is a Trustee of *Third Text* and co-Chair of the British Art Network's Black British Art Research Group. Her articles have appeared in *Art History*; *British Art Studies*; and *Nka: Journal of Contemporary African Art*.

What is Black Art?

Writings on African, Asian and Caribbean
Art in Britain, 1981–1989

Edited by Alice Correia

PENGUIN BOOKS

PENGUIN BOOKS

UK | USA | Canada | Ireland | Australia
India | New Zealand | South Africa

Penguin Books is part of the Penguin Random House group of companies
whose addresses can be found at global.penguinrandomhouse.com

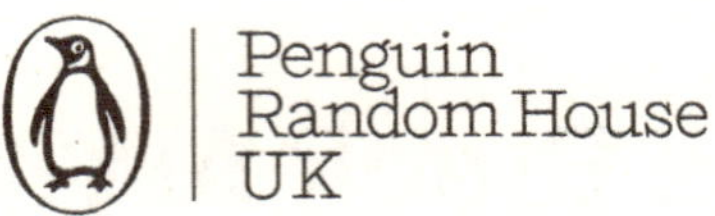

Penguin
Random House
UK

First published in Penguin Books 2022
004

Set in 9.68/12.1pt Dante MT Std
Typeset by Jouve (UK), Milton Keynes
Printed and bound in Great Britain by Clays Ltd, Elcograf S.p.A.

The authorized representative in the EEA is Penguin Random House Ireland,
Morrison Chambers, 32 Nassau Street, Dublin D02 YH68

A CIP catalogue record for this book is available from the British Library

ISBN: 978–0–141–99821–3

www.greenpenguin.co.uk

Penguin Random House is committed to a
sustainable future for our business, our readers
and our planet. This book is made from Forest
Stewardship Council® certified paper.

Contents

Contents

Contents

Introduction

As an Art History student in the late 1990s I learnt about the history of twentieth-century modernism and the way that white European artists including Paul Gauguin, Pablo Picasso and Henry Moore had appropriated Oceanic, African and South American art and visual culture in their work. But while it was clear that 'global cultures' were central to the development of modernist art in Europe, I also realized that I could name very few artists of colour. I had had a lecture on Cuban surrealist Wifredo Lam, and my father had told me about the Goan painter F. N. Souza, but what about the other African, Asian and Caribbean artists working in Britain? When Chris Ofili won the Turner Prize in 1998, much of the media coverage noted that he was the first person of African descent to win the prestigious award and there were suggestions that this was a momentous moment for multicultural Britain. However, amidst the celebrations it was apparent to me that the praise heaped on Ofili was unusual. Up to that point, I had never seen an art exhibition that reflected the diverse communities in which I had grown up, or my own mixed-race heritage. The realization that there were significant gaps in my knowledge of British art stimulated my subsequent research into what has become known as the British Black Art Movement of the 1980s.

The question posed by this book's title, *What is Black Art?* is deceptively simple, and yet what the texts assembled in this anthology reveal is that there is no single, universally agreed answer. The artists' statements, conversations and interviews, the conference papers, exhibition catalogue essays and reviews, all written between 1981 and 1989, address the definition of the term 'Black' and the form and function of 'Black Art' in Britain during the 1980s. What is critical to this anthology is an acknowledgement and understanding that during the 1980s 'Black' meant different things to different people, and that the debates and disagreements over the constitution of 'Black Art' simmered throughout the decade.

In Europe, the term 'Black' as a racial signifier has a long history dating back to fifteenth-century encounters between Portuguese and Spanish traders and Bantu peoples in sub-Saharan Africa.[1] Over time, it became a pejorative and discriminatory word to distinguish African and African diaspora peoples as 'other' from white people.[2] During the twentieth century the term was variously replaced with 'Negro' and 'Coloured', but by the 1960s it had been reclaimed, particularly by the Black Power and Civil Rights movements in the United States.[3] In Britain during the late 1960s and 1970s 'Black' was commonly – although not always – understood to include people of African, Asian and Caribbean heritage. Cross-cultural allegiances were fostered by organizations such as the Universal Coloured Peoples' Association, founded in 1967,[4] and during the 1970s, by the British Black Panthers whose members included Darcus Howe, Farrukh Dhondy, Linton Kwesi Johnson and Mala Sen.[5] Artist, and former Black Panther member, Rasheed Araeen argued in 1982 that 'we cannot understand the full significance of the word "black" outside the historical context of our struggle against racism, against cultural imperialism'.[6] By the end of the decade, cultural theorist Stuart Hall observed that the term 'came to provide the organizing category of a new politics of resistance, amongst groups and communities with, in fact, very different histories, traditions and ethnic identities'.[7] This collective definition of 'Black' encapsulated the strategic alliances and coalitions undertaken by a broad spectrum of people working in opposition to the marginalization, discrimination and racism they faced in white-majority Britain. In this book I use 'Black' as a historically situated political term, to denote people and communities of African, Asian and Caribbean backgrounds with common, albeit different, experiences of racism, rather than as a racial descriptor referring only to people of African ancestry; not all the texts I have included concur with this definition.[8] While the terms 'Black' and 'Black Art' were, and remain, highly contentious, what is certain is that the texts assembled here reveal the urgency, determination and resolve with which a generation of artists in the 1980s worked, even as their art was derided, marginalized or ignored.

*　　*　　*

. . . the Arts Council of Great Britain should now look into the possibility of organising a survey exhibition of the works of <u>black artists in Britain.</u> Although I'm aware of the pitfalls in approaching art from a point of view that may lead to separate groups based on sex, race, etc., the separateness already exists and it is not of our own making but a result of the attitude of the society. Moreover there doesn't seem to be any choice for us except in asserting now our historical presence here separately, till the cultural institutions of the country come to terms with the multi-racial aspect of this society by fully recognising the equal abilities of all peoples irrespective of colour and race.

Rasheed Araeen, letter to Andrew Dempsey,
Arts Council of Great Britain, 28 October 1978.[9]

At the start of the 1980s a generation of artists of African, Asian and Caribbean heritage were leaving art school: dynamic, aesthetically innovative and politically vocal, these artists are now collectively described as the British Black Arts Movement. This generation were the children of post-war migrants who had arrived in Britain during the 1950s and 60s. Born in Britain, or having migrated here as young children, this generation had grown up during the 1970s in a country beset with an education system that regarded Caribbean children as not only a 'problem', but often 'educationally subnormal'; where consecutive governments decried the 'breakdown of law and order' on British streets, but did little to prevent the 'Paki-bashing' enacted by racist thugs; and where industrial disputes, such as the 1976–8 strike at the Grunwick Film Processing Laboratory in North London, and rising unemployment laid bare the fragile alliances between Black and white working class communities.[10] In the lead-up to the 1979 general election, the leader of the Conservative Party, Margaret Thatcher, discussed the apparent fears of ordinary (white) British people that their country might be 'swamped' with foreigners should immigration remain at current levels.[11] Her comments 'were widely condemned as pandering to popular prejudices',[12] but she and her party went on to win the election, ushering in a decade of social unrest and political conflict.

As the 1980s progressed questions of race, patriotism and nationhood were braided into the political discourse. The introduction of more stringent immigration laws in the 1981 Nationality Act may be understood as part of a governmental response to the perceived threat of 'others' which also included the increased surveillance and policing of Black people.[13] The government's apparent disregard for Black life in the wake of the tragic New Cross arson attack in which thirteen children and young people died in January 1981 prompted the Black People's Day of Action.[14] On 2 March 1981 around 20,000 people, mainly from Caribbean and African communities, marched through the streets of London, protesting against the conduct of the police investigation and the 'media indifference to mass murder'.[15] The march did not effect changes to police procedure, or improve so-called race-relations, but rather resulted in 'Swamp 81', a massive stop-and-search operation organized by the Metropolitan Police in Brixton. During this initiative teenagers and young men of African and Caribbean heritage were particularly targeted under suspicion of loitering with intent. In protest, on 11 April 1981, rioting broke out on the streets of London and other British cities. After the riots of 1981, police powers were increased, and were put to use during the 1984 miners' strike. Riot police from across the country congregated in small Yorkshire and Nottinghamshire mining villages, leading to wider questions over whether the police were pro-active agents of the state government. Also in 1984, amidst public outcry, Margaret Thatcher became the first British prime minister to welcome the leader of apartheid South Africa in over twenty years.[16] Against this backdrop, artists including Sutapa Biswas, Sonia Boyce, Chila Kumari Burman, Eddie Chambers, Lubaina Himid, Keith Piper and Donald Rodney were making work that variously addressed the histories of British involvement in the transatlantic trade of enslaved African people; British exploitation of people and natural resources in its colonies; and the legacies of British colonialism, as manifested in everyday – often violent – racism in contemporary Britain. In their engagement with social and political issues, these artists reflected a wider cultural climate in which resistance groups from the 'margins' did much to challenge dominant modes of authority.[17] While larger organizations and events such as Rock Against Racism and the Artists Against Apartheid concert in London in 1986 would later bring the politics of race and racism to a mass audience,[18] during the 1970s and early 1980s, grassroots organizations such as the London-based socialist, pan-African Black Liberation Front, the Organization of Women of Asian and African Descent (OWAAD) and the Bradford-based youth protest group the United Black Youth League[19] worked from within communities to challenge the political discourse that cast 'blacks as an "outside" force, an alien *malaise* afflicting British society'.[20]

The 1980s was a socially turbulent and politically polarized decade, and as Lubaina Himid later recalled, she and her contemporaries faced 'diffidence, prejudice, hostility and hatred'.[21] But the story of this 1980s generation is one chapter in the longer history of the production, display and reception of art created by people of African, Asian and Caribbean ancestry in Britain during the twentieth century. It is a history of neglect underpinned by both subtle and overt institutional racism. Ronald Moody arrived in London from Jamaica in the 1920s, and his figurative wooden sculptures were in tune with contemporaneous ideas about 'direct carving' and 'truth to materials', as seen in the work of Henry Moore and Barbara Hepworth. Yet until recently he was entirely omitted from narratives of British sculpture in the 1930s and 40s. Similarly, F. N. Souza and Aubrey Williams, from Goa, Portuguese India, and British Guiana respectively, were celebrated by the London art world in the late 1950s and early 60s, but subsequent histories of post-war British painting minimized or excluded their contributions to that milieu. A comprehensive history of the Indian Painters Collective, formed in London in 1963, whose members included Balraj Khanna and Lancelot Ribeiro, and its subsequent incarnation as Indian Artists UK, established in 1976, has yet to be written.[22] The work of the visionary novelists, poets, artists and film-makers who became members of the Caribbean Artists Movement (CAM) in London, founded in the autumn of 1966 by Edward Kamau Brathwaite, John La Rose and Andrew Salkey, would, arguably, be largely forgotten were it not for the essential work of author Anne Walmsley.[23] David Medalla, originally from the Philippines, was a founding member of two radical exhibition spaces in London: Signals Gallery which opened in the mid-1960s, and Artists for Democracy, founded in 1974, but his work has largely been omitted from narratives of British Conceptual art.[24] The same can be said about the Chinese conceptual artist Li Yuan-chia, who established his LYC Museum and Art Gallery in Cumbria (1971–82) and made a significant contributions to artistic communities in northern England.[25]

Importantly, in 1996 Stuart Hall reminded us that these earlier generations of artists who migrated to Britain from across the globe:

came to London in a spirit not altogether different from that in
which Picasso and others went to Paris: to fulfil their artistic ambitions and to participate in the heady atmosphere of the most
advanced centres of artistic innovation at that time . . . they came
to Britain feeling that they naturally belonged to the modern movement and, in a way, it belonged to them. The promise of decolonization fired their ambition, their sense of themselves as already
'modern persons' . . . Their aim was to engage the modern world
as equals on its own terrain.[26]

But the reality of racism and discrimination in everyday life in
Britain, and the insidious primitivizing and orientalizing of their
work by gallerists and critics undercut those hopeful ambitions.
In post-war Britain, contemporary artists of colour from the
Empire, and later, the New Commonwealth found that opportunities to exhibit were sporadic, and often limited to particular
venues. Exhibitions such as those at the Commonwealth Institute
in London during the 1960s arguably siloed migrant artists from
contemporary avant-garde artistic contexts. When he was omitted from the *New Generation* exhibition of contemporary artists at
the Whitechapel Gallery in 1964, Frank Bowling, who had graduated from the Royal College of Art in 1962, was reportedly told
that 'England is not ready for a gifted artist of colour.'[27] He left
for New York in 1966.

By the 1970s curatorial and academic interest in the generation
of post-war migrant artists from Africa, Asia and the Caribbean
was nominal; Souza had followed Bowling to New York in 1967;
others such as South African painter Albert Adams, and Anwar Jalal
Shemza from Pakistan, forged teaching careers while attempting
to sustain their artistic practices in relative obscurity. Simultaneously, a new generation emerged: originally from Jamaica, painter
Errol Lloyd had been a member of CAM from its inception and
during the 1970s established himself as an award-winning illustrator

and children's author; born in St Lucia, painter Winston Branch graduated from the Slade School of Art, London, in 1970 and was awarded a prestigious Guggenheim Fellowship in 1978; while the Jamaican-born photographer Vanley Burke created important accounts of Britain's African and Caribbean communities, capturing events such as the African Liberation Day rally in Handsworth Park, Birmingham, in 1977.

In 1975, Rasheed Araeen staged his first solo exhibition at the Artists for Democracy space. The show included *For Oluwale* (1971–3, 1975), a conceptual text and image work that addressed the death by drowning of David Oluwale, a Nigerian man who, it is believed, was last seen alive being chased by two police officers near the River Aire in Leeds.[28] Following his arrival in Britain from Pakistan in 1964, Araeen had created minimalist sculpture and undertaken conceptual performance-based work, but *For Oluwale* marked a radical, and political, shift in his work. Subsequently, he produced work explicitly addressing neo-colonialism and the exploitation of the 'Third World', and his own status as a 'Paki bastard' in Britain.[29] David Oluwale's case was the first, and remained for decades the only successful prosecution of serving police officers for their involvement in the death of a Black person, and in 2019 artist Sonia Boyce identified *For Oluwale* as the first piece of 'Black Art' made in the United Kingdom.[30]

In 1976, cultural adviser and journalist Naseem Khan published her influential report, *The Art Britain Ignores*.[31] Khan argued that Britain's ethnically diverse communities had much to offer in terms of arts and culture and argued for better funding and access to support. But what ultimately resulted was not equal access within the existing arts funding structures, but dedicated funding bodies for 'ethnic minority arts' that prioritized community (understood as amateur) groups rather than the professional 'fine arts'.[32] As white institutional systems failed to recognize the aesthetic and cultural merits of art by Black artists, in 1978 Araeen published his 'Preliminary Notes for a BLACK MANIFESTO' in the radical arts magazine, *Black Phoenix,* which he co-edited with poet Mahmood Jamal.[33] Araeen refused to be marginalized and worked tirelessly to challenge the persistent, systematic omission of African, Asian and Caribbean artists from mainstream national narratives. He first proposed a 'survey exhibition of the works of <u>black artists in Britain</u>' to the Arts Council of Great Britain in 1978, pointedly noting that such exhibitions, selected and organized according to race, were a problematic necessity in the face of the white institutional exclusion of Black artists.

In 1979 the artists Eddie Chambers and Keith Piper met whilst undertaking a Fine Art Foundation course at Lanchester Polytechnic in Coventry. Both Chambers and Piper were interested in the writings of African-American political activists who gained prominence during the late 1960s and early 1970s; Larry Neal's essay, 'Black Art and Black Liberation' (1965) and Ron Karenga's 'Black Cultural Nationalism' (1968) were particular points of reference, informing not only their knowledge of the Black Power Movement in the USA, but also their understanding of radical Black activism. During the first year of his undergraduate course at Sunderland Polytechnic in 1980–81, Chambers undertook a typography exercise, and produced a visceral poster proclaiming:

Needed

Solemn Dedicated Black people to undertake the enormous task
of reclaiming the shattered psyches and culture of the Black race.
A race scattered over the continents of the world where they exist
in the mud of the floor of the foul dungeon into which the world
has been transformed by the white power structure.

In 2021 Piper recalled: 'Eddie wanted to create a support network for Black artists and minorities, to create visibility for these artists.'[34]

Chambers, with Piper, established a network of like-minded artists located in the West Midlands, and in 1981 staged the exhibition *Black Art An' Done* at Wolverhampton Art Gallery. The show marked the beginning of a remarkable sequence of exhibitions and events which showcased the anger and frustration, but also the creative aspirations and artistic innovations of the next generation of British-Caribbean artists. Chaired by Chambers, the Wolverhampton Young Black Artists group would evolve into The Pan-Afrikan Connection, and later The Blk Art Group. Membership was fluid, and during its period of activity between 1979 and 1984, included Piper, Claudette Johnson, Marlene Smith and Donald Rodney, amongst others. It is notable that although the writings of the American Black Power Movement were important touchstones for Chambers and Piper, and Smith and later Maud Sulter noted the importance of African-American women writers including Angela Davis, bell hooks and Alice Walker, this generation of African and Caribbean disapora artists were arguably more influenced by the ideas and possibilities proposed and embodied by African-American writers and activists than by specific artists or artworks associated with the American Black Arts Movement of the 1960s and 70s. In 2021 Marlene Smith recalled that as an A-level art student, she had been able to access limited amounts of material about the American Black Arts Movement and that at the start of her career, of greater importance to her were the connections she made with her peers and with older generations of British-based artists and photographers, including Vanley Burke, Frank Bowling and Ronald Moody.[35] On 28 October 1982 the Wolverhampton Young Black Artists group organized the First National Black Art Convention, staged at Wolverhampton Art Gallery; speakers included the artists Araeen and Johnson; film-maker Imruh Bakari (listed as Imruh Caesar), and designer and curator Shakka Dedi. Sonia Boyce later recalled the 'sense of relief and exhilaration when I walked into that first conference; seeing so many black artists there!'.[36]

While the organizers of the Convention had taken an open approach to who might be defined as 'Black', and Araeen argued for solidarity amongst artists of colour in Britain, disagreements and anxiety over who the term included remained. The Organisation for Black Arts Advancement and Leisure Activities (OBAALA), which established The Black-Art Gallery in London, used the term 'Black' in relation to a Pan-African world view. The Black-Art Gallery rejected any trans-racial definition of 'Black Art', stating that 'Black-Art is born and created out of a consciousness based upon experience of what it means to be an Afrikan descendant wherever in the world we are.'[37] As Mumtaz Karimjee recounts in this volume, 'while I consider myself part of the Black community, there are clearly occasions when the word Black does not include me',[38] while in 1989 Sunil Gupta conceded that not all South Asian people were 'at ease with' with the term.[39]

Nonetheless, by the middle of the 1980s, 'Black' was used regularly in exhibition titles. Shows such as *The Thin Black Line* curated by Lubaina Himid in 1985, and *Reflections of the Black Experience* staged at Brixton Art Gallery in 1986, included the work of artists from African, Asian and Caribbean backgrounds. Chila Kumari Burman's essay, 'There have Always Been Great Black Women Artists' detailed the shared experiences of women of colour and the obstacles and challenges they faced in establishing their careers. Maud Sulter's Blackwomen's Creativity Project encompassed exhibitions and writing, working with British-based women artists including Karimjee and Ingrid Pollard, and authors Bernardine Evaristo and Meera Syal. Artistic collectives including Black Audio Film Collective; the Manchester-based Black Arts Alliance; and the London-based Autograph: Association of Black Photographers, demonstrate that there were active collaborations and productive allegiances between what Araeen regularly described as 'Afro-Asian' artistic constituencies during the 1980s.

In 1988, Rasheed Araeen and Eddie Chambers each curated exhibitions of 'Black Art': *The Essential Black Art* (Chisenhale Gallery, London, and touring), and *Black Art: Plotting the Course* (Gallery Oldham and touring), respectively. Both artists used an open and expansive definition of 'Black' in their curatorial work, but where they differed was in their definition of 'Black Art'. In his exhibition Chambers took a looser, more inclusive view, including work that addressed subjects representing everyday Black life, broadly defined as the 'Black experience'. Araeen, on the other hand, defined Black Art stylistically:

> 'Black Art', if this term must be used, is in fact a specific historical development within contemporary art practices and has emerged directly from the joint struggle of Asian, African and the Caribbean people against racism, and the art work itself explicitly refers to that struggle. It specifically deals with and expresses a human condition, the condition of Afro-Asian people resulting from their existence or predicament in a racist society or/and, in global terms, from Western cultural imperialism.[40]

For Araeen, Black Art should actively engage with the contemporary politics of race – with early works by Chambers, Rodney and Piper exemplifying this position. But as the decade progressed, Black artists, and especially Black women artists such as Shanti Thomas and Maxine Walker, sought to address a range of themes and concerns, from the personal to the aesthetic. In the highly charged 1980s little space was given to those artists, such as Simone Alexander, Joy Gregory, Eugene Palmer and Veronica Ryan, whose work was not overtly political or confrontational. Issues of disability and sexuality were often overshadowed or excluded from debates as racial politics were prioritized, and as Sunil Gupta recounts, it often seemed that only one 'issue' could be addressed at a time.[41] Art historian Kobena Mercer would later describe the expectations placed on Black artists to address issues of race in their work as 'the burden of representation'.[42]

This book starts with statements from the exhibition pamphlet *Black Art An' Done* written in 1981. Following numerous rejections and setbacks, Araeen eventually staged his survey exhibition *The Other Story: Afro-Asian Artists in Post-War Britain* at the Hayward Gallery in London in 1989.[43] I conclude with reviews of that show published that year. Although these two exhibitions bookending the decade were very different, they shared an important characteristic: both were initiated by artists. Throughout the 1980s, Black artists found that to get their work seen and discussed they had to do it themselves. Many had been alienated or racially bullied within educational institutions, and upon leaving college found that curators in museums and galleries were rarely receptive to their work. Simultaneously, institutions arguably felt some pressure to 'deal with' Black artists in the wake of the 1981 Brixton riots and the subsequent Scarman Report, which according to Paul Gilroy initiated a period of 'municipal anti-racism'.[44] *From Two Worlds*, staged at the Whitechapel Gallery in 1986, which included the work of Zarina Bhimji, Denzil Forrester, Gavin Jantjes and others, exemplified the type of group survey show of Black artists that took place in public galleries in the mid-1980s. Generally, little connected the work exhibited in these survey shows except the diasporic backgrounds of the exhibitors. To their detractors, exhibitions such as *From Two Worlds* and *Black Art: New Directions* at Stoke-on-Trent City Museum and Art Gallery in 1989, were efficient ways of showing the work of large numbers of Black artists without jettisoning the regular – white – exhibition programme. Galleries were criticized for instrumentalizing the Black artists who curated or exhibited in them.[45] Nonetheless, some regional art galleries seemed more receptive to working collaboratively with Black artists, and throughout the 1980s important group and solo exhibitions were staged at Wolverhampton Art Gallery, the Bluecoat in

Liverpool, Rochdale Art Gallery and elsewhere. In London, smaller venues such as the Africa Centre, Horizon Gallery and 198 Gallery, most of which were founded and run by artists or Black cultural collectives, offered opportunities while mainstream institutions in the capital remained largely inaccessible.

As the 1980s came to a close, *The Other Story* opened at the Hayward Gallery. The culmination of more than ten years of work, the exhibition was a monumental achievement for Araeen, but was not without its critics. Concurrently, a new form of 'internationalism' emerged at the start of the 1990s, and the confrontational politics of the 1980s were arguably neutered by the twin forces of globalization and the evolution of a British youth culture that was simultaneously loud, brash, and regressively parochial.[46] While racism remained prevalent in British society, exemplified by the murder of teenager Stephen Lawrence at the hands of white fascists in 1993, and the Macpherson Report's conclusion in 1999 that the Metropolitan Police Force was 'institutionally racist', for Kobena Mercer, the cultural climate of 'multicultural managerialism'[47] in 1990s Britain enabled artists of colour to gain prominence within the art world, but only if their work was denuded of politicized racial discourse. Although Iniva (the Institute of International Visual Art), founded in 1994 under the directorship of Gilane Tawadros, organized and supported important exhibitions including David Medalla's *The Secret History of the Mondrian Fan Club II* (1995) and Aubrey Williams' solo show at the Whitechapel Gallery (1998), the majority of artists included in this book remained marginalized within, or excluded from, mainstream survey exhibitions of British art and art historical publications. During the 1990s some artists stopped working; some continued to make art alongside other jobs and careers. Some died without experiencing the acclaim their work is now generating.

The texts in this book are arranged chronologically according to their year of publication, or in the case of conference papers, the year of their presentation. This arrangement allows the debates regarding 'Black Art', identity politics and white institutions, to unfold and develop. Themes, issues and concerns overlap; texts build on and bounce off each other. Most were published in self-produced exhibition pamphlets; books and catalogues that are now out of print; or arts magazines, feminist journals and periodicals dedicated to issues of race and culture, most of which have ceased publication. From the early 1980s *Echo: Living Arts in Britain's Ethnic Communities*, a newsletter published by the Minorities' Arts Advisory Service (MAAS) run by Fay Rodrigues and Errol Lloyd regularly included exhibition reviews, as did *Race Today*, produced by the Race Today Collective. In November 1982, *Echo* was succeeded by *ArtRage: Inter-Cultural Arts Magazine*, which was later joined by *Bazaar: South Asian Arts Magazine*. The journal *Third Text*, founded by Araeen in 1987, was, and remains, a key publication specifically addressing Black cultural activity in Britain.

This anthology is one of a growing number of exhibitions, books and research projects reassessing the dynamism, power and criticality of the British Black Art Movement. In 2011 artists Claudette Johnson, Keith Piper and Marlene Smith established The Blk Art Group Research Project; in 2011–12 *Thin Black Lines* curated by Paul Goodwin and Lubaina Himid at Tate Britain revisited Himid's curatorial work of the 1980s; in 2017 the exhibition *No Colour Bar: Black British Art in Action 1960–1990*, organized by the Friends of the Huntley Archives was staged at the Guildhall Gallery, London, and contextualized Black visual arts practice through the activities of Eric and Jessica Huntley, who ran the important and influential Walter Rodney Bookshop in West London. In the same year Himid became the first Black woman to win the prestigious Turner Prize, with Ingrid Pollard and Veronica Ryan receiving nominations for the Prize in 2022. In 2022 Sonia Boyce became the first Black woman to represent Britain at the Venice Biennale, where she was presented with what many regard as the art world's highest accolade, the Golden Lion award for Best National Participation. At the start of the 2020s a succession of solo exhibitions of work by Chila Kumari Burman (Tate Britain, 2020–21), Sutapa Biswas (Kettles Yard, Cambridge, 2021–2), Lubaina Himid (Tate Modern, 2021–2) and Keith Piper (New Art Gallery, Walsall, 2022) have brought the work of this generation to new audiences. The popularity of shows such as *Life Between Islands*, an exhibition of Caribbean-British art at Tate Britain curated by David A. Bailey and Alex Farquharson (2021–2) demonstrated that there is an appetite for complex, trans-cultural stories of art in Britain, which reflect the diversity of British people.

In selecting this anthology, I have aimed to give an overview of the artistic practices and debates taking place during the 1980s. Many of the texts in this volume were written forty years ago. What is striking and disheartening is how relevant they remain. So many of the social and political struggles addressed in this volume – including institutionalized racism, the deaths of Black people at the hands of the police, homophobia and sexism – continue to dominate contemporary life. Inevitably there are omissions, and this book could easily have been two or three times as long. Artists including Pogus Caesar, whose photographs are now held in the National Portrait Gallery collection; Symrath Patti, who curated the landmark exhibition *Jagrati* at Greenwich Citizens Gallery in 1986; and the internationally acclaimed sculptor, Sokari Douglas Camp, are notable omissions.[48] Likewise, it has not been possible to include the writings of art historian Kobena Mercer, film-maker Pratibha Parmar and author Kwesi Owusu, each of whom have made hugely significant contributions to the debates on representation, race and British art.[49] However, what these omissions demonstrate to me is the intellectual depth and discursive breadth of this creative moment: there are many more books to be written and exhibitions to stage. In assembling these archival materials here, I hope that each text will prompt further research, and help new audiences question, challenge and expand how Black art, and its contributions to the creative culture of Britain, is written about and understood.

NOTES

1 See Hugh Thomas, *The Slave Trade: The History of the Atlantic Slave Trade, 1440–1870*, London: Simon & Schuster, 1997.

2 See Frantz Fanon, *Black Skin, White Masks*, London: Penguin, 1952; reissued 2021.

3 Ben L. Martin, 'From Negro to Black to African American: The Power of Names and Naming', *Political Science Quarterly* 106:1 (Spring 1991), pp. 83–107.

4 See Ambalavaner Sivanandan, 'From Resistance to Rebellion: Asian and Afro-Caribbean Struggles in Britain', *Race and Class* 23:2–3 (1981–2), p. 136.

5 See Kehinde Andrews, *The British Black Panthers*, BBC Radio 4, first broadcast 3 August 2019, https://www.bbc.co.uk/programmes/m0007boy

6 See this volume, Rasheed Araeen, *Art & Black Consciousness*, 1982.

7 Stuart Hall, 'New Ethnicities', in Kobena Mercer (ed.), *ICA Documents 7: Black Film, British Cinema*, London: ICA, 1988, p. 27.

8 See Reni Eddo-Lodge, *About Race* podcast (2018), 'Episode 4: Political Blackness', https://www.aboutracepodcast.com/4-political-blackness. For further discussion of the term 'Black' within British art during the 1980s, see Gen Doy, *Black Visual Culture: Modernity and Postmodernity*, London: IB Tauris, 2000, pp. 4–10.

9 Rasheed Araeen, letter to Andrew Dempsey, 28 October 1978, Asia Art Archive, https://aaa.org.hk/en/collections/search/archive/rasheed-araeen-archive-correspondence/object/letter-from-rasheed-araeen-to-andrew-dempsey-28-october-1978/sort/title-asc

10 See Centre for Contemporary Cultural Studies, *The Empire Strikes Back: Race and Racism in 70s Britain*, London: Routledge, 1982; reissued 1994, and Sally Tomlinson, 'Britain's racist 1970s education policies still resonate today', *Guardian*, 28 May 2021, https://www.theguardian.com/commentisfree/2021/may/28/britains-racist-1970s-education-policies-black-children-educationally-subnormal. For useful introduction to the Grunwick Strike, see https://www.striking-women.org/module/striking-out/grunwick-dispute

11 Margaret Thatcher, *World in Action*, 27 January 1978; full transcript available at http://www.margaretthatcher.org/document/103485

12 Zig Layton-Henry, *The Politics of Race in Britain*, Oxford: Blackwell, 1992, p. 94.

13 See Ian R. G. Spencer, *British Immigration Policy Since 1939: The Making of Multi-Racial Britain*, London: Routledge, 1997; and Adam Elliott-Cooper, *Black Resistance to British Policing*, Manchester: Manchester University Press, 2021.

14 See John La Rose, *The New Cross Massacre Story*, London: Black Rose Press, 1984; and Darcus Howe, 'Why I Still Think the New Cross Fire Was a Massacre', *New Statesman*, 12 February 1999, p. 16.

15 Peter Fryer, *Staying Power: The History of Black People in Britain*, London: Pluto Press, 1984, p. 398.

16 Gavin Evans, 'Margaret Thatcher's Shameful Support for Apartheid', *Mail and Guardian*, 19 April 2013, https://mg.co.za/article/2013-04-19-00-margaret-thatchers-shameful-support-for-apartheid/

17 See Sivanandan, 'From Resistance to Rebellion'.

18 For more on the intersection of music and youth protest, see Keith Gildart, Anna Gough-Yates, Sian Lincoln, *et al.* (eds.), *Youth Culture and Social Change: Making a Difference by Making a Noise*, London: Palgrave Macmillan, 2017.

19 See Anandi Ramamurthy, *Black Star: Britain's Asian Youth Movements*, London: Pluto Press, 2013.

20 John Solomos, Bob Findlay, Simon Jones and Paul Gilroy, 'The Organic Crisis of British Capitalism and Race: The Experience of the Seventies', in Centre for Contemporary Cultural Studies, *The Empire Strikes Back: Race and Racism in 70s Britain*, London: Routledge, 1982; reissued 1994, pp. 9–46, 26.

21 Lubaina Himid, 'Letters to Susan', in *Thin Black Line(s)* exhibition catalogue, Preston: Making Histories Visible Project, University of Central Lancashire, 2011, p. 9; available at https://makinghistoriesvisible.com/portfolio/letters-to-susan/

22 See *The Roots of the Indian Artists' Collectives*, exhibition catalogue, London: Grosvenor Gallery, 2019, https://www.grosvenorgallery.com/usr/library/documents/catalogues/therootsoftheindianartistscollectives.pdf

23 For more on the Caribbean Artists Movement, see Anne Walmsley, *The Caribbean Artists Movement 1966–1972: A Literary and Cultural History*, London:

New Beacon Books, 1992; and David A. Bailey and Allison Thompson (eds.), *Liberation Begins in the Imagination: Writings on British Caribbean Art*, London: Tate Publishing, 2021.

24 See Guy Brett, *Exploding Galaxies: The Art of David Medalla*, London: Kala Press, 1995. Medalla was omitted from the exhibition *Conceptual Art in Britain 1964–1979* at Tate Britain, 12 April–29 August 2016.

25 See the Li Yuan-Chia Foundation website, http://www.lycfoundation.org/

26 Stuart Hall, 'Black Diaspora Artists in Britain: Three "Moments" in Post-war History', *History Workshop Journal* 61 (Spring 2006), pp. 1–24, 5.

27 Frank Bowling in conversation with Rasheed Araeen, 24 July 1989, cited in Rasheed Araeen, *The Other Story: Afro-Asian Artists in Post-war Britain*, London: South Bank Centre, 1989, p. 40.

28 See *Remember Oluwale* website, https://www.rememberoluwale.org/

29 Araeen first presented his mixed media and performance work, *Paki Bastard: Portrait of the Artist as a Black Person*, at Artists for Democracy, London, on 31 July 1977.

30 Sonia Boyce, 'All the Rage: For Oluwale and Destruction of the National Front', in Nick Aikens and Elizabeth Robles (eds.), *The Place is Here: The Work of Black British Artists in 1980s Britain*, Berlin: Sternberg Press, 2019, pp. 113–36.

31 Naseem Khan, *The Art Britain Ignores: The Arts of Ethnic Minorities in Britain*, London: Community Relations Commission, 1976.

32 See Richard Hylton, *The Nature of the Beast: Cultural Diversity and the Visual Arts Sector. A Study of Policies, Initiatives and Attitudes 1976–2006*, Bath: ICIA, 2007.

33 Araeen's manifesto is reprinted in Jessica Lack (ed.), *Why Are We 'Artists'? 100 World Art Manifestos*, London: Penguin, 2017, pp. 245–85.

34 Melissa Chemam, 'Keith Piper: On the History of the Black Art Group', *Art UK* 25 October 2021, https://artuk.org/discover/stories/keith-piper-on-the-history-of-the-black-art-group

35 Marlene Smith in conversation with Alice Correia, 'She Is Not Bullet Proof', *Black British Artists and Political Activism*, Paul Mellon Centre for Studies in British Art, London, 9 December 2021; https://youtu.be/ZB4cT96MrIw

36 John Roberts, 'Interview with Sonia Boyce', *Third Text* 1 (Autumn 1987), pp. 55–64, 60.

37 See this volume, OBAALA (Organisation for Black Arts Advancement and Leisure Activities), *The Organisation* and *A Statement on Black-Art & the Gallery*, 1983.

38 See this volume, Mumtaz Karimjee, *Black and Asian: Definitions and Redefinitions*, 1987.

39 Sunil Gupta, 'Fabled Territories: An Introduction', in *Fabled Territories: New Asian Photography*, exhibition catalogue, Leeds: Leeds City Art Gallery, 1989, pp. 5–8, 6.

40 Rasheed Araeen, 'The Emergence of Black Consciousness in Contemporary Art in Britain: Seventeen Years of Neglected History', in Rasheed Araeen (ed.), *The Essential Black Art*, exhibition catalogue, London: Chisenhale Gallery, 1988, p. 5.

41 See this volume, Sunil Gupta, 'Desire and Black Men', 1986.

42 Kobena Mercer, *Welcome to the Jungle: New Positions in Black Cultural Studies*, London: Routledge, 1994, pp. 233–58.

43 The exhibition would later tour to Wolverhampton Art Gallery in March–April 1990, and Manchester Art Gallery and Cornerhouse in May–June 1990.

44 Paul Gilroy, *There Ain't No Black in the Union Jack: The Cultural Politics of Race and Nation*, London: Routledge, 1987; reissued 2002, pp. 177–94.

45 See Eddie Chambers, 'Mainstream Capers', *ArtRage* 14 (Autumn 1986), pp. 31, 33–4.

46 See Julian Stallabrass, *High Art Lite: British Art in the 1990s*, London: Verso, 1999; and Kobena Mercer, 'Ethnicity and Internationality: New British Art and Diaspora-Based Blackness', *Third Text* 13:49 (Winter 1999), pp. 51–62.

47 Kobena Mercer, 'Iconography after Identity', in David A. Bailey, Ian Baucom and Sonia Boyce (eds.), *Shades of Black: Assembling Black Arts in 1980s Britain*, London: Duke University Press, 2005, pp. 49–58, 51.

48 See 'Photographer in Focus: Pogus Caesar', National Portrait Gallery website, https://www.npg.org.uk/collections/about/photographs-collection/photographers-in-focus/photographer-in-focus-pogus-caesar; Alice Correia, 'Researching Exhibitions of South Asian Women Artists in Britain in the 1980s', *British Art Studies* 13 (September 2019), https://doi.org/10.17658/issn.2058-5462/issue-13/acorreia; and Lorraine Griffiths, 'Sekiapu: Sokari

Douglas-Camp', *Women Artists Slide Library Journal* (October–November 1987), p. 20.

49 See Kobena Mercer, *Travel & See: Black Diaspora Art Practices since the 1980s*, London: Duke University Press, 2016; Pratibha Parmar, 'Black Feminism: The Politics of Articulation', in Jonathan Rutherford (ed.), *Identity: Community, Culture, Difference,* London: Lawrence & Wishart, 1990, pp. 101–26; and Kwesi Owusu (ed.), *Storms of the Heart: An Anthology of Black Arts and Culture,* London: Camden Press, 1988.

A Note on the Texts

This anthology comprises artists' statements, articles, reviews, exhibition essays, interviews, and speeches, sourced from a range of magazines, journals, newspapers, pamphlets, books and catalogues. The texts have been reproduced whole, except in a very few cases where it was impossible to include the complete text due to length. Omitted text is marked by an ellipsis in square brackets [...]. In the main, editorial interventions to the texts have been kept to a minimum. Idiosyncratic phrasing, capitalization, punctuation and spelling have been retained, except in instances of obvious typos or where spelling mistakes inhibited comprehension. Where possible, corrections and amendments have been made in consultation with the respective authors and artists' Estates. All footnotes and endnotes are original to the texts, except in clearly noted instances. The texts are arranged in chronological order; in instances where the date of publication or presentation cannot be ascertained specifically, they are ordered by year according to the information available, such as Spring, Summer etc. Each text is preceded by a short introduction which provides some information about the author(s) and an outline of the context in which the text was written. Details of where each text was originally published can be found in the Sources and Permissions section at the end of this book.

1 *Black Art An' Done: An Exhibition of Work by Young Black Artists*, 1981

In 1981 a group of politically conscious young Black art students staged an exhibition of their work, *Black Art An' Done: An Exhibition of Work by Young Black Artists* at Wolverhampton Art Gallery from 9 to 27 June. The exhibiting artists were all of Caribbean heritage from the West Midlands: Eddie Chambers, Dominic Dawes, Andrew Hazel, Ian Palmer and Keith Piper. The group was mentored by local school teacher Eric Pemberton, and had been actively forging collaborative networks with other Black artists since 1979. During the period of its existence, the group's membership was fluid and it variously exhibited as Wolverhampton Young Black Artists, The Pan-Afrikan Connection and The Blk Art Group. In its early years the group was all male and inspired by the American Black Arts Movement of the 1960s and 1970s, and particularly the Pan-African writings of Larry Neal and Ron Karenga. Faced with institutionalized racism at art school, from teachers, curators and galleries, Chambers and his contemporaries staged their own exhibition, on their terms: *Black Art An' Done*. The title of the show provided a sense of forthright certainty: 'An' Done', is a colloquialism meaning, 'and that's an end to it'. The exhibition included work in a range of media, including painting, sculpture and printmaking, and addressed the civil rights of Black people in Britain and internationally. According to artist Rasheed Araeen, this exhibition was, arguably, the first time that the term 'Black Art' had been used to describe contemporary artistic practice in a British context.

*   *   *

INTRODUCTION

This exhibition of visual art work by five young black artists, is the first of its kind to be mounted in Wolverhampton.

It is a stride along the road to "sombodyness" for the black community.

These artists have all struggled to succeed in an adverse situation. We hope that they will "Keep on Keepin' on".

We hope that the exhibition will inspire other black youngsters to develop their creative genius.

ACKNOWLEDGEMENTS

We wish to thank –

1. Mr. Rodgers and all of the staff at Wolverhampton Art Gallery, expecially Mr. Flynn, for their help.
2. Mr. I Henry, President of the Afro-Caribbean Teachers Association (ACTA), for officiating at the opening ceremony.

ARTIST'S STATEMENTS

To me, the black art student cannot afford the luxury of complacency as enjoyed by many of his white counterparts. These people, finding little worth responding to in their decadent lives of leisure and pleasure seek out ever more obscure playthings amongst the self indulgent vogues of art 'for arts sake'.

The black art student, by his very blackness finds himself drawn towards the epicentre of social tension. He is forced to respond to the urgency of the hour. The aspirations of the British Black are ripe, and our time is 'NOW'.

So let us in our work undersign the logical mechanics of our greater struggle. Let us strive by any means to raise the revolutionary consciousness of each other as to the form and functioning of the social, political, and economic barriers which this man has placed all around us, and within our very minds.

KEITH PIPER.

I believe that this exhibition is a great opportunity for young Blacks to show another side of our character not quite so topical. My own work does not seek to make any great statements, mainly by choice, but also because, as may be obvious to some, I'm the Graphic Illustrator amongst Fine Artists. Because of this the majority of the work I've displayed is course work and thus somewhat predetermined. At the moment I'm at Kingston Polytechnic doing a Graphics degree, so I won't be at the Exhibition in person. However, I hope the few pieces myself and the others are exhibiting will at least give visual pleasure and hopefully initiate a few thoughts.

ANDREW HAZEL.

About my work? Well I do it to please me. I feel that if the work satisfies someone else's needs and not your own, you yourself are missing out on what it is trying to say.

Some may say there is little talent in my work. I would answer that may aim is to show that you need not be a master at painting and drawing to be in art. You don't need to have extreme skill with a brush. True, it helps, but it is not a condition to take an active part in creating an art form.

I sometimes wish I was better at what I do. The only thing I can do is to "rebel on". Thats what we all need to do. Go forward – never backward. The future must be seen with an aim in mind.

IAN PALMER.

I was asked to submit a statement about my work, but I feel that the work speaks for itself, so I'm limiting this statement to only a few sentences.

Inna Inglan

At the age of about 10 something hit me which, years later I was able to forgive, but never forget. It was an English dictionary. You see, for sometime around that period of my life, I was called many racist names, so I looked in a dictionary for reference to some of the names and their meanings.

I found out that "Negro" meant "of the African race". Then underneath, in smaller letters, it said "Nigger" – "A good hard worker". Since then, I became, and still am becoming more aware of how Black people have become victims of this Fascist society and white racist brutality.

Babylonian Blood

In our towns and cities, on your subway walls etc. and just as much in our minds, there is racial abuse: WOGS GO HOME, N.F. RULES, BLACK BASTARDS, ETC. but who made us the so-called "bastards"?

If man could only think as a child, he would not only learn more, but learn how to think peace. We fail to let our thoughts, noble though they sometimes are, move our bodies and not just our dreams.

DOMINIC DAWES.

Because of the fact that we, the 3.7% of the British population, have been and are being oppressed as a race and exploited as the working class: now more than ever before, the Black artist has a growing obligation to acknowledge (in and through his or her work) the fundamental elements that characterise our existence as Black British.

The work of the Black artist should be seen as having specific positive functions: a tool to assist us in our struggle for liberation, both at home and abroad, as opposed to simply reflecting the moral bankruptcy of modern times.

Black art, at the very least, should indicate and/or document change. It should seek to effect such change by aiming to help create an alternative set of values necessary to better living. Otherwise it fails to be legitimate art.

Generally speaking "Black Art an' Done" aims at raising the level of self-awareness and motivation amongst ourselves. The exhibition also hopes to encourage more youth to cultivate their creative tendencies (in music and literature as well as art), with a view to reclaiming the shattered psyches and culture of the Black race.

As individuals, and even more so as a group, we would like to thank Mr. Eric Pemberton for his constant and invaluable help, advice and encouragement during the months of planning that have gone into this exhibition. Without his help, this event would definitely not have been possible.

[. . .]

EDDIE CHAMBERS.

2 Rasheed Araeen, 'Paint it Black', 1982

Artist, writer and curator Rasheed Araeen is one of the leading figures in debates regarding Black art in Britain. In 1982 he wrote a review of *The Pan-Afrikan Connection* exhibition, held at the Africa Centre, 3 May – 4 June 1982. Established in 1960, the Africa Centre, then in Covent Garden, London, was a cultural venue which regularly staged book fairs, literary events and exhibitions of African artists in the UK. *The Pan-Afrikan Connection* was the second exhibition of the Midlands-based Black artists group and included work by Eddie Chambers, Dominic Dawes, Claudette Johnson, Wenda Leslie and Keith Piper. In his review, Araeen notes that all the exhibiting artists were still students and suggests that while some of the work may be regarded as 'rough', their energy and commitment to expressing themselves authentically should be admired and supported. He praises these young Black artists for refusing to conform to 'ethnic' expectations of white society, and commends the way that they each, in their individual ways, dynamically express the realities of Black life in Britain.

*   *   *

'Britain is not South Africa or Nazi Germany, whatever some of the artists represented here may believe. They should be thankful that it is not.'
'Art is inspired by love. Propaganda is fired by hate. Choose.'

These two remarks come from an unusually animated visitors' book to a recent exhibition of the work of five black artists. The artists were born in Britain, but describe themselves as descendants from 'Africans dispersed during the Atlantic Slave Trade'. The remarks could be seen as just two people's personal opinions. But they represent a kind of complacency (both towards what happens in this society, and towards art) already anticipated by the artists: They say: 'We feel for our brothers and sisters throughout the world who are victims of racial injustice. "Injustice anywhere is a threat to justice everywhere" – Martin Luther King . . . In developing our sense of "some bodiness", we are trying to avoid blind mimicry. We are trying to recreate and develop our humanity.' The artists were Eddie A Chambers, Dominic Dawes, Claudette Johnson, Wenda Leslie and Keith Piper.

Take a work by Eddie Chambers. It comprises four collage sequences in which Union Jack is seen as Swastika. But this vision is not consolidated or presented as an affront to anybody, but reflects a fear that is transformed into a hope by a radical action. As one's eyes move from one sequence to another, more and more cracks appear in the unified Union Jack/Swastika image, till finally the whole thing falls into small pieces. This may look like propaganda to people like Mrs Thatcher who apparently thinks that British people are 'still the same people who had built an Empire, and ruled a quarter of the world' (*Guardian*, July 5 1982). But, then, in that vision there is no equal or dignified place for all the people.

These artists are still in art school. How can they achieve the sense of 'some bodiness' in an educational context dominated by European artists? The stamp is there. The *visual* quality of the work is no different from what one would see in diploma shows. But there is a difference that separates them significantly from the rest. They use the available knowledge not in order to pay homage to 'their' predecessors or identify with prevailing perceptions, but to challenge what to them has become a 'blind mimicry'. Behind what may appear to be art school exercises, mixed with political slogans, there is evidence of a subtlety with which it attempts to turn the whole prevailing notion of art upside down.

John Berger once wrote about the difficulty of being a good artist in a post-war period, when the humanist values of Europe lay shattered in the rubble of its ruined cities. But the devastation did not stop. It continued somewhere else. And the difficulty of being a *good* artist is still there, and more so if you are a black person (i e Afro/Asian) living in a white society such as Britain. You not only encounter what goes on every day in a racist society, but your role as an artist is also prescribed and limited. These artists know very well that they will never be accepted as blue-eyed boys of the Bond Street gallery circuit. Can we really forget what we encounter in our daily lives, and then try to make art which has no relation to our own experience? How can we be insensitive to a social environment such as Dominic Dawes points out:

'In your town and cities, on your subway walls, etc, and just as much in your mind, there is racial abuse: WOGS GO HOME, NF RULES, BLACK BASTARDS, PISS OFF NIGGERS, etc. But who made us the so-called bastards?' Just the National Front? On May 23, Lord Denning, Master of the Rolls, was quoted in the *Observer* as claiming that 'black, coloured and brown' people have lower moral standards.

It would be easier if we adopted the standpoint of the two visitors, and didn't look at the work in relation to the culture in which it was produced. We could then look for the 'aesthetic dimension' without worrying too much about the real world. But even that might not be necessary: after a quick glance the whole thing could be dismissed as just angry rhetoric, without much substance or positive vision. But where would that lead us? To hack criticism. Seriousness of the matter demands we try to penetrate what to me is a rhetorical mask, for the work concerned questions the very foundation on which we normally based our critical judgements.

We are still trapped in the myth of the artist who transcends all hostile social conditions to produce masterpieces, without the sense of belonging to a continuity of history or without a history being sympathetic to one's role as a producer of ideas. Even radical aesthetics often presupposes that there is a history common to all and different people living in the same society. In fact, the language which was developed during the colonial period is still very much with us as part of art criticism. We have not yet developed a radical approach which comes to terms with what McLuhan calls 'a global village' or / and look at the conflicts and tensions of racially heterogenous societies of postwar period.

If the world has now become one, it is considered to be the West's world, and therefore its dominant perspective remains Eurocentric. There is no significant place in it for anybody other than European people, for it ignores the fact that African and Asian people now form an essential part of postwar Europe. This attitude is not though new: non-European peoples have been treated in a similar – if not more brutal – manner for centuries in the new world. Multiracialism is seen merely as an aberration to be put up with or is dismissed as marginal to the main struggle.

The position of black people can't be seen purely from the point of view of class analysis. There are ideas, values and attitudes which are inherent in the general make-up of this society which often escape questioning, even by those on the left. The struggle for a more equal society can't remove this stumbling block without the *critical* perspective offered by black radical self-awareness.

This white society in fact remains stubborn in its attitude, rejecting any idea that its Afro/Asian minority does actually have an important contribution to make to its humanising process.

Black woman living in a white society such as ours is doubly vulnerable. She stands opposite and exposed to what represents power and authority: white male. Claudette Johnson expresses this anxiety: 'My work is about the conflict and growth that has been the experience of the African woman born and raised in the West . . . It attempts to express the myriad aspects of oppression, racist and sexist, that have shaped us. It deals not with specific events but with our responses: anger, frustration, fear and depression . . . It charts the move towards relating to one another that we have devised for our survival . . .'

The issue here is not of alienation, as we understand it in the Western context. The alienation of a white person vis-à-vis contemporary Western culture may create similar psychological conditions or symptoms, but then there is no rupture between the individual and his/her own history. The rootlessness of a black person on European soil creates an entirely different condition, which is like being in a total void, cultural and historical. You are inside a space and the space is inside you, but without any mutual recognition.

This rootlessness has positive as well as negative aspects. Outside the culture, you are at the same time part of it. This gives you a broader perspective, beyond parochial and national interests. You become international. Alternately, you can escape into the nostalgia of your own past or far-away culture; which would amount to your shutting your eyes to reality.

It is this dilemma of belonging and not belonging to the same reality to which these artists address themselves, not through a mythical level or some phoney spiritual stance but with an awareness of their place and responsibility in the present world. They know that our present predicament is not the result of a natural process. It is a dire consequence of a global economic and cultural system commonly called Western civilisation.

Kenneth Coutts-Smith, an English critic and historian: 'the Fine Arts have, historically, fallen victim to a myth concerning the absolute and metaphysical nature of its activity, as a result of which its actions and its products have been used to justify not merely a criminal structure of social relations but also the world-wide edifice of imperialism upon which this structure still depends'.

What we see in Britain now is the increasing development of a kind of neo-colonial situation, with all its paraphernalia of Afro-Caribbean and Asian intermediaries and ethnic / exotic cultural activities.

Liberalism is desperately trying to resolve its dilemma, but without actually shifting its ground. It likes to think that the issue here is that of our culture looking nostalgically back to Africa, Asia or the Caribbean. Unfortunately this view is shared by many black people who find no other way but to accept ethnic categories in order to survive. But these black artists can't be put into ethnic bags. They have the integrity to resist all impositions. They are in fact quite scornful of those who are now going around the establishment's table with ethnic bowls in their hands and LOVE & PEACE on their lips in the hope of getting some crumbs. Art is now being reduced to an instrument of the race-relations industry whereby it is turned into an exotic entertainment for the sake of phoney racial harmony.

The seriousness with which these artists take their role deserves our utmost admiration. There is an acute sense of purpose generally lacking in the professional art world. It is significant that they are not worried about individual styles – although each one shows a distinct personality in the work. They use all kinds of material – paper collage, paint, photographs, plaster, images and words, either used individually or juxtaposed, in a genuine spirit of experimentation, exploration and reflection. The present result may be crude and rough, and even hybrid, but that is not important at the moment. What is really significant is the presence of tremendous energy, the sense of full commitment and definite direction which, it is hoped, will in time develop into a more significant visual articulation.

What is Black Art?

The work may be loud and noisy. But, then, it is partly deliberate: the attempt is to express anger and frustration. The situation is such that any sensitive human being would be angry. The furiousness is about the world in which hypocrisy, smugness, cynicism, self-exaltation, self-righteousness have become norms. While I'm writing this more than ten thousand men, women and children have been brutally massacred within a week in Lebanon. Where is the conscience of the civilised world? Why so much helplessness? . . . Are we to believe that there is no relationship between Apartheid and racism in the West? When South African troops kill and plunder in Namibia, when white soldiers rape young black women in front of their captured men, what do we do in the West? Is it difficult to believe that the daily suffering of millions of people in Southern Africa is being perpetrated not without the help of those who would send almost a full naval force to 'liberate' two thousand people?

The work of these young black artists represents not only an authentic black voice, but it is also a voice of humanity that refuses to be brutalised and insensitised. No masterpieces are being offered here, since conditions to make masterpieces do not exist. What is being expressed is more important and urgent. It is a critical consciousness, if not conscience, of our time. And we ought to pay a serious attention to it.

3 Rasheed Araeen, *Art & Black Consciousness*, 1982

On 28 October 1982, artist, writer and curator Rasheed Araeen presented a conference paper, 'Art & Black Consciousness', at the First National Black Art Convention, held at Wolverhampton Polytechnic. The Convention was organized by Wolverhampton Young Black Artists, a group of students including Eddie Chambers, Keith Piper and Marlene Smith, and aimed to discuss the form, function and future of Black art in Britain. In addition to Araeen, speakers included Claudette Johnson, who presented a paper titled 'Images of Black Women in Art', and Shakka Deddi, whose paper was titled, 'If Art is Art is Universal - then What is Black-Art?'. A series of film-screenings took place throughout the day, including *Riots and Rumours of Riots* (1981) by Imruh Bakari (listed as Imruh Caesar). In his paper, Araeen introduced his audience to ideas he had been developing as an artist, writer, and member of the British Black Panthers during the 1970s, and which had been published in his 'Preliminary Notes for a BLACK MANIFESTO', in January 1978, in *Black Phoenix*, the journal he co-edited with poet Mahmood Jamal. Araeen proposed a politicized understanding of the term 'Black', to denote people of colour who had a shared experience of racism and discrimination enacted by white, colonial and neo-colonial powers.

*   *   *

The main aim of my presentation today is to explore the meaning of the word 'black' as used in reference to people, particularly in Britain, and its relationship with art or cultural practices. This may appear strange or unnecessary as we all know what we generally mean by 'black' or black people. But I think this meaning is too often taken for granted. It does not mean the same thing for all the people, neither has the word 'black' been used and accepted all the time. It does not represent a fixed attribute of some people and culture. In fact we are in a danger of being defined as a fixed and separate category (or categories) if we do not consider the meaning of 'black' in its historical development, particularly in the context of postwar Britain.

What I'm trying to establish is that we cannot understand the full significance of the word 'black' outside the historical context of our struggle against racism, against cultural imperialism which exists not only globally but also inside Britain in relation to people of African and Asian origins; and only within this context can we understand the emergence of what I call black consciousness in contemporary art in Britain.

When we say we are black people, what do we really mean by this? If this only indicates the colour of our skin, our facial features, or our identity with our place of birth or origin, how does this define our place in the contemporary world? But if, on the other hand, this signifies our relationship with or difference from white / European people, what is the nature of this relationship? How and by whom is this relationship defined and how does our own awareness and understanding of it, critical or otherwise, affect our position in this society? If 'blackness' has been imposed upon us at various times in history, as functions of colonial domination, how can we now by calling ourselves black subvert this imposition? If our own assertion as *black* people represents a different position, a shift in meaning, a critical deconstruction of colonial relationship, what is its function in art?

These questions are complex and difficult, and there are no easy answers. Neither will it be possible to deal with these questions in some depth in this limited space. I'm merely outlining the issue here, so that we can discuss together its various aspects beyond its populist and rhetorical manifestations. I wish to propose no prescriptions or permanent solutions.

It is however imperative to seek and develop new 'terms of reference' to comprehend what is contextual, contingent and historical. The emergence and manifestation of black consciousness in contemporary art in Britain cannot be understood within the existing 'terms of reference' of the dominant culture or outside of it, neither can it be located within our own Afro/Asian traditions. To see ourselves outside the dominant culture, on the basis that it is white/European culture, will be to accept our marginal positions.

Another difficulty we face in trying to deal with the word 'black' is its perhaps rightful but confused connection with African people, its apparently inherent attribution to African race and cultures. So, when the word 'black' is also used by other non-European people, particularly by the people of the Indian subcontinent living in the West, it brings the whole thing to a complex ideological level which is not easily recognised or accepted. The simplistic and common approach which relates 'blackness' only to the colour of skin or racial features (particularly of African people), may underline an essentialism that often leads to racial categorisations and their separate functions in a racist society.

I therefore find it necessary to depart from the common definition of 'black', from its appropriation and monopolisation by African cultural nationalism or by those who see their salvation in the reintroduction of their past cultural traditions in the midst of modern technological culture. To see communal cultural traditions as an answer to alienating and dehumanising modern culture is to enter into the ghetto of nostalgia. In order that our own assertion of 'blackness' has any meaning in relation to our opposition to what is a racist culture, it must be located within the history or historical continuity of our struggles against colonial and neo-colonial domination. If 'white' means domination and exploitation, then 'black' must mean liberation from all kinds of domination. In other words, the question of race and racism must also enter into class struggle.

The history of the word 'black', as used to define certain people, is too long to go into its full investigation, which would in fact require a separate paper. It would take us right back into early history, more than two thousand years ago when Africans were taken away as slaves by both Europeans and Arabs. But my own starting point is modern history which starts more or less in fifteenth century Europe with the emergence of a new world-view that brought the whole world into colonial domination through successive European conquests and exploitations, and the socio-economic and political system that emerged with it is still with us today.

We all know that African people were taken to the New World in order merely to be used on plantations which were important for the emergence of modern European economy. But, the transatlantic slave trade was not an ahistorical phenomenon or an aberration resulting from the nastiness of some greedy and brutal individuals. Though personal greed and brutality did play their role in this slave trade, it was the result of an ideology or world-view that saw and still sees the world, both animate and inanimate, in terms of raw material (nature) to be exploited for Europe's development and the global expansion of its civilisation. However, it's my understanding of history that if there were enough people available in the New World who could have been effectively used, either through persuasion or force, on the plantations then perhaps the transatlantic slave trade would have not taken place. That does not necessarily mean Africa would have been spared from colonialism or that it would have a different relationship with the West today. The futility of the hypothesis is obvious:

how can we ignore what actually happened? The consequences and memories of what happened to African people as the result of their uprooting from their soil and subsequently their barbaric treatment in the New World are with us as part of African people's traumatic history. What I'm really trying to do is to place the transatlantic slave trade in its historical context, which is colonialism. The people who were enslaved or colonised were mostly non-European peoples, and thus racism became part of the ideology of white/European colonial expansion and imperialism.

Racism is of course directed at the colour of one's skin and racial features, because that is how one is recognisable and is recognised as different from European people. African people have been and still are the main target of racism, as in Southern Africa and to a lesser degree in America. It also now represents a continuation of colonial domination within the West, such as in Britain, in the form of metropolitan neo-colonialism. It is important that a distance is maintained between those who are supposed to rule and those who are meant to be ruled, physically and psychologically, so that the system could continue working as before and for the benefit of the privileged. In Britain, both African and Asian people are the target of racism, both being subjected to common abuse and attacks but also excluded from the centres of power – in cultural terms, from the mainstream of contemporary art. One shouldn't therefore be surprised that black consciousness in Britain is not confined only to people of African origin.

In South Africa racism is still being used as an overt ideological apparatus in order to maintain and justify a brutal system of white domination and exploitation, which of course provides power and privileges only to a small white minority. The brutal nature of Apartheid is apparent to most people, but it is not an aberration in the colonial system. It will collapse without the external support. It will not survive very long without the help of many Western countries or international capitalism, a system which is vigourously maintained and defended at all costs.

It is the same system which operates today in most parts of what we call the 'Third World'. While in South Africa it is overtly and brutally colonial, since a small minority of European settlers is still ruling the large African majority by the use of its vast technological and military power, in Kenya, for example, white/European ruling class has been replaced by a native (black) ruling class after the so-called independence but without much change in colonial relationship.

The Kenyan economy is now in the hands of multinational companies, and their control is maintained by the political/military power which has been passed on to the new rulers, those who are proud of their black African heritage, who often gather in international cultural conferences and art festivals to pronounce their 'blackness'. The Kenyan ruling class is so proud of its African culture that it puts it on display frequently by parading young African women in their traditional costumes in front of international dignitaries whenever they arrive at Nairobi Airport. Culture has thus been turned into an exotic entertainment for the internationally privileged classes. While at the same time, Kenyan people who are rightly opposing the hijacking of their country by the international exploiters are put behind the bars or are even forced to leave the country. And all this is done with international help. Otherwise why should there be British, American, Israeli, and, according to some rumours, South African troops stationed on Kenyan soil? Can we therefore consider the present Kenyan rulers as an embodiment or a representation of black consciousness? When African leaders, such as Banda, Mobuto, Moi, for example say that they are black, what does this really mean? Post-colonial demagogy and antiracist rhetoric of most of our leaders in Africa and Asia have nothing to do with our struggle.

Black consciousness has little to do with black faces. The system has become so sophisticated that it can now use black, brown or yellow faces to maintain its status quo. While many African, Asian, as well as Caribbean, leaders make pronouncements against racism in South Africa, against imperialism, they themselves at the same time oppress and exploit their own people on behalf of their international bosses.

Britain only recently ruled a large part of the world, a fact which we are frequently reminded of even today, and is now part of the system (neo-colonialism) that continues to dominate and exploit the world, with its support for Apartheid in South Africa, Zionist occupation of Palestine, and in general all those regimes which are against the aspirations and struggles of people for freedom and self-determination. In other words, Britain's role in the world today is not different from what it used to be when it ruled parts of Africa, Asia and the Caribbean directly, and its relationship with the world is determined by the same ideology which justified its colonial rule.

It is therefore important that we see our position in this society in a broad world context. We shouldn't really be surprised if Britain is a racist society, in which racism is not only overtly expressed but is also part of its cultural institutions. How could it be otherwise? British society would continue to be so as long as its outlook to the world is not radically changed, so long as it continues to entertain its imperialist ambitions (and fantasies), maintaining the division of the world between a powerful and privileged centre, the capitalist West, and its 'dependent' periphery, the Third World. Britain today also represents internally a microcosm of the divided world, with its Afro / Asian population being pushed to and kept at its periphery. Although this periphery can be defined and analysed in class terms, the predicament of AfroAsian people is really the result of extra-class factors.

Britain is of course a class society. But it seems that class divisions are no longer rigid enough to prevent movements across class boundaries as far as white people are concerned. A person from a working class background can now become a prime minister of the country, or to put it in cultural terms, can receive recognition as a great artist – such as Henry Moore or David Hockney. But can we apply this analysis to the position of AfroAsian people in Britain? In fact any AfroAsian person found entertaining an ambition to be a prime minister of this country would be considered an utmost lunatic, and that goes for an artistic ambition as well.

One of the functions of colonialism was to deny us our own historical developments, as a result of which we have been cut off from our own histories. We do not always have links with our own past historical achievements in the same way European people have in the form of unbroken historical continuity. John Berger says:

> A people or a class which is cut off from its own past is far less free to choose and to act as a people or class than one that has been able to situate itself in history. That is why – and this is the only reason why – the entire art of the past has now become a political issue.

The situation looks pretty discouraging. It seems that we do not have many choices. But let us not despair. We have not gathered here to talk about our being victims of history. People who continue struggling cannot be the victims of history, and it is our struggle that has brought us here.

The struggle is about power. It is about our position in this society and in the world. If the power to act in the world is denied to us, how to deal with our 'powerlessness'? To be specific, how to reject our marginality in contemporary society and demand our place in the mainstream of modern culture? If mainstream of modern culture, Modernism, is not sympathetic to our entry into it, what is to be done? It should be naive to think that the doors of Modernism are going to open for us as soon as we have started shouting outside its doors. It would be naive to believe that the dominant culture is going to change with itself by itself to accommodate us. The doors may not open, and they will not open by themselves, but that does not mean that we have to turn our backs to the dominant culture and take comfort inside the ethnic tents that we are trying to pitch outside the gate.

Centre-periphery relationship by its very structure represents a hierarchy, in which the dominant and dominated must stay *together* in a state of equilibrium. It is not necessarily a static state. A movement is allowed so long as it is within the system's ideological framework, so long as its fundamental ideas, values, attitudes, etc. are not threatened. However, its ambivalence provides us a space within which the dominant ideas, values, attitudes, etc. can be questioned.

We are concerned here with the specific relationship of domination which produces marginalisation on a racial basis. However, racism in art is not a matter of bigotry which can be dealt with by anti-racist slogans. It is a complex form of institutional power which is geared to 'automatically' maintain the historical primacy and centrality of white / European people in the development of modern / contemporary art. In other words, it is the presumed Eurocentrality of Modernism which provides a focus for our struggle, and only within this context the meaning of black consciousness in art becomes clear.

It is important to recognise the role of Asian people in the development of black consciousness in Britain. It forced the meaning of 'black' to a level whereby it could only be understood ideologically, a shift from the level of visible race and colour to that level which is complex but nevertheless provides us an opening through which the ideas which underpin Eurocentricity could be confronted. It is by no means implied that only Asian people understand the ideological meaning of the word 'black', but Asian participation in the struggle has been important in its reinforcement. In other words, Afro-Asian unity has been very crucial in combating the establishment's divide-and-rule tactics which it is using behind its promotion of ethnic minority cultures.

The establishment has in fact made an intervention, and in some respect quite successfully. There is a growing number of people who believe that racial and cultural differences are *fundamental* to their identities.

It was perhaps in the early Seventies when the establishment started realising that it should come up with its own solution to what it called 'black problem', in the face of growing black consciousness among *both* Afro-Caribbean and Asian communities. It was necessary to divert the struggle to a level where culture and cultural differences between various AfroAsian communities became central, recognising the importance of AfroAsian traditions to these communities. It was based on a view that the predicament of AfroAsian people in this country was not really due to racism (although liberalism does recognise the racism of the National Front, and is also opposed to all kind of racial bigotry) but cultural alienation, caused by the inability of these people to participate in a culture which is alien to them but which is also modern, technological and complex. And therefore the solution to their predicament would be to introduce AfroAsian cultural forms in Britain and also encourage AfroAsian communities to identify with their own specific cultural traditions. You do your own ethnic bit, stay at the periphery (the ghetto), and we will provide you special funds for your activities. Don't disturb the system by taking pot shots at its centre. You will only increase the conflict and antagonism between various factions of the society, which is not good for race relations!

It is not my aim here to dismiss cultural traditions altogether or to say that cultural differences don't matter. But it is not the issue, as far as art is concerned; and it is not the reason why

AfroAsian artists have no place in the history of modern/contemporary art.

The system is very good in taking U-turns, constantly changing its position to keep us defined and categorised so that we remain outside the centre of power. Once we were primitives, and the white man came to our countries to help us become civilised, to help us enter the modern technological age. And now when we are here, right in the centre of civilisation, we are being told that this would be too much for us. When we say that we are now part of this modern society, and that we are contributing to its development, and therefore we should also have an equal share of its pie, we are told that there is something wrong with us. We are suffering from cultural alienation, we have forgotten our role in our own communities. The new medicine will rejuvenate our creative energies, we will again be able to dance in the rhythms of our forefathers, we will again be able to produce pictures which will be understood by our communities. Hail mediocrity! Down with elitism!

To attribute all that rubbish which is being produced in the name of our community to our own cultures is to insult our great achievements, past and present. History does not move forward by looking at the past nostalgically. To use African or Asian cultural traditions in a way that turns them into exotic entertainment is to insult our own people. It has nothing to do with black consciousness.

I'm not dismissing nostalgia altogether. It can be part of an imagination and it can trigger off a creative process. But pure nostalgia prevents one to come to terms with one's present environment. It can and often does provide a feeling of comfort when one is in an unbearable predicament, but it has no significant use in art unless it is sufficiently transformed into a vision which can link both past and present critically.

To look at Jamaica, for example, only as an idyllic landscape is to deny Jamaica its reality. Jamaica is not a holiday paradise. It is a country inhabited by millions of people who are daily struggling against poverty and exploitation.

Our choice is not really simple. Black art can't be about the past. Black art can't be about magic. It is about our present reality and it is about the real world. It is part of our struggle for freedom and equality. To be black is to be political.

4 *The Pan-Afrikan Connection, 1983*

Between 1982 and 1983, a Midlands-based group of students organised a series of exhibitions under the title, *The Pan-Afrikan Connection*. Following the group's 1981 exhibition *Black Art An' Done*, which had included the work of Eddie Chambers and Keith Piper, artists Claudette Johnson, Wenda Leslie, Donald Rodney, Marlene Smith and Janet Vernon joined at various points. Exhibitions were staged at the Africa Centre, London, and the Ikon Gallery, Birmingham, in 1982. The texts reproduced here were originally published to accompany the group's sixth exhibition, *The Pan-Afrikan Connection*, at The Midland Group Arts Centre in Nottingham, in January–February 1983. The exhibition included work by Chambers, Johnson, Piper and Rodney, and the introduction and artists' statements reproduced in the accompanying pamphlet provide an overview of the group's activities and motivations. Significantly, the introduction identifies and explains the political motivations of the group as being informed by a pan-African understanding of the historical and continuing exploitation of African people by Western capitalist power structures.

*   *   *

THE PAN-AFRIKAN CONNECTION

This group exists as the brainchild of EDDIE CHAMBERS, who, from the late 70's saw the need to present a radical black alternative to the self-indulgent and apolitical brand of creativity being encouraged within art schools. Towards this end and under the guidance of his friend and mentor ERIC PEMBERTON, he assembled a group of young blacks from Wolverhampton who, like himself, were interested and active in the production of radical black art.

By the time he met KEITH PIPER at Lanchester Polytechnic in 1979, the group had already been founded and was about to begin preparations for the first exhibition at Wolverhampton Art Gallery in June 1981. The line-up of the group has always been a fluid one and of the original five exhibitors, only CHAMBERS and PIPER remain.

The second group show at the AFRICA CENTRE, Covent Garden, in May 1982 saw the inclusion of CLAUDETTE JOHNSON – then a final year Fine Art student at Wolverhampton Polytechnic – followed by DONALD RODNEY, a student at Trent Polytechnic, who joined in the Autumn of 1982 to complete the existing line-up with WENDA LESLIE, JANET VERNON, MARLENE SMITH and ERIC PEMBERTON forming an essential organisational back-up team.

The exhibition title, THE PAN-AFRIKAN CONNECTION, has been used by the group since their second show as an expression of the solidarity which the artists feel with the struggles of all oppressed peoples of the world; be they in Africa, the Third World in general or the ghettoes of the capitalist West. Despite the fact that they may be physically isolated from the centre of that struggle, insulated as they are within the liberal art school system, the group feel themselves to be connected to those struggles in so far that as long as international capitalism continues to use race as a basis for exploitation, then, all black people will remain its potential victims.

"The phrase 'Pan-Afrikan' means three things:

1. There have been eight dispersions of Africans at various times in history. These artists are descended from Africans dispersed during the Atlantic Slave Trade (1500–1833).
2. We feel for our brothers and sisters throughout the world who are the victims of racial injustice. "Injustice anywhere is a threat to justice everywhere." M.L. King, 1929–1968.
3. In developing our sense of 'some bodyness', we try to avoid blind mimicry. We are trying to recreate and develop our humanity.

We hope that this exhibition will encourage Black people to further develop their creative talents."

THE PAN-AFRIKAN CONNECTION 1983

[. . .]

ARTISTS PERSONAL STATEMENTS

Eddie Chambers

Foundation at Coventry Lanchester Polytechnic; final year B.A. (Hons) Fine Art at Sunderland Polytechnic

"Five exhibitions on, sees us presenting the fourth edition of THE PAN-AFRIKAN CONNECTION. The exhibition is loud, bold, direct and clear. But what does it all mean?

In simple terms it's a visual representation of the Pan-African ideology. In more intricate terms, it's an exhibition of work by four young black artists, each one producing art which gives definite indications of their individual perception of, and involvement in, black politics.

My own political stance is orientated to the said Pan-African ideology, but what about those Khomeini prints? These pieces of work are intended to raise questions more than provide answers – the saga of Iran has produced valuable observations for the radical black thinker. Now go away and consider them. Those prints are black art in a not so recognisable form. Black art, at the very least, should indicate and/or document change. It should seek to effect such change by aiming to help create an alternative set of values necessary for better living, stronger communities, contemporary cultural identity and so on... rather than merely reflecting the moral bankruptcy of modern times, as does the majority of white art.

That's black art at the very least; at the very most, it should and can do a whole lot more.

Black art, like everything else in the black community must respond positively to the urgent reality of revolution. Very necessary revolution.

The most positive thing that this exhibition can do is motivate more young black artists to produce more black art. Art which takes the white person to task and strengthens the blacks that remain!"

EDDIE A. CHAMBERS 1983

<u>Claudette Johnson</u>

Graduate Fine Art student.

"My work is about the conflict and growth that has been the experience of the African woman born and raised here in the West.

It attempts to express the myriad aspects of oppression, racist and sexist, that have shaped us. It deals not with specific events but with our responses; anger, frustration, fear and depression. Most of all it charts the move towards mobilisation, recognising the value of alternative methods of organising and relating to one another that we have devised for our own survival; for we have our own "business in this skin, and on this planet."

CLAUDETTE JOHNSON 1982

Keith Piper

Foundation at Coventry Lanchester Polytechnic, final year B.A. (Hons.) Fine Art at Trent Polytechnic.

"Basically, my principal motive is to raise an issue or a notion or an argument, and to confront you with it in the hope that it may shake you out of your complacency. Race based exploitation and oppression will not disappear simply because we choose to ignore it. The controllers of western capitalism have far too much of a vested interest in the perpetuation of 'divide and rule' to allow for that. The situation demands an active consciousness raising and collectivisation process and if we have chosen to hijack 'art' as another vehicle in that process, and this hallowed gallery as its temporary parking space, then so be it.

Understand also that we are not racists simply because race remains a factor in our analysis. A dialogue on racism will remain an issue in our struggle as long as its application remains a factor in their (or dare I say your) resistance."

KEITH PIPER 1982

Donald Rodney

Foundation at Bournville School of Art; second year B.A. (Hons) Fine Art, Trent Polytechnic.

What is Black Art?

"The work you shall see is fresh and cutting and black. The colour of our skin is the reason you are here; the colour of our skin is the reason that keeps us together and it is the colour of our skin that has made us produce this work.

TO OUR WHITE READERS:
Through this group we have attempted to show some indication of our idea of being black, being a minority and being used.

I was told that one man's meat is another man's poison, but don't let this poison kill, let it shock you into enlightenment to our cause.

TO OUR BLACK READERS:
I joined this group as a way of continuing the struggle started by the dead and forgotten. This is my contribution albeit small.

Our work is good and the organising team within the group is very professional. We are united and dedicated in our commitment to our work.

I haven't been in the group long; I am in fact the most recent exhibiting member. During this time I have seen the group become a loud voice in the cheer of the Black Art Movement. A powerful approach will see us become stronger and better. Nothing can keep us from our goal."

DONALD G. RODNEY 1983

5 Bhajan Hunjan and Chila Kumari Burman, 'Mash it Up: Chila and Bhajan talk about their art', 1983

In 1981 Bhajan Hunjan and Chila Kumari Burman curated *Four Indian Women Artists* at the Indian Artists (UK) Gallery, London. At the time of the exhibition, Hunjan had recently completed her postgraduate studies at the Slade School of Art, London, and Burman was undertaking her MA in Fine Art there. Although both artists specialized in printmaking at the Slade, the subject matter of their work was quite different. Hunjan explored the expressive use of colour and texture through the depiction of symbolic shapes and natural forms, while Burman's pioneering work actively engaged with contemporary social concerns and the political realities of life faced by people of colour, including economic and class inequality, anti-nuclear protest and police brutality. Despite these differences, what united Hunjan's and Burman's work was a shared desire for more accurate – full, rounded – representations of South Asian women in mainstream British culture. In 1983 Hunjan and Burman were interviewed by the majority-white feminist magazine *Spare Rib*. In their responses reproduced here, each gives an overview of their career to date, outlining their approach to art making and the challenges they faced, as well as the support they received. When we talked in 2022, Hunjan reflected that the question proposing that she existed 'between two cultures' was indicative of the insidious racism she regularly faced; she also suggested that the discussion of her family betrays her own youthful inexperience. Nonetheless, both interviews, in different ways, demonstrate how Hunjan and Burman were driven to challenge gender-based inequality and violence. Burman's statement concludes with a rallying cry, encouraging other women to join the struggle and change the world.

*   *   *

Bhajan Hunjan

Why did you become interested in art?
Coming from a very strict / traditional Indian family it was very important to have an education, to have a degree so that I could marry a man of equal status. My family did not mind what subject the degree was in. I went to art school to be educated, and once I was there I began to find out more about myself, about where I came from and to question myself through my work.

Can you explain exactly what is your idea of art?
I do not start with an idea and see the idea through. I usually give my work a title after I have done it. I use different images to put across different feelings and emotions, which create symbols in my work. One has to be fully aware that a 'symbol' cannot be fully explained or translated – similarly I can only partly explain what my work is about.

In 'Unity', the two shapes in the half left-hand side confront each other, they are related, attracted, yet they are in their own respective spheres – represent female and male. In the middle a spiral-like shape (that is ever-growing, ever-evolving, ever-decaying, unfolding) could represent growth and time. This shape is enclosed by snares, thorns, taboos, restrictions which give it hardly enough air to breathe and survive. On the extreme right an organic structure of growth, death, continuation, sensualness, continues through from top to bottom. It represents nature. In 'Female and Male', the figure of a woman and a man are overshadowed by a thorny, evil-shaped, sharp structure pointing upwards and downwards while in a horizontal position. The snakelike shape within the woman's womb could represent her as a body for reproduction. It is her womb that projects her outwards and inwards. It is the physical medium between her physical inside and the outside. The image of a man exists alongside as part of existence.

It is my search into myself, into my unconscious. I question my dreams when I work as they are an inlet into my unconscious. I feel driven to express myself when I am undergoing emotional crisis personally and especially when it is something to do with women. I feel that I have an emotional outlet, doing what I do makes me think I can solve things.

What was art school like? Did you meet with any racism?
I did my graduate course at Reading University and a post-graduate course at the Slade School of Art in London. I was the only Indian girl on the graduate course. It was very strange and cold in the first two years, I often felt left out. At the time I felt it was due to my shyness. Later on I realised that generally the English are very reserved and cold even within their own society, though there are exceptions. I have a difficulty in explaining my experience of racism, I am ignorant of it directly affecting me, though I can see it in a historical context and understand why it occurs. The nearest I have come to it has been on holiday jobs where I have come across people who have stereotype ideas and false interpretations about immigrants and their way of life. It would help if people had open minds and hearts.

How does your family feel about you studying art? Did they ever oppose you?

They are pleased that I will be able to support myself. My mother comes from a very small village and has undergone many changes in her life. She cannot understand what I do, but is happy for me because she knows I can take care of myself. As far as my father is concerned, his ambition to see all his children educated has been fulfilled. He does see a woman's role as a housewife and bringing up a family. I come from a large family with elder brothers and an elder sister. They normally all see a woman as a housewife, married and with a family, as she is an 'asset' to the reputation and prestige of the family. I can only communicate with them on a certain level. On the whole they are pleased that I can continue working. It's strange, before I started studying art they had a certain idea about what art should be, but now they are more accepting to the idea that art can be what you want it to be.

There is something which I feel is very important to understand with Indian girls who have had a strict upbringing, that is a concept of fear. It is so inbuilt within you that you can never be fully yourself, never let go. You are so paralysed with this fear that you can rarely make a decision for yourself. You are conditioned to always respect and consult Indian elders. For instance, if I were anywhere accompanied by a man (irrespective of my relationship with him), I would be conscious and somehow scared, in case somebody in the community saw me! I have made a conscious effort to conquer this fear in my work. For instance it has taken me a year to come to terms with the image of a naked man. It's like a challenge to myself. Am I being morally wrong and untrue to myself?

Do you feel as if you are between two cultures?

I feel I am between two cultures, yes, and I feel I have every right to be there. I do not know what it feels like to belong to a culture.

I was born and brought up in Kenya, as an 'Asian' in Kenya. I never ever felt I belonged there. When I came to England I never felt the need to belong. I wanted recognition as an individual, I wanted to feel comfortable, within my own community and the other. Talking about two cultures, I must tell you something which happened in a classroom situation.

There was a project for the class to do their own self-portrait. One Indian girl did her self-portrait in which she had blonde hair and blue eyes. It was an incredible and pitiful experience for me. Was it because she wanted the rest to see her as part of them or was it her thriving wish to be accepted as one of them? I wish there was more understanding from other people and just a little more awareness. Some white people do care, so do a very small proportion of teachers in schools, but others don't even try a little.

Chila Kumari Burman

Hiya Sisters . . .

When asked to be interviewed by *Spare Rib*, I thought to myself, 'Well, you ask the questions, and I'll answer after you'. I first started making prints when I was at school. There weren't any facilities, but you could still manage to make mono prints from old spuds or even by inking different parts of your body and then pressing against the paper or screen . . . magic. Right from my early days I was printmaking, early woodblock printing, etching and engraving. They really fascinated me. And at art school there was space to experiment with new ideas.

Me Mum and Dad are traditionally Hindu-Punjabi, and weren't really into the idea of me going away from home, because of what all the relatives and the community would say. But 'cos me dad worked all his life as an ice-cream man and me mum worked hard to bring us up healthy and strong in this strange land, they wanted us to have a good education, 'cos they never had the opportunity to go to school. Me Dad's a brilliant tailor too and a very gentle man – he teaches me about respect. And me mum is a really amazing, strong woman. They're both very loving and caring. There were hassles at home, like when I wanted to bring English friends home, and go out.

There was racism at school and university: comments were passed like, 'you are like curry with a suntan', or 'all you Pakis take our jobs'. There is a helluva lot of ignorance and stupidity. I did have some hassle with some tutors and students. There were of course the difficulties with 'class', which really stood out. So, you see, through my work I'm trying to expose some of these things. It also helps me to understand what is going on in the world. I use different sorts of print techniques. The infinite possibilities intrigue me, it's kinda orgasmic!

Many different thoughts flow into my works; my feelings – political, spiritual, philosophical; women's issues, sexism, racism and the media's con. None of these are developed exclusively. They all interact and change. My work doesn't encompass any rules or regulations. It's about freedom. A lot of my ideas flow from happenings and emotions. Other ideas come from the environment, love, compassion, dear friendships, respect, knowledge and discipline, (that's hard sometimes), and, above all, mostly through living. Being aware and conscious of the women's movement has taught me a lot of what I am doing now.

Some of the most recent stuff, is what you could say social, political, if you want to give it a label, 'cos sometimes art should have a social and political function. The recent stuff comes from within, naturally. It describes what I feel, the desires, fears, suffering and anger as shown in the image, *One Race the Human Race*. The gas mask is used to symbolise war and it's all about anti-nuke stuff.

The images shown are different. Indian women, women under apartheid and as mentioned, anti-nuke stuff. The ideas/issues/

subjects, plus my own culture have determined the content and form. They represent a consciousness and a culture. When I express personal thoughts, I try and create something which is more direct and harmonious. I try to bring about an awareness of what is going on. It sort of reflects the changes the women's movement has attached to the personal in the political world. They both merge. Other ideas come from music, eating, sleeping, thinking, Zen, friends, reading. Miro, Mum and Dad, brothers, Billy, Sean and Peter (Achar, Ashan, Ashok), Ashra and many other sisters, especially Meena.

I don't always use images of men – if I do, I try and subvert them or to put a new perspective on them. It would be good to move towards a demystification of art within the present system. Everyone should be given the space and opportunities to realize their full potential, not just the privileged or those who go through the system.

When asked by *Spare Rib* to define art, I thought well, 'ere goes. First of all I'd like to say that art is an activity, a development of oneself in this mad world. It never seems to be understood, allowed nor appreciated. There's some good stuff around, exciting, in performance, video, film, painting and music. Art is a way of getting in touch with oneself, with the visible world and nature. You could go on forever and ever. But here is a really nice quote from a book called *The Zen of Seeing and Drawing*. Here goes: 'Art is the unspoilt core in everyone, before being choked by schooling, conditioning, and training, until the artist within shrivels up and is forgotten.' Even artists who go to art school can still be damaged by becoming competetive or in a rush towards a personal style, or to be "in". It can be easy to let this happen to you unconsciously. 'You gotta be aware', 'Natural Progression'.

Sona from *Spare Rib* asked me what I felt about being between two cultures. I don't think I am between, I hate that phrase, it's more like beyond two cultures. All this labelling is something the media has conjured up. The media doesn't arf go on about stereotyping us: 'Mash the Media Up'. We have to entangle all this and take control of our lives. Challenge and transcend, transform and reveal these issues – like the imbalance of power relations that exist between men and women, and violence against women. We must do this through whatever medium, films, writing, talking, print, sound, science and living . . . the world would be a better place to live in then.

To other sisters, it ain't easy. We can stand up for our rights. Be strong. The world is full of shit and pollution. Let's clean it up Sisters. Challenge and transform and become aware of what is going on. We are strong and dynamic.

Namesta Benji's

6 John Akomfrah, 'Black Independent Film-making: A statement by the Black Audio Film Collective', 1983

The Black Audio Film Collective formed in 1982 and comprised seven fine art, sociology and psychology students from Portsmouth Polytechnic. Members included John Akomfrah, Reece Auguiste, Eddie George, Lina Gopaul, Avril Johnson, Claire Joseph and Trevor Mathison, with David Lawson joining in 1985. Members came from diverse backgrounds, and the use of the term Black in the Collective's name signalled political allegiance rather than racial specificity. The Collective organized screenings of avant-garde world cinema and created their own films, videos and slide-tapes which addressed the lived experience of African, Caribbean and Asian people in Britain, and globally. In this statement, Akomfrah explores the parameters of Black independent film-making in the context of white, Western cinema. He goes on to identify what the Collective believed should be the priorities of Black independent film-making, namely to challenge racism and racist stereotyping, and the misrepresentation of Black people on film.

* * *

The area of black independent film-making will soon see the growth of a number of workshops established with the specific aim of catering for black film needs. We will also see a growth in the number of films made by members of these workshops. As in any other field of cultural activity and practice such a development calls for collective debate and discussion. Some of the important issues to be raised will be around the relationship between the workshop organisers and participants in the course. The others should obviously be about the nature and structure of the courses themselves.

Prior to this debate, however, is the task of accounting for the specificity of black independent film-making. What, after all, does 'black independent film-making' mean when present film culture is a largely white affair? And does this posture of independence presuppose a radical difference of film orientation? If this is the case how does one work within this difference?

The Black Audio Film Collective has chosen to take up these issues in a very particular way and this is around the question of the 'figuration of ethnicity' in cinema. Our point of entry is around the issue of black representation. The Collective was launched with three principal aims. Firstly, to attempt to look critically at how racist ideas and images of black people are structured and presented as self-evident truths in cinema. What we are interested in here is how these 'self-evident truths' become the conventional pattern through which the black presence in cinema is secured.

Secondly, to develop a 'forum' for disseminating available film techniques within the independent tradition and to assess their pertinence for black cinema. In this respect our interests did not only lie in devising how best to make 'political' films, but also in taking the politics of representation seriously. Such a strategy could take up a number of issues which include emphasising both the form and the content of films, using recent theoretical insights in the practice of film-making.

Thirdly, the strategy was to encourage and emphasise collective practice as a means of extending the boundaries of black film culture. This would mean attempting to de-mystify in our film practice the process of film production; it would also involve collapsing the distinction between 'audience' and 'producer'. In this ethereal world film-maker equals active agent and audience usually equals passive consumers of a predetermined product. We have decided to reject such a view in our practice.

Underlying these aims are a number of assumptions about what we consider the present priorities of independent film-making should be. These assumptions are based on our recognition of certain significant achievements in the analysis of race and the media. It is now widely accepted that the media play a crucial role in the production and reproduction of 'common-sense assumptions' and we know that race and racist ideologies figure prominently in these assumptions. The point now is to realise the implications of these insights in creating a genuinely collective black film culture.

Such a programme is also connected with our awareness of the need to go beyond certain present assumptions about the task of black film-making. We recognise that the history of blacks in films reads as a legacy of stereotypes and we take the view that such stereotypes, both in mainstream and independent cinema, should be critically evaluated. This can be connected to a number of things that we want to do. We not only want to examine how black culture is mis-represented in film, but also how its apparent transparency is given a 'realism' in film. It is an attempt to isolate and render intelligible the images and statements which converge to represent black culture in cinema. The search is not for '*the* authentic image' but for an understanding of the diverse codes and strategies of representation.

It could be argued that all this is stale water under a decaying bridge and that we know all this stuff already and that black film-makers already accept their responsibility and are aware of these problems. There is a lot of truth in this. Others may say that as long as we are making films and gaining exposure of our work we are keeping black film culture alive.

To place our discussion in a relevant and meaningful context the Black Audio/Film Collective in conjunction with Four Corners cinema will be organising a number of screenings to run with the Colin Roach photography exhibition at Camerawork Gallery.

The series of films and discussion will run under the title of *Cinema and Black Representation* and will deal specifically with the complexity of black portrayal in films. The main aim here is to see how film can contain 'information' on race, nationality and 'ethnicity' with (Presence) or without (Absence) black people in films. With this in mind we hope to cover a number of films and themes ranging from prison movies like *Scum* to Hollywood social criticism films like *Imitation of Life*. What we will be attempting will not be to push all the films into one category of racist films but rather attempting to examine what specific responses these films make to the question of race and ethnicity.

In the end we realise that questions of black representation are not simply those of film criticism but inevitably of film-making. These issues need to be taken up on both fronts. With this in mind we are also making preparations with the GLC Ethnic Minorities' Unit and the Arts and Recreation Committee to organise a number of courses on some of the themes outlined in this article. Neither the dates for the screenings nor film courses have been finalised – both will be advertised when they are.

I am indebted to 'The Core' – Eddie George, Lina Gopaul, Claire Joseph, Trevor Mathison – for discussion which led to this transcription.

7 Imruh Bakari, 'Open Art: The First Open Exhibition of Contemporary Black Art in Britain, organised by Creation for Liberation', 1983

Creation for Liberation was the cultural arm of the Brixton-based Race Today Collective. The Collective, whose members included Farrukh Dhondy, Leila Hassan, Darcus Howe and Linton Kwesi Johnson, published the magazine *Race Today* which became a prominent voice in anti-racism campaigns throughout the 1970s and 1980s. The press release for the 1983 open exhibition of Black art, which ran from 20 to 30 July, explained that the show sought to champion the work of all Black artists – whether trained or self-taught – whose work expressed the dynamism, vibrancy and innovation of Black people. The Collective regarded cultural events, including art exhibitions, as important contributions in the struggle to break free of the constraints placed upon Black people by the existing political order. In this review, film-maker Imruh Bakari discusses the range of work on display, highlighting the work of painters Denzil Forrester and Thomas Joseph, now known as Tam Joseph. Significantly, Bakari discusses Joseph's painting, *Has Anyone Seen Tony Berbeck?*, which addresses the life and death of Anthony Berbeck, who, having survived the New Cross fire in 1981, committed suicide on 9 July 1983.

* * *

In Brixton, St. Matthews Meeting Place is an elephantine structure marooned on an oval island in the midst of a sea of traffic. Once a church, it has in more recent times been given a new lease of life as a multi-purpose community centre. This was the venue for The First Open Exhibition of Contemporary Black Art in Britain organised by Creation For Liberation.

Black artists were generally asked to submit their work which was then put into the exhibition without any specific selection process or value judgement. This 'open' approach brought some pleasant surprises, and the exhibition assumed a rare and unique quality which was not missed by the many visitors. Immediately apparent was the diversity of styles, influences and emphases. The overall level of artistic excellence was high although expressed at varying levels of maturity.

The exhibition began outside of the building. For its duration one side of St. Matthews Meeting Place was camouflaged with sheets of corrugated iron. An awesome sight to the casual passerby, but on reflection, an appropriate symbol of the environment within which the artists taking part in the exhibition have been working.

For people in the Third World, corrugated iron is a familiar sight. As a result of the urban uprisings experienced in places like Brixton not long ago, corrugated iron has gained significance as a symbol of some aspects of the Black condition in Britain. At this exhibition, according to the programme notes, the pieces which hung on the front of the building were meant to 'depict the idea of corrugated iron being blown away . . .' A significant thought after having seen the exhibits.

The main exhibition was most definitely an inspiring experience. It provoked much reflection and, as the Creation For Liberation forum on 27 July proved, much heated debate.

What is Black Art? Who are Black Artists? What should be their role? . . . The questions of the moment seemed to be vividly expressed in a work by Thomas Joseph titled *Ei! Who Are You?* This is a piece made up of bits of scrap iron welded together. It assumed an angular mask-like form. It stood upright with a stoic presence at the exhibition entrance.

In an exhibition such as this, how can these questions be resolved? What comparison can be made between Joseph's piece and the work of textile designer, Leslee Wills, for example? Maybe the clues are to be found in the interpretation of names like 'Creation For Liberation' and 'Art for Uhuru' (another organisation of black artists in Britain) and the implications which become apparent when related to the individual artist, their work, the black community and British society as a whole.

It is important to note that all the artists participating in the exhibition have worked almost entirely in Britain. Some are 'self-taught', but the majority have had formal art tuition. Their works however, all have a distinct quality of authenticity and vibrant self-expression. As well as outstanding individual exhibits, there are artists whose work have a style and a feel which reflects a certain maturity.

Thomas Joseph is one such. Apart from *Ei! Who Are You?* his canvasses *Spirit of Carnival* and *Has anyone seen Tony Berbeck?* are forceful political statements. *Spirit of Carnival* is a bare canvass depicting a masquerade ringed with police officers and a snarling dog straining on its leash. The message is clear.

Denzil Forrester's *Orange Dub*, *At The Control* and *Dub Echoes* depicts the Blues Dance and Sound System elements of black youth culture. Forrester uses images of their intimate, secluded and energised environment contrasted by the imposing oppressive exterior to explore the urban predicament.

Johney Ohene's work has a spatial quality. His figures are placed in masses of sharply contrasting colours. The effect is one of understatement and even parody.

For sheer evocative quality it is worth noting the works of Susan

McFarlane (*Reflect* and *African Woman*), Muemue Jiyane (*Jazz Players, Man Reading Newspaper, Township Scene*), Shaheen Merali (*Nataraj For Shiva, Water Ceremony, Satna Market Place*), and Errol Lloyd's *Portrait of Joan Ann*.

The exhibition firmly establishes the presence of a new and dynamic generation of black artists in Britain (with the exception of Errol Lloyd and Dam X who are of the older generation – just about). Of course many questions provoked by the exhibition works have not been answered and many contradictions have been highlighted in the continuing debates. These issues cannot be resolved by contrivances. The development of black art in Britain, or put another way, the works of black artists seem tied to the development of the black community.

It seems desirable that similar open exhibitions should take place periodically in the future.

8 Extracts from Lubaina Himid (ed.), *5 Black Women: Exhibition of Drawings, Paintings and Sculpture*, 1983

In September 1983, *5 Black Women: Exhibition of Drawings, Paintings and Sculpture* curated by artist Lubaina Himid opened at the Africa Centre in Covent Garden, London. The contributors to the exhibition were all Black women living in Britain: Sonia Boyce (born in the UK), Lubaina Himid (born in Tanzania), Claudette Johnson (born in the UK), Houria Niati (born in Algeria) and Veronica Ryan (born in Montserrat). This exhibition was the first major all-women show to be staged at the Africa Centre, and Himid sought to champion the work of each artist, individually. She recognized that while strength could be generated and harnessed by working collectively, each artist also worked in their own individual ways, and conveyed messages differently according to the materials that they used. Rather than select an exhibition in which each work conformed to a particular style, theme or political position, Himid presented the work of each artist in its own right. As such, the exhibition sought to demonstrate both the varying and shared concerns of Black women. A small photocopied pamphlet accompanied the show that included the poem by Houria Niati and the short statement by Claudette Johnson which are reproduced here. In 1987 Lubaina Himid reflected on the reception of this exhibition in her essay 'We Will Be' (see Chapter 21).

What is Black Art?

*   *   *

The greasy and dark streets where the intoxicated hearts vanish
into the slack magics of the atomic world
Mysterious island
Forbidden city which the keys are given up to the geometric holes
that the passer-by leave lonely and mysterious
Crazy side
Undecided dreams inadequate dreams
A/political dreams sensual dreams
Flexible irritations of the keeps that dominate the uncertain
powers

The multitude of the dried up fountains
The cascades waterless where my feet find neither the bottom
nor the freshness
Crazy side
The scream rises and gets lost in the malefic square of the golden
universes
The scream explodes and meets the barrels
The scream recoils into the inscrutable entrails
It's echo rejoins the silence of the closed doors
The upsetting scream of the rocks
The refusal
The nails of the TORTURE

HOURIA NIATI

MUCH ART IS NOT EASY OR ACCESSIBLE. THE ART
OF BLACK WOMEN HAS BEEN BURIED, HIDDEN AND
DISGUISED.

BURIED: BENEATH A DELUGE OF WESTERN IMAGES
AND IDEAS THAT STIFLE ITS TRUTH.

Extracts from Lubaina Himid (ed.), *5 Black Women*, 1983

HIDDEN: BY A HIERARCHY OF DEFINITIONS THAT HOLD IT PINNED AND CAGED WITHIN THEIR BARBS OF "PRIMITIVE, NAIVE, GAUDY, ETHNIC".

DISGUISED: BY THE GARBLED MISREPRESENTATIONS OFFERED AS UNDERSTANDING BY CRITICS, WHO HAVE STEPPED OVER IT IN THE STREET, OR BRUSHED IT, AS A FLY, FROM THEIR DESKS, WITH MINDS TOO CLOSED AND SMALL TO FATHOM ITS DEPTHS.

THIS ART HAS NO ONE FORM. THE VEHICLES OF EXPRESSION ARE BOUNDLESS. IT CANNOT, WILL NOT BE CONTAINED WITHIN THE COLD FORMALITIES OF GALLERIES, CONCERT HALLS, BOOK COVERS. THE HISTORY AND STRUGGLES OF BLACK WOMEN ARE CONDENSED AND CONTINUED IN OUR WORK.

SOUGHT OR DENIED, RECOGNISED OR IGNORED, BLACK WOMEN'S ART CONTINUES AND EVOLVES . . . .

. . . . FOR THOSE WHO HAVE EYES TO SEE IT.

CLAUDETTE JOHNSON

9 OBAALA (Organisation for Black Arts Advancement and Leisure Activities), *The Organisation* and *A Statement on Black-Art & the Gallery*, 1983

The Black-Art Gallery opened in Finsbury Park, North London in September 1983. Run by OBAALA, the Organisation for Black Arts Advancement and Leisure Activities, it had a specific remit to exhibit the work of artists of African descent. The gallery's founders, Shakka Dedi and Eve-I Kadeena, championed a broad range of creative activities, and 'art' was understood to include not only painting, sculpture and photography, but also textiles, batik, weaving, and other forms of creative practice. The catalogue for the gallery's first exhibition, *Heart in Exile*, included an introduction to OBAALA and the organisation's manifesto, which presented its definition of 'Black-Art', reproduced here. Dedi was director of the gallery from 1982 until 1990. During its period of operation, the gallery staged numerous solo shows, including those by Sonia Boyce, Eddie Chambers, Donald Rodney, Maud Sulter and Leslee Wills, as well as important themed group shows such as *Craftwork?*, *Starring Mummy & Daddy*, *Heroes & Heroines* and *From Generation to Generation (The Installation)*. These exhibitions were supported by educational activities with local schools, and an annual Summer Arts School for 6–16-year-olds was taught by practising artists. The OBAALA Poetry Theatre gave voice to leading spoken-word artists of the era, such as Jean Breeze, Oku Onoura, Afrikan Dawn, Sweet Honey in The Rock and Anum Iyapo, who were all deemed to be performers of Black-Art. The gallery received its core funding from Islington Borough Council, and in September 1992 the Council's Leisure Services Committee voted for the immediate withdrawal of its grant. Despite a campaign to overturn the Council's decision, the recently renamed Black Art Gallery closed shortly thereafter.

* * *

OBAALA – THE ORGANISATION

OBAALA, the Organisation for Black Arts Advancement and Leisure Activities, has been founded to promote Black art in all areas and to encourage its greater appreciation, greater participation and higher regard within British society.

For too long, Afrikan-Caribbean Lifestyles and traditions have been regarded merely as a sub-culture – just another 'exotic' commodity to be given spasmodic bouts of recognition and praise. OBAALA will seek to rectify this by providing a forum for the expression of Afrikan arts in all its rich and varied forms. OBAALA regards all areas of creativity, whether it be literature, dance, visual art, drama or music as having an important and worthy function in our community.

The organisation will be presenting various activities such as concerts, film shows, workshops, recitals, dance performances and festivals, with the aim of giving talented and little known artists opportunities to perform before audiences which they might not otherwise have reached.

On 22nd January this year, OBAALA staged a highly successful evening of 'Afrikan Roots Expression' at Islington Town Hall in London. In this show, OBAALA brought together an Afro-Caribbean dance group 'Yaa Asantewa', who performed traditional

Ghanaian dances; the Roots poets Benjamin Zephaniah, Frederick Williams, Anum Iyapo and the Sounds of Simba, and Shakka Dedi. James Danton, the solo saxophonist, and the band 'Tribesman', also provided musical vibrations. In contrast to Yaa Asantewa, Steppaz Unlimited, a new group of young reggae dancers formed with OBAALA's guidance made their first inspired stage performance. This show was an example of the type of future events which OBAALA will be organising.

The Black-Art Gallery has been OBAALA's most notable achievement to date, and this first exhibition, 'Heart in Exile', marks the first fruit of much hard work, perseverance and faith.

It is our aim to provide the support and encouragement so badly needed by Black artists, not only in the U.K., but also internationally, and are continually on the look-out for both traditional, and new and original forms of expression.

OBAALA are presently engaged in the provision of an educational resource unit, and the compiling of a National Register of Artists and Craftpersons. With the continued support of the community and of bodies such as the GLC, GLAA, Islington Council, and the CRE – support which we gratefully acknowledge, and through our own fund-raising efforts, OBAALA intends to achieve its goal of assisting the dynamic development of Black creative expression, and to ensure its accessibility and relevance to both the Black and wider community.

A STATEMENT ON BLACK-ART & THE GALLERY

As the name of the gallery makes clear, OBAALA intends to provide a location where the majority of work exhibited will be of a particular type.

In the main, the exhibits will have a criteria applied to them which is based not simply on the imagery alone but equally on the consciousness and cultural identity behind the imagery.

We believe that Black-Art is born and created out of a consciousness based upon experience of what it means to be an Afrikan descendant wherever in the world we are. 'Black' in our context means all those of Afrikan descent: 'Art', – the creative expression of the Black person or group based on historical and contemporary experience.

Black-Art should provide an historical document of local and international Black experience. It should educate by perpetuating traditional art forms and by evolving and adapting contemporary art forms to suit new experiences and environments. It is essential that Black artists aim to make their art 'popular', – that is expression that the wide community can recognise and understand. We also believe that artistic creativity should extend itself to functional and common usage artifacts (eg, household furniture and artifacts).

Overall honesty should be the mark of Black-Art. Therefore, it cannot afford to be elitist or pretentious. We believe that Black-Art can, should and will play a very important role in community education and positive development, and that it is by having their work recognised by the general community that Black artists draw their strength. OBAALA exists therefore, to stimulate and implement discussion and activity which will bring about the desired close relationship between consciousness, art and positive community development.

OBAALA COMMITTEE

THE BLACK-ART GALLERY – IT'S DEVELOPMENT

The Black-Art Gallery is now a reality. On Friday 2nd September 1983, the premises housing the gallery and its supporting projects, were spiritually blessed in a traditional Afrikan Blessing Ceremony, by the Brothers Koka and Shange. Brother Shange, who is a direct descendant of Shaka, the great Zulu warrior, was warmly received by OBAALA members, exhibiting artists, and guests from the Black community – on what was an historic occasion.

Sunday 4th September saw the Public Opening of the gallery. The Opening ceremony was performed by Sister Mollie Hunte, and was attended by some three hundred people.

The original idea for the gallery was developed in 1981, by Shakka Dedi and Eve-I Kadeena. It came about as a response to the scarcity of space and lack of opportunities for Black artists to exhibit their work. It was recognised that there were very few venues where work by Black artists could be exhibited on a regular basis. The few venues that did exist, such as the Commonwealth Institute, Africa Centre, and at one time, the Keskidee Centre, were not well situated or suited to attract the audiences that many Black artists wished their work to reach. Some artists had tried to get their work exhibited in the established commercial art galleries, – which are dominated by white, private enterprise. Owners of these establishments argue that they can only handle work that is commercially viable, and that the work produced by Black artists does not fall into this category. When they do display any interest, it is only in the stereotypical images of what they expect and believe Black art to be – i.e. palm trees, beaches, smiling fruit-women, etc. Others, aware of the way in which British society views Afrikan peoples and their culture, spared themselves the frustrations of seeking exhibition space in the private gallery arena.

This lack of exhibiting venues and opportunities had the effect of stifling artistic expression – thus, preventing its development and progress. Many artists and potential artists ceased to produce work, – having little motivation in this dead-end situation. OBAALA intends The Black-Art Gallery to act as a catalyst, and provide an incentive for artists to continue and to take up producing work.

Another important aspect involved in the creation of The

Black-Art Gallery was the situation regarding the generation of Black youth and adults, who had either been born or brought up in Britain, and as a consequence of inadequacies in the British school system, knew little about their immediate cultural backgrounds, or of their historical past as Afrikan-Caribbean peoples. A major aim of the gallery is to provide a physical environment in which Black people – particularly the young, can learn about and gain a greater understanding of their artistic and cultural heritage, and to identify themselves with this inheritance. The gallery will enable people to see, and to perhaps possess works of art, depicting images of themselves, and which reflect their lifestyles and culture. Further, society at large will be better able to learn about Black art and culture, and to appreciate its intrinsic value, with the aim of redefining the negative stereotype images of Afrikan-Caribbean cultures which have existed in the West.

Importantly, the idea for The Black-Art Gallery evolved not simply as a response – albeit a positive one to a negative situation. It arose too out of the conscious recognition that Black people need to establish institutions and structures in Britain, which they are seen to administer and control – in order to best suit the needs and demands of the community.

The establishment of the Black-Art gallery seemed a logical development. Over the last twenty years, there had been numerous attempts by members of the community to set up permanent exhibition space for Black artists. For a number of reasons, such as lack of experience, lack of support, and perhaps more importantly, lack of finance, these attempts amounted to little in terms of lasting impact or significance.

After drafting up the main elements of the proposed project, a small-scale, local survey was conducted amongst members of Islington's Black community, – in the area where the gallery was to be situated. The response was very encouraging. Full details of the project were then presented to Islington Council, in June 1982, and it was at this time, that the Organisation for Black Arts Advancement and Leisure Activities was formed. The people chosen to make up the OBAALA committee were already active members of the Black community. They brought together a variety of backgrounds, knowledge and skills necessary to carry out the aims of OBAALA and to continue its development as an effective organisation in the field of Black arts advancement. The OBAALA committee now consists of the following members; Lorna Chin, Shakka Dedi, Beverly Francis, Anum Iyapo, Michael Jess, Eve-I Kadeena, Joel Woodley.

10 Rohan Jayasekera, 'Art Under Attack', 1985

In February 1985, the Arts and Recreation Committee of the Greater London Council allocated funds for a large-scale public art programme, as part of the Council's anti-racism initiative; the project became known as the *Anti-Racist Mural Project*. Four major murals were commissioned, and created in Notting Hill, Brixton, Southall and London's East End – all areas that have an historic Black population and/or that had experienced contemporary racist violence. The murals were intended to provide a record of past struggle, and offer visions for the future. Eight artists, working in pairs, were commissioned: Shanti Panchal and Dushka Ahmed; Keith Piper and Chila Kumari Burman; Gavin Jantjes and Tam Joseph; and Lubaina Himid and Simone Alexander. In this report, journalist Rohan Jayasekera, who was then working as a press officer for the ill-fated Roundhouse Black Arts Centre in Camden Town, gives an overview of the evolution and reception of the mural by Panchal and Ahmed.

*　　*　　*

"This mural does much more than speak of the struggle against racism, it holds out a promise of hope and harmony." Artist Shanti Panchal talking about his work in Tower Hamlets, the second of four street murals commissioned by the GLC's Anti-Racist Mural Project 1985.

Like the other three it was designed as a living testimony to the black community's contribution to London life; but the finished article in Tower Hamlets testifies to much more.

In Tower Hamlets the art itself is under racist attack, threatened, yet proud, if sometimes a little fearful, just like the community that gave it birth.

Shanti sketched six grim skinheads into the mural's original design, yet they were whitewashed out on the final version. The people feared the skins' nameless models would return with hammers and spray cans and repeat an earlier attack on the Lowood Street wall painting.

On the draft sketches Shanti depicted the thugs smashing at the door of a Bengali family. On the finished mural they are replaced by the painted figure of a bland, indifferent white man.

The brilliant Panchal and his talented assistant artist Dushka Ahmad had their own ideas, but by its brief this was art by consensus – artistry approved by public meetings and vetted by a whole community. There was too much at risk, they said. Each brushstroke was the product of too much suffering, too much experience, to be lost in a moment's mindless hate.

An artistic triumph that lasts a day before a thug smears it with excrable graffiti is no kind of triumph.

Thus the skinheads were painted out, and while the aforementioned bland, indifferent white man is one reality, another, perhaps more pervasive reality was pushed behind the scenes.

But what has been left unsaid, in fact says much about the community that created the mural.

Fearful, threatened and under attack, so too is that community's art. Art reflecting life.

"I got as many people, especially the young ones, to join in, painting flat areas of colour," said Shanti. "That way it became their project as well. If it's theirs, they will look after it."

Shanti, born in Gujarat 34 years ago, studied in Bombay. He

claimed first class honours right through his studies finishing as a fellowship award winner in 1976 and a lecturer up to 1978.

Then a British Council scholarship brough him to London where he now lives and works. Last year he added the Countess Enid Driscoll-Spalletti Memorial Prize to his already lengthy roll of honours.

Shanti has exhibited across Britain, Europe and India and has been feted at dozens of top art galleries. And like many Asians living in London, Shanti has first hand experience of racial harassment and attack.

So Shanti, clearly qualified for the job in many ways, was swiftly recruited by GLC Race Equality Unit head Parminder Vir to join their Anti-Racist Mural Project.

He started work in February under project co-ordinator Sheila Seepersaud-Jones. She saw a project that would have taken anyone else a year completed in six months despite the vandalism.

Assisted by 23 year old Dushka Ahmad, a London born ex-Chelsea School of Art student, Shanti studied photos, documents, newspaper articles, then talked to the people.

They talked and talked, listened and understood. Then there were the public meetings, the debates, the revised designs, the deadlines, the 18 hour days.

"Would I do it again?" muses Dushka. A definite yes. She was one of four new black talents matched with experienced artists like Shanti specially for the mural projects.

The point of including her in on the project, she said, was to expand her knowledge and experience. She thought it had.

The mural is painted on the east facing wall of a former Victorian school turned community centre in Lowood Street, and BBC TV cameras were there for a September reception to celebrate its completion.

Special guest Ken Little, chair of the GLC's Ethnic Arts

Sub-Committee, echoed the words of GLC Arts and Recreation Committee chair Peter Pitt: "These murals will provide a living testimony to all Londoners of the multi racial composition of the capital city and the contributions made by the black and ethnic minority communities."

Then Sheila Seepersaud-Jones, organiser of the well attended reception, laid on Indian dishes and dances for the audience – the members of the community who in various ways shared in its creation.

After the speeches, the dancing and the dishes, the community went outside and looked on their work. Children played in the yard under Shanti and Dushka's vibrant depiction of a people living with hate and fear.

A wall mural is as strong as bricks, mortar and concrete. Yet each person looked on it as if it was as fragile as gossamer, as though tomorrow it would be gone, blown away by a single puff from a spray can.

But what ever happens to the art, the artists and their community will go on.

11 Colin Prescod, 'Black Artists/White Institutions', 1985

Colin Prescod is a British sociologist, film-maker and cultural activist. In November 1985 he was the keynote speaker at the conference *Black Artists/White Institutions*, organized by the Race Equality Unit of the Greater London Council. The conference sought to address the role of mainstream, publicly funded arts institutions in the development and support of 'Black art'. The organizers recognized that there was a racial imbalance within mainstream organizations, both in terms of which artists were offered opportunities to exhibit or perform, but also with regard to the diversity of those employed within those organizations. The conference sought to enhance awareness of Black artists amongst white directors, managers and administrators, while also identifying strategies for promoting Black participation at all levels within the arts sector. In his speech, Prescod addresses the ways Black artists might engage with mainstream institutions whilst outlining the ways dominant culture is based upon racist ideologies. Prescod concludes with some thoughts on the ways Black art might be harnessed as not simply a record of historical injustice or act of contemporary resistance but how it might also be regarded as an expression of a radical and creative culture.

* * *

What's on the agenda of a conference in which Black artists confront white institutions? There are, of course, the obvious points of negotiation – (i) that there should be greater access for the work of Black artists to be on public display and on the major stages, (ii) that there should be more Black artists working in the major companies, and as directors and planners in the executive of major art bodies, (iii) that there should be properly funded opportunities for apprentices and raw talent out of our communities, (iv) that there should be funding support for 'independent' Black arts. And the conference will doubtless discuss ways of establishing networks to press on and to monitor on all these fronts.

But I want to suggest that if Black artists are not to be easily compromised in all these negotiations, they must clarify the basis on which they will negotiate. What 'line' will Black artists take, if they are not to be compromised by the culture of 'equal opportunities' masquerading as the answer to Black demands? I want to talk then about something that artists are notoriously loathe to discuss – although less so people who call themselves Black artists. I want to talk about the political perspective that sets one of the tones of the Black artists' confrontation with white institutions.

BLACK AND WHITE

In order to do this we must remind ourselves of some basics. The first is, that Black and white, as they are used in the title of this conference, are not natural colours. In fact they exist only in relation to each other. And I want to talk about this, to see what it implies for this conference.

By Black I think we must mean to refer to Black and Third World people. And by Black I think we must mean to refer to a political colour, and not a skin colour. Black, then, is the colour of an historical experience – of racist oppression and exploitation, and of resistance and survival. (Just so white is evidently not a skin colour, but the colour of an institutionalised racism, and of those who work for it and benefit from it.) So I want to argue that the Black artist cannot be an artist who just happens to be Black-skinned – but someone whose artistic expression or imagination is delivered out of Blackness, out of the Black experience. The black artist is, in this sense, a commissioned artist! And I want to argue further that the Black artist in Britain today has a very specific commission – kind of an imperative.

In our time the grand project to which Black artists in Britain must make a specific contribution might be called a cultural awakening 'out of the ghettoes'. And I want to suggest that *all* activists and organizations for Black liberation in Britain must face up to this challenging, difficult and new imperative of Black struggle in the 1980s.

The history that brings us to this moment is well known. From the colonies in Asia and the Caribbean, out of populations that were even then, in the 1950s and 1960s, struggling for 'independence', came hundreds of thousands of ambitious Black workers. Ambitious, not for themselves directly, more so for their children. By the 1970s the children had begun to become young adults, and it was this 'Black youth' which first led the call 'out of the ghettoes'. And Black youth have been making that call, non-stop, (to put dates to it) from 1975 to the present, 1985. (British politicians, recently, have been crying shame and condemning Botha's TV and press bans on news of Black uprisings in Azania – yet the British state has organised, and succeeded in large part, since 1981 (indeed since 1975) in doing exactly this with regard to the 10-year long rebellion of Black youth and their communities in Britain).

THE YOUTH

The youth could see, and were saying, from the 1970s, that state schools were failing to serve them properly, and that the jobs they were being offered were fewer and fewer, impossibly low-paid, and came with intolerable conditions. They were saying that their lives on the streets and in their clubs, and more and more even in their homes were lives of terror (harassed by the police, hounded into courts, criminalised when they defended themselves against racialist attacks). They could see that they had precious little cover or immediate hope coming to them from their elders (their beleaguered parents; the struggling existing community organizations; the authorities; the big politicians). And most of all they were the first, 'the youth', to point out that in as much as all this was happening to them it was happening to us all – and that sooner or later we'd all see the direct truth of this.

And because no-one outside of the ghetto would understand or listen, while no-one inside the ghetto could suggest real hope – they screamed their protest, they rioted. They wanted 'out of the ghettoes'.

THE GHETTO

The ghetto, then, is not merely an urban-geographical location. It is an economic, political, legal and ideological domain. In the ghetto, economically, we are considered to be the workers who work less and less, in poorly paid jobs; who suffer the most massive unemployment, some say never-employment, and we suffer, therefore, poverty and corruptibility in a wage-money economy. In the ghetto, politically, we are restricted, by a numbers-game, to powerlessness in the legitimised power games. In the ghetto, juridically, we are restricted from appeal and justice in a legal system that defines us as people with suspicious rights to citizenship, and as people with doubtful rights to protection under the law; and as people against whom the agents of the law must be given a free hand, since, *by our very presence*, we can constitute a threat to law and order. In the ghetto, ideologically, we are the people who make it necessary for Britain to become more and more a police-state – because we *will* insist on rejecting the rôles and the statuses given to us. We will insist on striking back when we are struck. (Some sociologists might say – in the "ghetto" we are "organised".) And here's the twist – the white institutions have a confusing and tricky way of restricting the ghetto. They can be downright repressive, or they can be liberally tolerant – and from where we stand, those positions work hand in glove.

So, in the economic institutions, the genetic racists say that we are more unemployed because we are culturally 'unemployable'. (We lack discipline, brains, morality and responsibility.) The liberal racists on the other hand, offer us job-training schemes to nowhere, and ghetto leisure centres, and a few 'equal opportunities' jobs in the existing unequal scheme of things, hoping that this will compromise and so quieten the rest. And, maybe more of us could come to be like the Black Asian shopkeeper class!? In the political institutions, the white supremacists say that we are a minority, and that it's not our country anyway, so we'd better accept the will and dictate of the majority. While the social democrats say that we may have a cause, *but* we are too impatient for political change, and must work more slowly through the well-tried, existing political set-up – through the parties, colourlessly if possible!

In the law and order institutions, the authoritarian racists say that we have a tendency to be criminals and possibly should be arrested before we commit the crimes rather than after. While the liberal racists acknowledge our complaints against the courts and police (there *are* records after all), *but* as principled supporters of the rule of law, they will denounce our acts of challenge and resistance to unjust courts and illegal policing as *criminal*!

In the ideological institutions, the social scientific racists say that we come from uncivilised cultures and so lack proper respect for authority and civilised traditions – and possibly need short, sharp shocks to humble us to reality. While the liberal racists sympathise with our predicament as culturally destabilised, ex-colonised, ex-slaves and coolies, new arrivants making difficult adjustments – with perhaps a little too much suspicion and paranoia though – and they push varieties of multi-cultural programmes for the dissolution of our 'differences'. We must beware the liberals.

IMAGINATION

The first act 'out of the ghettoes' must be an "act of the imagination" then. It must be to turn the understanding or the meaning of *how* and *why* we are restricted to the ghetto. In this turning over of our experience – from the economic ghetto, we've come to see that full-employment since the "technological revolution" is in fact a thing of the past, for all workers, Black and white – and this is a startling new feature of society. From the political ghetto, we've come to realise that when we are co-opted, through 'equal opportunities' for Blacks, women and working class people, into the existing institutions – this is in large part opportunity to become part of the problem and not of the solution. From the ghetto of injustice, we've come to see that the law we live under (the Police Powers Act, the Nationality Act, the Industrial Relations legislation, the proposed Public Order legislation, for instance) is increasingly law against the people, all the people. From the ideological ghetto where the white institutions define what we are – we've come to know that although we do indeed have specific cultural practices, we are not a people apart from the white imperialist centres, since we've participated directly in the last 400 years or more of making the rich but very unequal contemporary world system. And we know that merely acknowledging the existence of many cultures without combatting the sophisticated barbarity of the dominant culture will change nothing fundamentally.

These are the plain truths of Black resistance culture – and they are not destructive but creative truths. They reach out to touch all the people.

Now it is from this creative, resistance culture that the Black artists in Britain get their imperative – their commission. These acts of the imagination – of truth – which are the first step in escaping or turning the trick on the white institutions, make artists of us all. And these acts of imagination connect the Black community to its specialist artists, and connect Black artists to their communities.

*"The artist, like any other individual, intellectual or otherwise, belongs to the community, not the community to the artist. And what the artist conveys is not so much of her or his personal experience of truth as the collective vision of a society of which the artist is part, expressed not in terms private to the artist and her or his peers, but in familiar language – or in symbols, the common language of truth" A. Sivanandan, 'The Liberation of the Black intellectual'**

THE "COMMISSION"

My point is then, that if the Black artist is to deliver on this commission, the artist's mass community requires (a) that the Black artist must avoid the diversions of self-indulgent individualism; (b) that the basis on which the Black artist challenges the status quo is the authority of the Black experience; (c) that the Black artist's expressions of the imagination are necessarily and powerfully constrained historically and contemporarily by this experience (unless that artist pretends to colourlessness); (d) that the Black artist must avoid being co-opted by the white institutions in the comfortable 'folk art' or the colourful 'ghetto art', or the exotic 'ethnic art' bags. And this is the challenge that Black artists bring to the white institutions (and not just to the white *art* institutions). And this is the position from which they negotiate.

* From A. Sivanandan, 'The Liberation of the Black Intellectual' in *A Different Hunger*, London: Pluto Press, 1982.

What is Black Art?

Those who call themselves Black artists have recruited themselves to be specialist workers or activists on the cultural terrain – where Black culture and its imaginative expression meets white culture. Here cultural actions, if they are Black, are acts of record, of resistance, and of vision, all at once. As matters of record, they are acts in and of the whole history of the Black and Third World experience. As resistance, they are acts against the arrogance, elitism, and exploitation of racism and Imperialism, in art as elsewhere. And as acts of vision they are acts of imagination for the liberation of all – Black and white – from the domination of white institutions. Acts out of Blackness, out of the bantustans, out of the colonies – acts out of the ghettoes.

And so, if the title 'Black artists' is to mean anything in this conference, it cannot be crudely separatist and narrowly culturalist. It should be used to signify an intention to let loose Blackness out of the ghettoes – to turn on Blackness in the Black and the white masses. To work from this perspective, far from being a limitation for the Black artists, is to be given licence to practice truly radical and creative arts.

12 Extracts from Lubaina Himid (ed.), *The Thin Black Line*, 1985

The Thin Black Line was an exhibition curated by Lubaina Himid at the Institute of Contemporary Arts (ICA), London, and staged between 15 November 1985 and 26 January 1986. Following protracted negotiations, Himid was allocated the concourse corridor and one gallery space for her exhibition of contemporary Black women artists. The exhibition aimed to present an expansive collection of artists working in painting, photography, sculpture and installation, and included work by Brenda Agard, Chila Kumari Burman, Claudette Johnson, Ingrid Pollard, Jennifer Comrie, Lubaina Himid, Marlene Smith, Maud Sulter, Sonia Boyce, Sutapa Biswas and Veronica Ryan. The title of the exhibition knowingly acknowledges the way in which Black women are marginalized to liminal spaces within arts institutions. The exhibition quickly became a significant moment in histories of the representation of Black women artists. Himid's preface and statements by Agard, Comrie and Smith are reproduced here from the exhibition's catalogue.

*   *   *

PREFACE

All eleven artists in this exhibition are concerned with the politics and realities of being Black Women. We will debate upon how and why we differ in our creative expression of these realities. Our methods vary individually from satire to story telling, from timely vengeance to careful analysis, from calls to arms to the smashing of stereotypes. We are claiming what is ours and making ourselves visible. We are eleven of the hundreds of creative Black Women in Britain. We are here to stay.

LUBAINA HIMID

BRENDA AGARD

I first want to draw our attention to the documentation of the black image, believing that we as black people of African origin document wherever possible and by whatever means ourselves.

Perhaps one of the most important documents to have come out in recent times, after five years of dedication to the work, has been a publication entitled *Heart of the Race* and I quote – *"Using history and analysis as well as interviews, this powerful book describes the black women's celebration of their culture and their struggle to create a new social order in this country"*

I too am able to draw on the designs of my history and in turn to understand where I myself am coming from.

Understanding that Western Society's stereotyped images of us are how they believe we are – not how we believe we are.

Photography as a means of documentation and recording has been taken on board by a number of black photographers in this country.

It means that our children will have the true account of how it was for us – not just the lies perpetrated by western media.

It means that when we take our work to other parts of the world, in particular other parts of the west – that we do not remain invisible in our achievements, as western media would have it.

It means that when western media creates a false picture of events that we have been involved in – we too have records to emphasise what it was and is really like . . .

Example, the resistance of 1958, 1976, 1977, 1981 and 1985.

Example, Colin Roach.
Example, sixteen dead – New Cross fire
And there are many more.
In our fight back, therefore, we must continue to document, we must continue to reconstruct, we must continue to demobilise those institutions that attempt to conceal our understanding of ourselves.

In summing up –

> There's a hunger burning inside of me
> A struggle wanting out
> And though my struggle is as different
> As it is seen to be
> Of my patience there can be no doubt
> Britain our country breathes fire
> We must let it burn to our desire
> No stone must go unturned
> Every crevasse is to be explored
> until found that which I look for
> I must open all doors and more
> I must let the fire burn
> Through my Desires I will learn
> My struggle will be freed.

This piece was prepared in September 1985 apart from the 'In Summing Up' Section which was written in 1981, and is intended to suggest that the work continues

JENNIFER COMRIE

I was born in Leeds, England, where I attended the Jacob Kramer College of Art and completed the one year Foundation Course.

What is Black Art?

At present I am a third year student at Goldsmith's College studying on the Three Year B.A. (Hons.) Degree Course in Fine Art.

Using a thought from an African intellectual, Alpha.I.Sow, I would like to believe that my work has emerged from the cry within me and the black community.

My 'blackness' and 'spiritual awareness' are important elements within the work. With a sense of 'black consciousness', I am able to speak as a black woman who feels that her sexuality within this society is reduced to 'rabidity', whose intelligence, confidence in herself is still being reduced in inefficiency. Unable to keep a home together let alone a man (hence the over emphasis of the black woman falling victim of a one parent family), rarely speaking of her success within the 'struggle for survival'; yet when it does it reinforces the myth of the 'Black Superwoman'.

The point in question is not a moral issue, but illustrates how one factor can be used against the victim, wrongly.

Spirituality, is also of utmost importance, as it causes me to realise that life is a school,

> *"providing man with an explanation about his origins and a rule of conduct governing his relationship with the dead, with intangible and in themselves inexplicable forces and with the eternal Being, as well as an answer to the questions of man's existence on earth and its ultimate purpose".*
>
> (SOW)

Hence from these convictions the work has emerged, articulating my thoughts and becoming, for me, critical, conscious pieces; acting as, *"a force trying to work against the humbug and deceit . . . (sharing) hopes and anxieties, giving them vent".*

The work offers hope and strength, as it tries to identify the problem, warning any innocent sojourner on life's journey. It acknowledges solidarity with the individual, who has experienced or is experiencing the alienation, hurt and conflict expressed within the work to draw support from the fact that they are not alone. As well as the hope of transcending stereotypes as one allows one's true self expression.

The feeling of conflict, within oneself, is one that can be identified by all human beings; but as I am black, my point of reference is from a black experience – my own.

Though others of a different racial group may be able to intellectualise and rationalise the problems I face as a black person, experiencing similar problems, one is only truly comforted when one's own 'kind' states, 'I understand . . . I have been there myself!'

MARLENE SMITH

> Not seen
> (unless exotically un/dressed)
> Not heard
> (except our bittersweet,
> ohsosadbutharmless? songs)

Originally this piece of writing started *"Racist/Sexist Myths about black women abound"*, but I struck that line out because the myths are not in abundance. Perhaps it is a measure of the White Establishment's contempt for us that the invention of caricatures into which we might be squeezed has, up until now, been so limited. Or is it in recognition of our revolutionary potential that the attempt at defining us is made? Caricatures are an attempt to define us. Those that define control.

As Black artists, *"The nature of our art is predetermined by the nature of our existence."*

As Black women artists our work revolves around and evolves out of an experience which is our own. As a black woman I feel a responsibility to address that experience, to embrace it, to explore it. In so doing many of my images deal with brutality and violence.

What is Black Art?

It is important to point out here that such work is about the continued *attempt* to dehumanise us – My work is not about dejected people nor does it portray a degraded black womanhood. I seek to contribute to the building of a material culture that might have been denied were it not for the struggles of my people.

> the thin black line
> is long
> is slender (but not delicate)
> is cord, not thread
> is a long, slender cord
> taut when stretched

13 Eddie Chambers, 'The Marginalisation of Black Art', 1986

In this article, published in the radical magazine *Race Today*, artist Eddie Chambers comments on the upsurge of exhibitions by Black visual artists in British galleries and institutions during the mid-1980s. Writing in February 1986, he contrasts the current situation with that of the start of the decade, when exhibitions of Black artists were rare. However, he raises a note of caution and questions whether the recent flurry of group shows and public commissions should be regarded as a positive development. He goes on to argue that the patronage majority-white institutions proffered to Black artists was exploitative: a way of demonstrating the anti-racist credentials of curators and galleries, while simultaneously defusing Black art's revolutionary potential. In this article Chambers decries the way that Lubaina Himid's exhibition *The Thin Black Line* (1985) was crammed into an unsuitable corridor at the ICA in London, while also arguing that commissions such as the GLC's 1985 *Anti-Racist Mural Project* coerced Black artists and co-opted their work; such projects, Chambers suggested, only served to further marginalize Black artists.

* * *

Throughout the twenties, as Langston Hughes has said, "The Negro was in vogue". White interest in black people, especially black artists, writers and performers, became a national pastime. **John Henrik Clarke.**

Faced with the militant peoples of the ex-colonial territories, imperialism simply switches tactics. Without a qualm it dispenses with its flags . . . this means, so it claims, that it is "giving" independence to its former subjects, to be followed by "aid" for their development. Under cover of such phrases, however, it devises innumerable ways to accomplish objectives formerly achieved by naked colonialism. It is this sum total of these modern attempts to perpetuate colonialism while at the same time talking about "freedom", which has come to be known as neo-colonialism. **Kwame Nkrumah**

Mind your motion, black people, You're heading for sudden destruction. **Black Slate.**

In an article written nearly a year ago, I stated the increasingly-held view that "art by black people is being acknowledge and recognised". Taking this observation further, the press release for the recent Black Visual Arts Conference held in Birmingham, opens with this paragraph:

There have been enormous strides made in recent years in the raising of the profile of black artists and their work. Community and mainstream galleries are showing increased interest in the promotion of exhibitions by black artists and there has been increased press and media coverage of their work.

With statements such as these frequently being made, one could be forgiven for holding the mistaken belief that black artists have finally been accorded the respect and status for which they have been struggling.

However, the recent police shooting of Cherry Groce, and the death of Cynthia Jarrett are tragic reminders that as black people, we remain oppressed, exploited, and brutalised. And we are deluding ourselves if we believe that our artists are receiving better treatment. This article then, is another look at the so-called "recognition" being given to black artists.

1985 has of course seen an increase in the number of temporary outlets for the work of black artists. An undisputable fact. My suspicion and dissatisfaction however, centre around the motives and reasons for the existence of such exhibitions. I would, if I may, like to advance the argument that many (if not most) of these exhibitions are on a par with what John Henrik Clarke and Kwame Nkrumah observed. Namely, that most exhibitions of work by black artists exist because of inclement, patronising white interest. Furthermore, such exhibitions represent the re-appropriation, the rendering impotent, of black (and therefore socio-political) creativity.

In 1978, with a perception and clarity acquired through bitter experience and thoughtful observation, Rasheed Araeen offered what, at the time, must have been considered a wholly unpalatable view. Addressing some of the issues raised by an exhibition of Afro-Caribbean Art, he wrote:

> There will in fact be many such exhibitions, supported by the establishment, taking place under various ethnic titles during the coming years . . . which will attempt to re-ethnicise the black artist and thereby marginalise further his/her role in this society.

It goes without saying that Araeen was correct. But why *should* he have been correct? After all, the late 70's and early 80's were heady, progressive times for black artists. In particular, two examples of this spring to mind. Firstly, black art students up and down the country were putting pencil to paper, squeegee to silkscreen, and brush to canvas to make a new kind of mark. A mark that wasn't reluctant to draw from, and address, the struggles of black people. And in London, a small group of black cultural activists were seriously considering, and working on, the idea of a black art gallery. An American term, defiant in its simplicity, was increasingly being used to describe the work of British-based black artists. "Black Art" was emerging.

So, faced with progressive, restless, and assertive black artists, who demanded that their new-found voices be heard, the white art world simply switched tactics. For years it had ignored and marginalised the work of Britain's pioneer black artists, but with a crop of articulate, art school trained black artists to contend with, the art world went for the time-honoured European practice of re-appropriation. Without a qualm it dispensed with its hostile, indifferent attitude, and began making liberal, accommodating noises and gestures. A previously unknown type of creativity, "Ethnic art", was encouraged, and suddenly became a familiar and widely practised art form. The white establishment created a type of person known as an "Ethnic Arts Officer". Black arts administrators were trained, and bodies were established to oversee and guide the emergence of black art. And white art critics began to pay lip service to their "favourite" black artists.

The (white art) establishment claimed that it was "assisting" black artists. This "assistance" was followed by "grant aid" for their development. Metropolitan and provincial local government provided funds, workers, and schemes for "Afro-Caribbean" or "Ethnic" art. (For months now, I've been meaning to write an article titled "How the GLC undermined and subverted black creativity".) Under cover of such gestures however, the establishment devised innumerable ways to accomplish objectives formerly achieved by blind prejudice and racism. It is the sum total of these modern attempts to subvert militant black creativity, while at the same time talking about the "Vision and Voice" of black visual arts, that has led to the ethnicising (and at the same time marginalising) of black art.

It should also be remembered that the present white "interest" and support for black artists is little more than a temporary vogue, and will pass, just as surely as night follows day.

Take for example, *The Thin Black Line*, an exhibition by black women artists in the heartland of the white art world, the ICA. Whilst the bulk of the work deserves much respect and recognition, the exhibition itself serves as a good example of re-appropriation and compromise. Here we have a situation in which the work of a dozen or so of our strongest women artists is marginalised in the most obvious of ways, hung as it is along a pokey, cramped, altogether unsuitable corridor and stairway. If the ICA can play host to the likes of artists such as the racially offensive Robert Mapplethorpe, then why are the likes of Claudette Johnson, with her stunningly powerful drawings of black women, unable to gain access to the same space? Furthermore, the implications of so many black artists being crammed into such a difficult and unsuitable space are not pleasant.

But the betrayal and re-appropriation of our art has never been a one-sided process. All too often, and all too quickly, black artists themselves have become involved with various projects that have had words such as "tokenism", "careerism", and "paternalism" stamped all over them. In the case of the so-called "GLC Anti-Racist Murals" one assumes that the supposedly lucrative sums of money offered were the incentives used to coerce black artists into what can only be described as an ill-conceived and hollow project. At other times one assumes that an increased profile in art circles (again, supposedly) is what attracts black artists to take part in the neutralising of their own creativity.

It was Marcus Garvey who commented on the seriousness of collusion (conscious or otherwise) with the white power structure when he wrote "The great stumbling block in the way of progress in the race has invariably come from within the race itself." Or, to put it another way, the biggest single factor that prevents black art from taking up its rightful place amongst the cultural vanguard of the people has invariable been the lack of self-confidence and political integrity amongst black artists themselves.

This then is something of the situation of black artists in Britain at the present time. It is black artists alone who determine the form, functioning and future of black art, for better or for worse. The final word goes to Araeen: "The choice for us is clear. Either we accept our marginalised separate categories or reject them. The rejection will entail hard thinking and commitment. It would require us to look deep into our reality as black people in this country . . ."

14 Gavin Jantjes, *Art & Cultural Reciprocity*, 1986

In his paper, 'Art & Cultural Reciprocity', presented at the East Midlands Art Conference on 12 April 1986, South African artist and curator Gavin Jantjes reflects on the inequalities experienced by Black artists in Britain and institutional responses to diversity. The conference was organized by the East Midlands Arts Council visual arts committee and its regional director Anthony Everitt, who later became the Arts Council of Great Britain Secretary-General. At the time it was, arguably, the most significant conference to address the Black arts struggle because for the first time a number of gatekeepers and institutional leaders were forced to attend. Although other conferences addressing 'Black art' had been staged during the early 1980s, there had been a notable absence of gallery directors and top-level decision makers from those events. Writing in 2022, Jantjes recalled that 'this was the first time decision makers could directly engage with the anger of artists who were being discriminated against'.[1] Significantly, it was at this conference that Rasheed Araeen met Joanna Drew face to face. At the time, Drew was possibly one of the most powerful people in the UK art world. She served as Director of Exhibitions and then Director of Art at the Arts Council, with oversight of national funding, between 1975 and 1992, and she was Director of the Hayward Gallery, London, from 1987. The meeting between Araeen and Drew in 1986 ultimately resulted in the Hayward Gallery agreeing to stage his exhibition *The Other Story: Afro-Asian Artists in Post-War Britain* in 1989.

Jantjes' participation in the conference led to his appointment as a council member of the Arts Council. During his tenure between 1986 and 1990, he chaired the Council's newly formed Monitoring Committee which was charged with not simply overseeing but also developing a national policy for cultural diversity. 'This resulted in significant organizational and policy changes within the Arts Council, including Black representation on all boards and committees; an annual review of spending; and an important increase in funding dedicated to the issue of diversity from £250,000 in 1986 to £8.5 million over the following four years'.[2]

* * *

I was brought up in a country where people were segregated into groups along the lines of race, religion, skin-colour, wealth, social status and political belief. My life and work are caught up in the struggle to prove segregation wrong and equality to be right. So I've attempted to bring to my work, and my profession, a sense of morality upon equality.

The visual arts have a reputation for being immoral, even decadent. Yet it has always claimed to be the upholder of humanitarian freedoms. The freedom of expression and the freedom of the individual today are synonymous with contemporary visual art. But what about equality? Is there equality in the visual arts? In theory, yes! In practice, no!

I believe in cultural reciprocity; in enjoying all those things human beings offer each other. For when cultures rub shoulders, or even better, when they engage each other, it is then that humankind develops, progresses, finds solutions to problems. This is a hallmark of all human culture; for I will know more about you by appreciating your visual expression for what it is, rather than evaluating it against a strata of other expression.

The inequality in the contemporary British art scene is there for all to see; or better said, it's what is *not* there that is so conspicuous.

A clear radical and cultural bias, prevalent in the dominant consciousness, has become recognisable even to the 'dominant' themselves. Not through their own introspective investigations, but due to pressures from those denied equality. It would be true to say that the art institutions of this land have had no vision of solutions to the problem of inequality in the arts; nor have they allowed those who suffer the inequality to have a voice in the solution-finding process. Cultural reciprocity finds no favour with them and I am saddened and frustrated by that fact.

Institutionalised inequalities have led to polarisation and segregation. It seems hypocritical that in order to gain equality in the arts, we do the opposite and tear art apart along national borderlines and ethnicity. The Alice in Wonderland bureaucracy surrounding contemporary visual arts has created this situation. My personal belief in cultural reciprocity, equality and the power of art to transcend cultural and other borders, has difficulty with this approach. The resulting frustration calls for my constant reaffirmation in these beliefs. For it would be so easy to throw them overboard and go for a more radical, short term belief, as so many have before. The simplistic solutions are segregationalist. It's what the bureaucrats want! The institutions have created the categories and bureaucrats have had neither the patience, the fantasy, the commitment to alter those categories.

In the early fifties the arts aspired to universality, internationalism even the Commonwealth. Today we have multi-culturalism, ethnicity and national heritages – all concepts which aim to separate, segregate and deny cultural reciprocity. The institutions have designed, for the visual expression of certain people, the labels 'Ethnic', 'Minority' 'Heritage', 'Asian' and 'Black'. I find all of these categories difficult if not impossible to accept – for two reasons.

How can I accept categorical separation when I believe in cultural reciprocity? And how can I allow someone else the prerogative of categorising or defining my work, without any true knowledge of my aspirations, history and culture? Do I not have a *voice* with which to name the world and tell the truth? Do I not have a *vision* with which to evoke consciousness?

There is another category of course which the institutions use all the time. It's never used as a label. It never appears in policy papers. It's never put down in writing. It is Eurocentrism. It is present at every level of institutional work and permeates their thinking and decision-making within them.

It is the unwritten, invisible category which is responsible for the inequality in the Arts. *For Eurocentrism believes in inequality*. It believes in the inferiority of other cultures, and it can deal with those cultures only by placing them in a separate ethnographic niche, with the label 'ethnic', or marginalising them and labelling them the minor arts; or, by distancing itself from them in historical time through the term 'heritage' or 'traditional'; or by separating them geographically from the West and Europe through the use of national titles; or, even by using the terminology of its opponents in the cultural debate, as a label, so as to avoid any alteration to its position.

The term 'minority' defies all logic. Its reference is not numerical but cultural. So we find in this category the kind of plurality lacking in the dominant mainstream. The term 'heritage' is applied liberally to both the artistic production of the past and the contemporary production of certain artists.

The question has to be asked: What is contemporary non-Western visual art? It's certainly not heritage nor traditional nor ethnic nor minority. And the question of its nationality is certainly more complex than the artist's passport or the general geographic region of the artist's cultural root.

Western Eurocentrism has popularised its art as free, dynamic and expressive of its time (even when it's using non-Western and non-European visual imagery, methods, ideas and philosophies). It considers all other visual art as *time-bound* – trapped in the past – and incapable of meaningful, innovative expression to liberate itself and deal with the contemporary world. It therefore believes that nothing other than the phenomenon of its *own* creative expression is capable of sensitising it, of moving it emotionally and intellectually.

Western Eurocentrism has the audacity to equate its art history with world art history, thereby denying the majority of the world a contributive part in the progress of human culture. And to crown this Western Eurocentrism does not think of other people as contemporary! It cannot recognise either art or artist as being anywhere else except in the shadow of their respective traditions or caught between the worlds of tradition and contemporaneity, in a state of suspended animation.

So this invisible category which so dominates world art, is equally unacceptable to me. I'm after a pluralist world view – one which recognises the difference of cultures the world over but which does not use those differences to create a ladder of priority with which to equate cultures.

There's more to be had in terms of awareness by listening to Indian ragas, Villa Lobos, the National Orchestra of Mali and Gustav Mahler than just the latter. Or, the fat and felt objects of the late Joseph Beuys, the pressed pigment forms of Anish Kapoor or the string-bound wooden fragments of Sokari Douglas-Camp's mechanised sculpture than just the work of the former.

Now, about the term 'black visual art'. I do not see black as an adjective to describe the skin pigment of the artist. Were I to do that I would also have to accept the category 'white art' and that to me does not exist. A black art finds its meaning in the substance of the arts' images in the creation of a work. Put another way, not all art made by women is feminist; there is a contextual difference. It would be equally correct to say that not all art made by black people is a black visual art.

A black visual art is an innovative expression of a particular reality – a reality set in the framework of specific cultural and historic forces. These are: cultural domination by Western Eurocentrism and marginality to it; the experience of exploitation, appropriation, slavery, inequality and racism; and the long abominable history of colonialism. A black art emerges from this framework and is vitalised by these forces. They give it its liberatory character – make it a creation for liberation. Just like the tight constricting mantle around gunpowder turns it into an explosive, the constricting framework confining black visual expression, activates the energies for its liberation.

What the institutions want to do is to hide the framework, take the gunpowder of black visual expression and ignite it on an open surface, where it becomes a harmless, colourful, entertaining display and just another part of their great ethnic parade.

So for me a black visual art is a creative response to the inequalities in society and the Arts. Similar to movements in art history, it has emerged to broaden our understanding of the world. To sensitise us emotionally and intellectually, and bring blackness to our consciousness; to challenge the status quo. And, like all movements, it will cease once it has achieved its goal.

If those who are being discriminated against have rallied under this term, then it has been to generate a change towards equality, to crack the Eurocentric stranglehold on the development of world culture. And – in some cases – to create a working space for themselves within the dominant mainstream.

A contemporary black visual art is an innovative synthesis of two worlds. The first holds the artists' traditional roots; the second, the contemporary world of the artist. So a black art is rooted in tradition but not bound to it. It is a contemporary art in that it is addressing the realities of the present. It therefore has to create a new visual language – a new voice – a new set of conventions within visual art which articulates, expresses and creates consciousness, Black consciousness, not African, Asian, or Latin

American. The art from these cultures have their own visual languages with which they express their own internal dynamics – before colonialism, before cultural domination. A black visual art is therefore not simply a copy of a traditional, heritage art form. It has to be a synthesis of both. It has to be something new, created out of the experiences and understanding of both worlds and within an understanding of the media of visual art.

If the category black art is used and understood to mean what I've just described then it's an acceptable, valid and constructive premise to work from. But if it's to be part of the ethnic parade, then I want no part in it. Neither would I accept it as a contribution to world culture if it only aimed to sell slogans and pedal protest. For art is an expression of our culture – the whole of it. The good and bad; the positive and the negative; the urgent, important things, as well as the less pressing, the things that arrest and the things that signify progress.

What has to be understood by those concerned with the presentation, interpretation and promotion of the arts is that there has been, particularly over the past few years a dynamic shift in artists' thinking away from all the incorrect definitions and tacky labels, toward a pluralist cultural understanding. Amongst artists the debate has progressed from criticism of the institutions and diversified to a critical appraisal of artistic production and the aesthetics of a black visual art. The institutions trail far behind in their thinking and have a lot of catching up to do. The problem of equality in the arts is not going to be solved with yesterday's solutions. So all those ready-stick labels destined for artists and their work must be discarded.

And the solutions to equality in the arts is not to be found without consultation and the direct involvement of the artists who still bear the brunt of inequality.

We do not want to see non-Western art set aside from the mainstream in separate special exhibition programmes. Such exhibitions should only be done if their aim is to clarify structures of the art through thematic presentation. What is needed is integration.

A significant step toward the achievement of such a goal would be for the Arts Council to lead the way toward a plural cultural awareness – to lead in the finance it gives; in the way it brings this art into its collection and exhibition programmes; in the way the way it assists the promotion of this art both here and abroad. The British Council too has a significant role to play – one it has previously ignored. For it can bring to Britain and take from it new visual experience. It can make the vital link to the world outside; a link needed to comprehend the contemporary developments and the historical roots of our art. It can give a new British art an international arena to prove itself in, and it can help to remove the stigma of racism from Western Eurocentrism.

The institutions are not the only makers of our future agenda. There is a contribution artists must make. I would like that contribution to be understood not just in terms of bureaucratic engagement, but also, and more importantly, in what we create in our studios. To rid all art of marginality requires a dedicated input in both fields. But it is not our skills in bureaucracy, but our skills in visually expressing our world that make cultural reciprocity and a plural world-view possible.

NOTES

1. Gavin Jantjes, email correspondence with the editor, 19 April 2022.

2. Ibid. For more on Arts Council of Great Britain policy, see Richard Hylton, *The Nature of the Beast: Cultural Diversity and the Visual Arts Sector. A Study of Policies, Initiatives and Attitudes 1976–2006*, Bath: ICIA, 2007.

15 Sunil Gupta, 'Desire and Black Men', 1986

Sunil Gupta is a photographer, curator, writer and activist, whose work has consistently addressed the discrimination and marginalization faced by gay and lesbian people both in Britain and internationally. In this essay, originally published in the photography magazine *Ten.8*, Gupta outlines the way in which racial identities and sexuality are often put in competition by curators and institutions, with exhibitions only allowing space for the expression of one 'issue' at a time. Following a brief discussion of his own work, Gupta provides a critical analysis of the way that Black men were represented as objects of desire within 'fitness' magazines of the 1940s and 1950s. He then discusses the work of American photographer Robert Mapplethorpe, whose work in the 1970s and 1980s fetishized the Black male body. Gupta concludes with a discussion of his own photographic portraits of gay men in New Delhi, India, proposing that the depiction of Black homosexual desire can and must move beyond stereotyped images of physicality and the phallus.

*   *   *

The discourses around desire and Blacks very rarely overlap, and even less so in terms of photographic representation. There are several reasons for this: The theoretical discussions around desire / sexuality have limited themselves to a white discussion around sexual difference rather than a discussion of the *difference* of sexual orientation; and from a Black perspective, sexual orientation is viewed as a white issue and Black gays are seen to have turned their backs on Black struggle. Furthermore, in the current climate against "pornography" and the AIDS scare, to want to reconstruct a positive image of Black gay male desire is a delicate matter.

Several recent events in London, sponsored by the Greater London Council, have begun to tie these disparate elements together. A conference held at the Brixton Recreation Centre in mid-February 1986 titled "Black Communities: Living & Struggling Together" addressed itself to the differences within the Black community, principally of sexual orientation. Black lesbians and gay men came together with Black heterosexuals to discuss the issues that divide us. Although the heterosexual turnout was very small, one vociferous man reminded us all day how we had "caught a white disease."

In March, two photographic shows opened: one titled *Reflections of the Black Experience* at the Brixton Art Gallery, and one titled *Darshan* at Camerawork. I participated in both these shows. The Brixton show was commissioned work and, while I got lesbian and gay issues on the agenda, there was only one photograph that referred to a gay presence, out of a hundred. Faced with a choice of making ten photographs around the Black gay male experience or ten around key issues facing people of South Asian descent in the UK, I chose the latter. I admit, in this instance, to have given in to the pressure to marginalize sexual politics in favor of communal politics within the Black framework.

The Camerawork show was organized out of existing work, and since it was by and about South Asians, I felt freer about presenting a set of photographs representing the sexuality of Indian men. In this show, I was literally the one in ten, but I felt comfortable, as the cultural identity of the show had already been defined.

Both these shows are being read as historic and as first steps to establishing a Black presence within the British photographic community. Having been through these experiences, I would like to concentrate my work on the reconstruction of a Black gay male image of desire, keeping in mind that the audience is not only going to be the photographic community but also the Black community at large. One of the lessons learnt by Black gays after more than a decade of working for gay liberation is that not only does the movement marginalize Blacks, in a mirror image of society, but there is a pressing need to educate the Black community that we exist, and a wish to reintegrate ourselves with the communities that we came from. In my own work, it has meant returning to the city that I grew up in, Delhi, in order to make photographs that reflect the gay experience over there. Here in Britain, I would like to work on a series of photographs that allow Black gay men to construct an image of themselves as both producers and consumers of sexual desire.

Historically, Black men have appeared in popular picture magazines as objects of desire. For the purposes of this article I'll begin with the "physique" and "fitness" magazines of the '50s and '60s.[1] These follow a European tradition of photographing the male nude in classical settings. They appeared in North America and Britain, although it was in the US that repressive laws surrounding representation were successfully fought and won. The European tradition of setting out to the Mediterranean countries to find examples of idealized youth and beauty[2] also fitted the photographers who were able to distance themselves from their Northern homes. Black models begin to appear in the '50s, perhaps to coincide with the first wave of migrants from the West Indies. Curiously, the only Asians to make an occasional appearance are East Asians. I assume that South Asians either were not interested in bodybuilding or, more likely, that there was no demand for them. Although clearly aimed at a male gay audience, these magazines assiduously avoid revealing any part of male genitalia. This was due to the political climate of their times, an atmosphere of sexual repression which was not challenged till the late '60s and prevails to this day in Britain.

The '40s and '50s – best known for postwar reconstruction in Europe, the Cold War and McCarthyism in the US, and independence and hope in the colonized countries – are not normally thought of as a time of debate around sexual representation. It was a time when men were men, and women were women, and Blacks were meant to be kept in their place. Still, the climate allowed for the production and distribution of these magazines emphasizing the body beautiful, gay male sexuality, and desire. In the '50s, in the US, the magazines won a significant legal battle to allow them distribution through the US Postal Service.[3]

It must be pointed out that the magazines were produced by and for a white audience. The images of Blacks blend in with a popular reading of white classical treatments. So we have "Howard Hunter" leaning against a Greco-Roman pillar, as we have "George Paine" doing something similar. "Leroy Colbert – a smiling young Titan: by Lon" gets the full treatment in an extended piece titled "A Modern Hercules," prefaced by a reproduction of the *Farnese Hercules*. Leroy is described as a happy person with no complexes and, in case we read a gay subtext into the piece, he is reported to just have fathered Hercules III. Other photo-captions describe him as "Massive Power in Controlled Repose" or "The Strength of the Hills is His Also." *Modern Man* in 1959 brings us "From Jamaica, Neville Chisholm," who leans against a pillar and gazes up with a slight expression of bewilderment. Perhaps he was surprised at his facing page, which offers us two stereotyped pictures of "Natives": one from the Pacific and one from the Bahamas. "Noel Chaffey," it tells us, "sends these startling pictures of untrained men." No doubt untrained in the sense of weight training, but with a clear reference to untrained as in "uncivilized."

Sometimes the images have a camp sensibility like "Cecil

Addison," who looks like a Black incarnation of Errol Flynn, complete with sword. By the '60s in the US, both color and penises began to appear, although, in accordance with the rules, erections were still not allowed. Where more than one man appears in the photograph, the rule limiting contact to a straight wrestling variety has been relaxed to introduce definite gay iconography, such as overtones of S&M, uniforms, and touching. Now the photographs are clearly made for a gay male audience. In one "David O'Boyle & Jim Davis" gaze into each other's eyes, with their thighs touching in a romantic outdoor setting shot in a studio. An ideal cover shot for a gay Mills & Boon romance, Jim Davis is Black. Romance has overtaken beefcake. An even more amazing picture, since the Black man appears to be literally on an equal footing with the white man; if anything, the Black man appears in a dominant position, as he leans towards the white man whilst offering his thigh for support. In 1969, Black drag queens were in the forefront of the riots around the Stonewall Inn in New York that marked the birth of the Gay Liberation Movement.

In the '60s and '70s, "deviants" appeared as "appropriate subject matter for art photographers" (Susan Sontag).[4] Diane Arbus's show at the Museum of Modern Art in New York, of 120 photographs, attracted a sizeable audience; and since her death in 1971, her book has been the best-selling monograph in the history of photographic publishing.[5] Roll film, square format, and deviant subject matter combined to produce two of the best known gay photographers, Robert Mapplethorpe and Arthur Tress. By the late '70s and early '80s, Mapplethorpe's work had gained widespread notoriety by representing marginal and extreme forms of sexuality, particularly homosexuality and Black men. This happened against a background of ever-increasing gains by the gay community in the US, the legalization of male homosexuality in the UK for people over twenty-one in 1967, and a growing number of pictorial publications aimed at the gay male market.

The physique poses have given way to a variety of macho styles: cowboys, construction workers, and clones. Every conceivable kind of gay male sex has been photographed; the debate around representation within the gay movement has revolved around the need to stimulate desire and the desirability of limiting sexual role models to just a few stereotypes.

As the political climate changed with Reaganism in the US and Thatcherism in Britain, the agents of sexual repression restarted their work. Clean physique poses reclaim our attention, as in the work of Bruce Weber. Ads for permanent hair removal litter the back pages of the US's gay magazines. And AIDS has emerged, in the eyes of some, as retribution. We have seen the gains of the '70s swept away, we are under attack from the anti-"pornography" lobby, we have been returned to the laboratory by the medical researchers.

In this climate exist the photographs of Robert Mapplethorpe,[6] author of an exhibition and catalogue titled *Black Males*. Following Western art traditions, Mapplethorpe is a sculptor by training; he has photographed Black men essentially as objects. While this may make formalist sense, for us as Black consumers, he continues in the tradition of white photographers who have appropriated the Black image in order to reinforce the mythologies surrounding Black men; that in terms of desire they are limited to physique and big dicks. Initially, I was very interested in Mapplethorpe's work as an art student in the UK, as there seemed little or no work that seemed of specific interest to me. The nearest we got to exposure to his images was in a history lecture where his work was referred to but not shown; the student body was deemed too young or impressionable. I found this coyness very irritating, since we were constantly bombarded by the nudes of Edward Weston and Bill Brandt.

Eventually, I used some of his imagery in an audiovisual work about the history of London Gay Switchboard in an attempt to punctuate the narrative with a discourse about gay male art photography. This resulted in a ban on showing it after I showed it to members of the Switchboard collective. Several very vocal members found the images very offensive. I realized that if members of the gay community were offended, I could hardly expect my college (Farnham) to enter into a discussion around gay male desire, let alone Black gay male desire. Throughout my experience as a student and then a postgraduate student, I have found the issues that I specifically wanted to deal with marginalized. The all-white, heterosexual staff had, at best, formalism to offer.

It is on these grounds that Mapplethorpe has gained widespread acceptance. A recent article in *Aperture* follows that line as it traces the "human geometry" in Mapplethorpe's work. *Jimmy Freeman* (1981) shows a Black man sitting on his haunches with his forearms crossing his ankles; he wears a white skullcap, and his dick hangs down and intersects with his ankles or, as *Aperture* puts it, "The phallus forms a plinth for the nude, intersecting a triangular white space and penetrating ankles and forearms. Here the abstracted head is made contiguous with the abstracted phallus (a Black line)."[7] Is Jimmy a dickhead, masquerading as a Black line?

Man in Polyester Suit (1981) and *Jack, Fire Island* (1982) carry on in a similar vein. Headless Jack offers us his dick, since handily it lies at the apex of the geometry of his body. "Fire Island" suggests a gay venue; "The Pines" would have clinched it. Assuming then that Jack is gay and that the image, with its outdoor location and Jack's boots, refers to a gay pictorial tradition, the audience for this work must be gay males and the art world cognoscenti. This relentless offering of the nude Black male as a sacrificial figure can become tedious. Sometimes though, he does offer us a photograph with more meaning. *Man in Polyester Suit*, for me, sits on the edge of being yet another big Black dick, and a more complex reference to Black men in culture. We have seen images of Black men in suits, but the emphasis on polyester defines their position in society. I have to admit that in this instance, the contrast of textures between the artificiality of the material and the softness of the skin, the parallel veins in the penis and the hand, and the caress of the white shirt over the penis, works for me. *Abbraccio* (1982) depicts a Black man and a white man locked in an embrace with their pants on. "David Boyle" and "Jim Davis" no longer have to reveal their genitals and are allowed to carry their touching into an embrace suggesting an emotional life. Progress.

During three trips to India over the last few years, I have been trying to develop a pictorial scheme that could begin to relate the experience of gay men there. There was a time, growing up in Delhi, when I thought that only Indian men had sex with each other. Arriving in the West in 1969 in the wake of Stonewall, I found the Gay Liberation Movement an easy way of working out my identity. It was a time when you thought that everyone was working together towards the common goal of liberation. Cultural and generational gaps with one's family were relatively easily sorted out as one built bridges within the gay community. In the long run, the family and cultural differences have proved to be very resilient, and the gay movement and the expansion of the gay scene have shown themselves to be primarily aimed at a white middle-class male audience. Returning to photograph in India gave me a great sense of purpose. Here, at least, I was not marginalized by skin color, and the issues seemed very clear on a range of problems. I set about contacting the gay community there and discovered, first of all, that as a very complex society, India would only allow me access to urban middle-class men vis-à-vis a discussion around sexuality. And then, to take photographs in a society where your social identity is paramount was very threatening. The only public face of the gay network there is the variety of public meeting places, since there is no "scene" as in the Western model. The solution I have come up with is to work with men who are prepared to volunteer for the project. We pick a particular known location and reconstruct a scene. This gives me the chance to pick suitable light conditions and to try out a variety of angles. I hope, eventually, to cover the range of people and places that comprise a facet of the gay experience in India. The models are anonymous to both protect their identities and also to emphasize the invisibility of gay men in India.

Humayun's Tomb (1982) was first published in the *Guardian*, and I wrote an explanatory text to go with it. It was also, most recently, the basis of my contribution to the Camerawork show about South Asians.[8]

Happily the question of doing "physique" type nudes does not arise in India since the body is not idealized in quite the same way. Clothing and other cultural signifiers work to stimulate desire. Although there is a demand for imagery from the West and a history of erotic sculpture, the current climate is very repressive in terms of sexual desire. In any event, a direct representation of sexuality in India can be easily sensationalized by the media here in the UK, as Mary Ellen Mark's work on the "cages" in Bombay was in the *Sunday Times*.[9]

In the UK, my work in response to Mapplethorpe and others has been to investigate the other possibilities of meaning that being gay and/or Black might suggest. The photograph of the bodybuilder in Battersea works because of the two white men who hover in the background, who act as his trainers or possibly "civilizers," and who define the limit of his possibilities. Recently, a white commercial agent suggested making a poster out of the image by leaving out the two white men to make it commercially viable. Here, always, there is the dichotomy of race.

A recent issue of the *New York Native* contains an invaluable document of the voices of Black brothers and sisters.[10] Although they live in another country and have had quite different histories to ours, what they have to say holds in general to our experiences as well. We left our homes and cultures in the belief that within the gay movement, we would find a just cause in which we could participate as equals. But in the end, we discovered that white gay men suffer from the racism that permeates society at large. We now must return to the cultures that we came from with the news that we are gay. We must begin a dialogue with our own communities. *We have to conquer our fear of organizing in our own communities.* Black lesbians are saying to the women's movement that, *if you want us, you must take our men too.* The biggest challenge is to gain acceptance of the fact that being gay is not a white disease. As the writing on a piece of artwork puts it, "they say there were no gays in Africa before the white man, well then where did I inherit this Black male gay spirit?"

One of the unfortunate legacies of colonialism has been the criminalization of male homosexuality. These codes remain in India and in most other countries, and although "homosexual acts between consenting adults were decriminalised in Zaire in 1984, [it] hasn't stopped the arrests and blackmail of men assumed to be gay. Cops have virtually unlimited powers to keep people imprisoned indefinitely without charge or trial."[11]

Now, there is a new scourge to haunt us. AIDS. In the debate over whether it originated in Zaire or the bathhouses of New York and San Francisco, Black gay men find themselves the unfocused centre of attention. Initially identified as a gay disease, AIDS educators ignored the Black communities, whereas in fact, the rates of AIDS for Blacks in the US have been disproportionately high. There are twice as many AIDS cases among Blacks there than the proportion Blacks make up of the total population.[12] With the attack on gay sexuality under the guise of AIDS education in full swing, it's going to be important to fight to retain our right to define our own identity, and to fight the legal and censorship battles now going on in the UK.

Victor Burgin has argued for a "politics of representation"

rather than a "representation of politics."[13] He has also argued for showing the meaning of sexual difference and desire as a process of production: as something mutable, something historical, and therefore something we can do something about. I'm arguing, then, that given the emerging framework of a Black gay presence within a racist and homophobic society, it's time we reconstructed images of desire by ourselves and for ourselves.

Thanks to Simon Watney

NOTES

1 *Modern Man*, March 1959; *Men and Art*, May 1958; *Star Models*, 1954; *Man's World*, May 1956; *Body Beautiful*, 1956–60; *Physique: A Pictorial History of the Athletic Model Guild*, ed. Winston Leyland (San Francisco: Gay Sunshine Press, 1982).

2 Paul Lewis, "Men on Pedestals," *Ten.8*, 17 (January 1985): pp. 22–29.

3 *Before Stonewall: The Making of a Gay and Lesbian Community*, directed by Greta Schiller and Robert Rosenberg (New York: First Run Features, 1984), 87 min.

4 Susan Sontag, *On Photography* (New York: Farrar, Straus and Giroux, 1977).

5 Diane Arbus, *An Aperture Monograph* (New York: Aperture, 1972).

6 *Robert Mapplethorpe*, ed. Germano Celant (Venice: Comune di Venezia, 1983); *Robert Mapplethorpe 1970–1983*, ed. Sandy Nairne (London: Institute of Contemporary Arts, 1983).

7 Mike Weaver, "Mapplethorpe's Human Geometry: A Whole Other Realm," *Aperture*, The Human Street, Winter 1985, p. 44

8 Sunil Gupta, "They Dare Not Speak Its Name in Delhi: Sunil Gupta on the Secret Suffering of India's Homosexual Community," *Guardian*, November 26, 1982.

9 Mary Ellen Mark, "The Life of a Bombay Cage Girl," *Sunday Times Magazine*, May 24, 1981.

10 *New York Native*, A Heritage of Black Pride (supplement), March 3, 1986.

11 In the 2022 edited version of this essay Sunil Gupta's editor Theo Gordon notes: "Gupta sourced this quotation from the gay press in London in 1986. The Democratic Republic of the Congo (DRC) was named the Republic of Zaire from 1971 to 1997. This quote is partially erroneous: homosexuality has never been illegal in the DRC, even as the Penal Code's restrictions against "crimes against family life" are used to persecute gay people, who enjoy limited protections against various forms of civic discrimination."

12 Philip M. Boffey, "Blacks Alerted on Risks of AIDS," *New York Times*, October 23, 1985, p. 28.

13 Victor Burgin, "Man-Desire-Image," in *Desire* (London: Institute of Contemporary Arts, 1984).

16 Errol Lloyd, 'Caribbean Expressions in Britain', 1986

The exhibition *Caribbean Expressions in Britain* was held at Leicestershire Museum and Art Gallery in Leicester, in August–September 1986, and later toured to the Central Museum and Art Gallery in Northampton and Cartwright Hall in Bradford. It was part of a larger programme of cultural events, *Caribbean Focus '86*. Initiated by the Commonwealth Institute in London, *Caribbean Focus '86* comprised exhibitions of visual art alongside music, theatre, dance and literary events, which were staged at venues across the UK between March and November 1986. As part of the programme, Leicestershire Museum and Art Gallery invited the photographer Pogus Caesar, sculptor Bill Ming and painter Aubrey Williams to select a cross-generational exhibition showcasing artists of Caribbean origin working in Britain. *Caribbean Expressions in Britain* presented work by Simone Alexander, Frank Bowling, Sonia Boyce, Pogus Caesar, Denzil Forrester, Anthony Jadunath, Errol Lloyd, John Lyons, Bill Ming, Ronald Moody, Colin Nichols, Eugene Palmer, Veronica Ryan, Gregory Whyte and Aubrey Williams. Painter Errol Lloyd was commissioned to write the catalogue essay, reproduced here, which provides a perceptive and personal history of Caribbean-British artists and their contributions to British cultural life. Lloyd had arrived in London from Jamaica in 1963 to study law but was involved with the Caribbean Artists Movement from its inception in 1966; during the 1960s and

1970s he worked as an artist, illustrator and art critic, and from the early 1980s was an arts administrator at the Minorities Arts Advisory Service.

*　*　*

INTRODUCTION: AN HISTORICAL PERSPECTIVE

'Caribbean Focus 86' and its resultant visual arts exhibitions have provided a unique opportunity for an appraisal of Caribbean art in a broad international sense. The **'Caribbean Art Now'** exhibition of contemporary painting and sculpture from the Caribbean which opened at the Commonwealth Institute (a selection of which is also being shown at Leicester) has served as a timely reminder that there is a growing tradition of painting and sculpture in the Caribbean – albeit a relatively recent one. It also allows us to make a direct comparison with the work of those artists in Britain who are of Caribbean birth or descent whose work is shown here in this exhibition **'Caribbean Expressions in Britain'**.

It is of course difficult to use the phrase 'Caribbean artists' when referring to those artists who have been working in the Caribbean – in some cases without ever having left it, as well as to those artists who have either spent most of their working lives in Britain or were born here. There surely must be a stage when the latter cease to be considered as primarily belonging to the British outpost of a scattered expatriate Caribbean community, and are accepted as an integral part of contemporary British art. This is especially so in the case of the new crop of British born artists of Caribbean descent who are now emerging from British art schools and whose world view is shaped by conditions and experiences which are quite distinct from those of the Caribbean based artist. This stage is brought a step closer by the fact that many of these artists have forged links with artists from Africa and Asia, often subordinating their specific Caribbean identity in search of wider Black British identity.

There is, however, no precise moment at which such a transition is made, and the issues are too complex to employ a simple test such as nationality or domicile. The maintenance of strong cultural ties with the Caribbean will ensure that any period of transition will be a long one, and a shared historical experience of slavery and struggle has created strong bonds of kinship which will, no doubt, persist amongst people from the Caribbean, wherever they are to be found.

It seems quite appropriate at this point of time that Leicestershire Museums Service should take advantage of **'Caribbean Focus 86'** to mount an exhibition of the work of artists in Britain who have a Caribbean background.

It is generally acknowledged that slavery in the Caribbean severed any continuous development of African visual arts traditions, which are dependent on tightly woven social and religious structures. However, the early Caribbean settlers in Britain did not arrive devoid of any visual art traditions of their own. Each Caribbean island has its own peculiar art history, (largely under-researched and unwritten) but seen together they show a broad picture of a gradual creolisation, in which a Western sensibility in art established itself. This was aided by the presence in these colonies of amateur European watercolourists and imports of examples of books showing reproductions of European paintings and sculpture. The 1920s and 30s, however, saw the emergence of indigenous artists and art groups, particularly in the larger territories. This coincided with the growth of national consciousness and struggle for political independence, which invariably had as one of its aims, (often unstated) the forging of a Caribbean aesthetic which addressed itself to the changing cultural and psychological needs of the region.

This was also a period during which the foundations were laid for the emergence of Caribbean literature. Writers were eager to throw off their dependence on English literary models and instead to reclaim aspects of black cultural heritage, sometimes involving the use of local speech patterns or African oral traditions. The absence of comparable living traditions in the visual arts meant that developments in this area have not been as spectacular as in the field of literature, where writers such as Claude McKay, Edgar Mittleholzer, V.S. Naipaul, George Lamming, Eddie Braithwaite, Derek Walcott and many others have established international reputations and projected the new Caribbean personality on the world stage.

This was the broad cultural background to Caribbean emigration to Britain in the decades following the war. Many of the aspiring artists in the Caribbean had no choice but to go abroad if they wanted training, and some artists were attracted by the prospect of an improved work environment, the opportunity for broadening their own horizons and the wider recognition that travel to Europe promised.

Those artists who came to England met artists on a similar quest from Africa and Asia and together they formed a new grouping of artists from the 'New' Commonwealth. The early fifties to the mid-sixties was a very expansive phase as far as attitudes to black artists are concerned and many of these artists enjoyed tremendous critical and financial success. Artists like Iqbal Geoffrey, Avinash Chandra, Francis Souza from India, Sam Ntiro and Ben Enwonwu from Tanzania and Nigeria respectively, and many more, were lionised by the critics and had access to galleries: a position which many of them who are still alive or working in Britain have not since enjoyed. The bulk of purchases made by the Arts Council of non-Western artists seem to have been made at this time.

It is difficult to speculate why conditions were so favourable during that period, compared to the present day. No doubt there was a certain post-war euphoria in the air, combined with an idealism which saw the Commonwealth as part of the future world order, with Britain at the helm. It may also have been due to the fact that Britain had not yet joined the EEC or passed any anti-immigration legislation and that there was no National Front. It may also have been due to subtle changes in the work of the artists themselves who were, perhaps, becoming less inclined to create work which could be regarded as exotic, and many were in the process of exchanging their status as 'honoured guest', for the less certain status of immigrant.

For some reason there were no Caribbean artists among those mentioned who enjoyed high levels of material success at this time. The most likely candidate, Ronald Moody, was unable to capitalise on his early pre-war successes because he contracted tuberculosis soon after the war which limited his career as a sculptor. Yet none of the other 'successful' Commonwealth artists created work of more lasting importance than Ronald Moody. He came to Britain from Jamaica in the mid 1930s and was a pioneer, not only in being the first the first recognised Caribbean artist to settle in Britain, but also by adopting a new non-European aesthetic for his art. His work rejects the modern thirst for sensation in art and does not attempt in any way to chronicle or reflect the concord, discord and fragmentation of daily life so characteristic of a European approach to art. Instead it has a transcendental significance like that of the timeless art of the East. At its best, his work is an act of meditation which draws us into the world of certainty and immobility; a world reminiscent of the ancient Egyptian sphinx or pyramid. His concern with Pre-Columbian history and mythology was also reflected in his sculpture, particularly in his creation of the mythical bird, **Savacou**, which is profoundly Caribbean in its imagery and re-establishes the geographical and cultural links that the Caribbean has always had with Central and South America.

Another artist who shared this same spiritual nexus with the South American continent is Aubrey Williams, who came to England from Guyana in 1952 and eventually settled in London. Although he has lived in Britain for much of his working life, he has maintained strong ties with the Caribbean and his paintings are exhibited in Guyana and Jamaica (and North America) from time to time. His work has shown steadfast development—partly due to the fact that he avoided the temptation of 'overnight success' that many of the Commonwealth artists of the 1950s and 60s fell prey to. As with Ronald Moody in the field of sculpture, so in the field of painting, any chronicle of the development of black painting in Britain should figure Aubrey Williams as one of the earlier pioneers.

A remarkable feature of the 1960s was the presence in England of an influential group of novelists, poets, playwrights, actors, painters and sculptors from the Caribbean. In 1966 the **Caribbean Artists Movement** (CAM) was formed, with Jamaican novelist Andrew Salkey, Barbadian poet Eddie Braithwaite and Trinidadian poet and activist John La Rose as the founding members. This was perhaps the most remarkable cultural organisation of its sort formed by black people in Britain. It attracted many of the leading artists who were either already established in their respective fields, or who have subsequently established themselves. It was, however, a broad-based organisation and in addition to Caribbean artists and intellectuals attracted membership from a wide cross-section of the population, including interested white people. The **Caribbean Artists Movement** met regularly and organised exhibitions of paintings and sculpture, poetry readings; short plays as well as lectures, conferences and seminars.

CAM was instrumental in bringing artists from different Caribbean territories together and helped foster a sense of common Caribbean consciousness which had hitherto only been achieved in cricket. It played a significant part in mounting the **'Caribbean Artists in England'** exhibition of painting and sculpture, which was held at the Commonwealth Institute Gallery in 1971. **'Caribbean Artists in England'**, established a clear public demand for an exhibition of this nature; not simply to introduce the work of Caribbean artists to a wide public, but also to satisfy the needs of an increasing black population in Britain in search of its own cultural identity. Some of the artists featured included Althea Bastien (Trinidad) Winston Branch (St. Lucia) Daphne Dennison (Jamaica) Carl Craig (Jamaica) Art Derry (Trinidad) Errol Lloyd (Jamaica) Althea McNish (Trinidad) Ronald Moody (Jamaica) Ricardo Wilkins – now Kofi Kayiga (Jamaica) and Aubrey Williams (Guyana).

Research is now under way into CAM and the role it played in fostering the development of Caribbean art in Britain and at home, no doubt shedding more light onto its impact on the growth of a black art in Britain. The field of black art however remains seriously under-researched with only a handful of publications on the subject.

It soon became clear that artists of Caribbean origin living in Britain needed to organise themselves as British citizens, and to clarify their relationship to the state funding institutions and arts establishment. The formation of the **Minorities Arts Advisory Service** (MAAS) in 1977 following the publication of Naseem Khan's report 'The Arts Britain Ignores' was a natural development from this need, and united a wide range of 'Third World' and ethnic minority artists under its umbrella.

Apart from representing a broad ethnic range of artists, MAAS was also concerned with the whole spectrum of arts disciplines, making its specific contribution to the visual arts necessarily limited. In spite of this limitation, however, the publication of a national register of black artists certainly helped bring to the attention of the British public the existence of a range of practitioners in the field. In addition the 'Inter-cultural' magazine published by MAAS (**Artrage**) has been instrumental in highlighting developments in black visual arts through its exhibition reviews, and features on individual artists.

Perhaps one natural consequence of the limitations of MAAS, has been the creation of a number of black visual arts groups in recent years. One such group which made an impact was the **Pan African Connection**, a group of young black art school graduates in the North of England who mounted joint exhibitions of their work as well as lectures, seminars and conferences, to help forge a new black perspective for their art. The similarities with the Caribbean Artists Movement are quite clear, and unfortunately because of lack of information and documentation of the CAM years, many of the same problems have had to be faced anew, without benefitting from the experience of this earlier generation. This lack of documentation still continues to be a serious problem facing the black artist. The emergence of the **Pan African Connection** underlined the shift that had taken place from a Caribbean to a British perspective. Additionally the work of the artists involved sought to tackle pressing social and political issues: a feature common to many young artists working today. What is somewhat surprising, however, is that young black artists who have been born in Britain and passed through British schools and Art Colleges, should show so few signs of assimilation. If this can be interpreted as a sign of future developments, it seems that there is likely to be a distinct and powerful art expression: a black dimension in British art, which cannot be ignored. This exhibition shows that this process is well under way.

Another noteworthy phenomenon over recent years, is the emergence of black women artists as a force to be reckoned with. There have, of course, been black women artists working in the past and although there is an understandable suspicion in some quarters that both their numbers and the quality of their contributions have been downgraded, I do believe that recent developments mark a quite distinct new phase.

The preponderance of men as writers and researchers will always put into question the past involvement of women in the arts, however a more serious problem to address is the underlying social and economic factors that have in the past militated against women making the level of contribution of which they are capable. Women are now stepping out, and for the first time in Britain black women artists are exhibiting together, as well as exploring issues of common concern and creativity together, without the sometimes stifling intervention of men.

It is perhaps just as well that the contribution of the Greater London Council to the development of black visual arts is left to this stage, as some people have mistakenly assumed that there was no black creativity before the advent of the GLC. The GLC was instrumental, however, through its funding policies, in liberating some of the dynamism within the black community by providing much needed resources. Perhaps the most important contribution in this sphere by the GLC has been the funding of black galleries. **The Black Art Gallery** in North London and the **Westbourne Art Gallery** have been established with the help of the GLC finance, although the conception, programming and personnel of the galleries have come from within the black community. Although these are small-scale community oriented galleries, they have been instrumental in bringing into sharp focus both the existence of a neglected body of work and some of the issues concerning black artists. With the changing social and political climate in Britain generating a growing acceptance that we are living in a multi-cultural society which demands a pluralist approach to matters to culture, these specialist galleries will no doubt feed into the mainstream galleries; already we are beginning to see exhibitions transfer from the **Black Art Gallery** to galleries nearer to the mainstream.

Another significant role of the GLC in the visual arts has been the funding of murals in London to commemorate 'Anti-Racist' year. This has meant that, for the first time, the work of black muralists can be seen by the community at large; the contents of the murals and the message that there is a black community in Britain that demands to be visible, cannot be escaped. No less important has been the funding of a number of publications on visual arts—the most relevant of which is a book on the photographs of Armet Francis entitled **'The Black Triangle'**.

The role, too, of black cultural, social and political organisations in the development of the visual arts cannot be ignored. The mounting of group exhibitions of art to coincide with events of one sort or another has helped to provide useful and much needed outlets for the work of black artists. Many of these exhibitions have been ill-defined both in terms of concept and the space they occupied, but they have played an important role nonetheless. The danger to visual artists is that many current group shows have continued to be the work of well intentioned amateurs, long after the artists needs have changed.

The present exhibition I believe will bring together many of the strands that have gone into making up the evolving mosaic of Afro-Caribbean painting in Britain with the hint of a distinct black milieu in contemporary British art to come. Artists like Ronald Moody, Aubrey Wiliams and Frank Bowling as the earliest exponents of a unique expression in art are linked with the new generation of British painters like Claudette Johnson, Denzil Forrester and Veronica Ryan, with artists like Anthony Jadunath and myself occupying the middle ground.

There is also no easily identifiable line of development that can be discerned from bringing together the work of several generations of Caribbean artists. Those who do not understand the complexities of the Caribbean might come to an exhibition such as this expecting to see in the work a gradual progression from the simple naive images of a backward people, to more advanced expressions, as the process in 'westernization' makes its mark. Numerous commentators have however pointed to the unique geographical and historical circumstances that make up the Caribbean with its strong links with the continents of Africa, Europe and America—both North and South. C.L.R. James has made the point that even from the earliest days of slavery the black slaves were part of the modern world, and were responsible from beginning to end for the highly complicated technological process of turning cane into sugar—one of the most advanced industries at the time. This has helped to shape a modern people who are accustomed to absorbing influences from a variety of sources, and by the time an artist like Ronald Moody arrived in Britain, the gravitational centre of Western art had already started to shift from Paris to New York—and this was well after the Harlem Renaissance had made its impact!

The current exhibition at the Commonwealth Institute of the work of contemporary Caribbean-based artists helps to underline the point. For one can see in much of the work ideas which are as sophisticated as those to be found in the most cosmopolitan art centres in the world. One has only to look at the chair sculptures of Francisco Cabral of Trinidad for evidence of art works which are thoroughly modern, yet profoundly Caribbean.

Together, the **'Caribbean Art Now'** and **'Caribbean Expressions in Britain'** exhibitions celebrate the resilience and vitality of the Caribbean spirit. The British side of the equation is only now beginning to surface after years of neglect and discouragement. The emergence of an artist like Denzil Forrester, whose work so effectively mirrors the preoccupations and concerns of black British youth culture, is proof of the confidence of the new generation in the validity of the black experience, and I am sure will be an indication of the future fidelity to be shown in this experience.

The greatest benefit that could be gained by black artists in Britain, is that the current interest in its cultural expressions will carry on long after **Caribbean Focus '86** has come to an end.

17 Chila Kumari Burman, 'There Have Always Been Great Black Women Artists', 1986

In October 1986, Chila Kumari Burman gave a talk entitled 'There Have Always Been Great Black Women Artists' at the *Black Visual Arts Forum*, held at the Institute of Contemporary Arts in London. Her paper had originally been produced for the Greater London Council Race Equality Unit, and draws on her personal experiences of art college as well as interviews with other Black women artists to describe the barriers and exclusions that they faced individually and collectively. In her paper, Burman adapted and extended the arguments made by feminist art historian Linda Nochlin in her celebrated essay, 'Why Have There Been No Great Female Artists?' (1971), which identified and discussed the obstacles to female artistic success. However, Burman argued that white feminist artists and critics have been complicit in the oppression of Black women artists, stating that even in feminist narratives of art, Black women 'simply do not exist'. In order to challenge such pervasive omissions, she argues that Black women need to work collectively – for example in all-Black women exhibitions – to carve a space for themselves, on their own terms.

* * *

We face many problems when trying to establish the very existence of Blackwomen's art, and a strong social and political base from which to develop our study of it. Firstly, we have to struggle to establish our existence, let alone our credibility as autonomous beings, in the art world. Secondly, we can only retain that credibility and survive as artists if we become fully conscious of ourselves, lest we are demoralised or weakened by the social, economic and political constraints which the white-male art establishment imposes and will continue to impose upon us.

This paper, then, is saying Blackwomen artists are here, we exist and we exist positively, despite the racial, sexual and class oppressions which we suffer, but first, however, we must point out the way in which these oppressions have operated in a wider context – not just in the art world, but also in the struggles for black and female liberation.

It is true to say that although Blackwomen have been the staunchest allies of black men and white women in the struggle against the oppression we all face at the hands of the capitalist and patriarchal system, we have hardly ever received either the support we need or recognition of our pivotal role in this struggle. Blackwomen now realise that because of the specific ways in which we are oppressed by white-male dominated society, we must present a new challenge to imperialism, racism and sexism from inside and outside the established black liberation movement and at a critical distance to the white-dominated feminist movement. It is this realisation which has a lot to do with many second generation British Blackwomen reclaiming art, firstly as a legitimate area of activity for Blackwomen as a distinct group of people, secondly as a way of developing an awareness (denied us by this racist, sexist, class society) of ourselves as complete human beings, and thirdly as a contribution to the black struggle in general.

Having said this, Blackwomen's ability to do any or all of these three things is restricted by the same pressures of racism, sexism and class exclusivity which we experience in society in general. The bourgeois art establishment only acknowledges white men as truly creative and innovative artists, whilst recognising art by white women only as a homogenous expression of femininity and art by black people (or, more accurately, within the terms of reference used, black men) as a static expression of the ritual experience of the daily lives of their communities, be they in the Third World or the imperialist hinterland. In this system of knowledge, Blackwomen artists, quite simply, do not exist.

Nevertheless, if we look at the way in which these assumptions have been challenged to date, particularly by white women, we can still see nothing that acknowledges that Blackwomen exist. Art history is an academic subject, studied in patriarchal art institutions, and white middle-class women have used their advantageous class position to gain access to these institutions by applying pressure to them in a way which actually furthers the exclusion of black artists in general. White women's failure to inform themselves of the obstacles faced by black artists and in particular Blackwomen artists has led to the production of an extremely Eurocentric theory and practice of 'women's art'. It seems that white feminists, as much as white women in general, either do not attempt to or find it difficult to conceive of Blackwomen's experience. Some of those who do not attempt to may claim that they cannot speak for Blackwomen, but this is merely a convenient way of sidestepping their own racism. The fact remains that in a patriarchal and sexist society, all black people suffer from racism, and it is quite possible for white women to turn racism, which stems from patriarchy, to their advantage. Black men are unable to do this and, theoretically, are unable to turn sexism to their advantage, although they can do this for short-term gains which in the long term will never benefit black people as a whole. This has happened to a certain extent in the art world, where black men have failed to recognise Blackwomen artists or have put pressure on us to produce certain kinds of work linked to a male-dominated notion of struggle. However, because of their race and class position, black men have been unable to use the resources of art institutions in the same way that white middle-class women have.

THE STRUGGLES OF BLACKWOMEN ARTISTS

The first stage of most Blackwomen artists' encounter with the art establishment is their entry into art college. There are hardly any Blackwomen attending art colleges in Britain, and those who do, according to a survey of Blackwomen artists I carried out, seem to have experienced a mixture of hostility and indifference from their college. Because their white tutors work within an imperialist art tradition, using the aesthetic conventions of the dominant ideology, they are unwilling to come to terms with Blackwomen art students and their work. This resistance manifests itself in many ways – some Blackwomen students have found themselves asking why they as individuals found it easy to get into art college, only to realise that they are there purely as tokens, and in general it appears that Blackwomen's very presence in white-male art institutions is frequently called into question. Apart from denying us the support and encouragement that white art students receive, art colleges make us feel as though we don't belong inside their walls by the way in which our work is looked at. Those of us who have done more overtly political work have made white tutors very uncomfortable and, as a result, hostile, whilst students who have done less obviously challenging work have been questioned for not producing the kind of work which tutors expect black people to produce. Class differences amongst Blackwomen are significant here, for working-class Blackwomen have generally been quicker to reject the ideology of the art establishment and have therefore found it difficult to accept any kind of token status or to produce work of a more acceptable nature. Those who have not taken such an oppositional stance have still suffered from having their work analysed within a very narrow framework because their tutors have expected them to produce 'ethnic' work which reflects their 'cultural origin' using, for example, 'bright carnival colours', and white tutors and students alike have expressed confusion when such work has not been forthcoming. Another tendency of white tutors, irrespective of the type of work they are presented with, is to discuss art from the Third world with Blackwomen in a patronising and racist manner.

Of course, the assumption that Blackwomen will produce work with 'ethnic' or 'primitive' associations is one that white tutors make about black men as well, but it is important to point out that male <u>and</u> female white tutors are more inclined to see black men as having a more prominent role in this misconceived tradition. One Blackwoman student at Bradford art college commented:

'Funny how they always refer to you as some sort of bridge or crossing point between two things. Black meets woman. That's handy. As if you don't have an experience which is your own, but borrow from the brothers and sisters in struggle.'

It seems then, that when art colleges and universities give places to Blackwomen, which is in itself a rare event, all the forces of the dominant aesthetic ideology are brought to bear on us. Blackwomen artists are ignored, isolated, described as 'difficult', slotted into this or that stereotype and generally discouraged in every conceivable way from expressing ourselves in the way that we want to. This system of oppression and exclusion extends well beyond our time as art students. There are no full-time lecturing posts at art colleges and universities filled by Blackwomen in the entire country – instead we are offered 'freelance' work as visiting lecturers, which will never be enough to initiate a critique of contemporary art practice which is so desperately needed in every single art department in the country.

In addition, Blackwomen artists are denied the opportunity to develop their work as individuals in the same way that white artists can through grants from sources such as the Arts Council, the Greater London Council, regional arts associations and the Calouste Gulbenkian Foundation. Even though some of these sources such as the GLC and the Greater London Arts Association have recently begun to realise how much they have neglected Black visual arts, on the only occasion that a Blackwoman has received funding from the GLC as an individual, this has still been on unsatisfactory terms which differ significantly from the terms on which the only black man in this position has been funded. The man in question has been funded without any preconditions except that he produces a certain amount of work, whilst the woman was funded by the Arts and Recreation Department of the GLC for a year on the condition that she was attached to a community arts centre as a 'community artist', and the stipulation was made that the work she produced should not reflect her desires as an individual but 'the interests of the black community'. The GLC had ignored the importance to the black community of the experience of individual Blackwomen and had funded her on the basis of an ahistorical notion of 'community' or 'ethnic minority' arts, but when it came to applying to the Arts Council, it appeared that the role she had been pushed into was not individual enough. The rejection of her application to this body read:

'We do not think that your proposed project fits the terms of reference for this training scheme which is specifically aimed at developing the individual's skills, and is not to assist with research projects.'

If even the GLC funded a Blackwoman artist only as a 'community artist', this illustrates our position in a kind of funding no-woman's-land, because the Arts Council, racist and sexist as it is already, will continue to see our work as unfundable research projects and, as was the case with the application mentioned, refer us to bodies such as the Association of Commonwealth Universities, further relegating us to the marginality of the 'ghetto artist', completely outside of the British art world.

BLACKWOMEN ARTISTS FIGHT BACK

The resilience of Blackwomen artists in the face of oppression has manifested itself in the art world through our ability to produce and exhibit work despite all the social, economic and political constraints described above. The first all-Blackwomen's show at the Africa Centre in 1983 was not just a beginning; Blackwomen artists have been actively involved in exhibitions with white artists and Black men artists for several years, but this all-Blackwomen's show and the ones that have taken place since then – Blackwoman Time Now, 1985 International Women's Day Show, Mirror Reflecting Darkly, etc. – represent a significant new direction which has much to do with the development of what Barbara Smith describes as 'our own intellectual traditions'.

It is obvious that the majority of Black artists see their work in opposition to the establishment view of art as something that is 'above' politics, and Blackwomen artists see their work as integral to the struggles of Blackwomen and black people in general, but although Blackwomen's own culture plays a large part in determining the content and form of our work, we often concentrate on different issues to black men, who, as one Blackwoman artist points out, often believe that 'artists who are making through their works a collective, aggressive challenge to cultural domination are "real" black artists and making Black Art. But some male artists fail to understand or comprehend the struggles women artists go through to assert their identity and survive'.

Alice Walker illustrates the difference between these two ideas of Black Art in 'In Search of Our Mothers' Gardens', and goes on to put forward an alternative way for the black artist to operate:

'I am impressed by people who claim they can see everything

and every event in strict terms of black and white but their work is not, in my long contemplated and earnestly considered opinion, either black or white, but a dull, uniform gray. It is boring because it is easy and requires only that the reader be a lazy reader and a prejudiced one. Each story or poem has a formula, usually two thirds 'hate whitey's guts' and one-third, 'I am black, beautiful and almost always right.' Art is not flattery, and the work of every artist must be more difficult than that'.

'My major advice to young Black artists would be to shut themselves up somewhere away from all the debates about who they are and what colour they are and just turn out paintings and poems and stories and novels. Of course the kind of artist we are required to be cannot do this (our people are waiting)'.

Alice Walker's advice is important here, for she is not suggesting that we cut ourselves off from the outside world, because we cannot forget the mark our oppressions as black women have made on us, or the fact that 'our people are waiting'. The point is that what we need as artists is the opportunity to create the situation she describes so that we are allowed to develop an understanding of ourselves and of the struggle we have to wage within British society for recognition and respect. If we are able to do this by having adequate resources put at our disposal, we hope to share our experiences with, awaken the consciousness of and impart our strength to the whole society.

18 Yasmin Kureishi, 'Reworking Myths: An interview with Sutapa Biswas', 1986

Sutapa Biswas studied Fine Art at the University of Leeds, 1981–5, and would later undertake her postgraduate studies at the Slade School of Art in London, 1988–90. When this interview between Biswas and critic Yasmin Kureishi was published in the feminist magazine *Spare Rib*, in 1986, she had already participated in the exhibitions *The Thin Black Line* (ICA, London, 1985) and *The Issue of Painting* (Rochdale Art Gallery, 1986, touring to the AIR Gallery, London). Biswas' early figurative works were deliberately large, created using oil pastels in a vibrant colour palette. She often combined South Asian visual imagery and symbolism, such as the Hindu goddess Kali, with Western art historical references, including Fluxus and the work of US painter Robert Rauschenberg. In her painting, *Housewives with Steak-knives* (1984–5) Biswas included a reproduction of Artemisia Gentileschi's painting *Judith Beheading Holofernes* (c. 1620) in order to draw attention to the universal experience of patriarchal violence towards women, and the need for a collective feminist resistance. In this interview Biswas discusses her career to date, and the importance of representing South Asian women as active agents in their own lives, challenging Western stereotypes through humour.

* * *

Through the ages, women artists have become closely associated with the use of pastels to paint quiet, delicate images. Sutapa Biswas continues to use pastels, but rejects traditional techniques and notions, by producing huge, strikingly colourful, and assertive images. Sutapa told me, when I met her recently, *'I never realised the kind of effect my work would have, because I never made my work to last – it was never precious – I thought, oh well if it gets a hole in it, it gets a hole in it.'*

Born in India in 1962, Sutapa came to Britain at the age of four. She studied Fine Art at Leeds University and was the only Black woman in her department at college. Though several of her lecturers were supportive, Sutapa experienced a great deal of racism. *'It was not the kind of racism you can pinpoint, it's insidious. At the time I didn't know of any other Black artists and I felt very isolated.'* Since then, her work has seen the light of day at the ICA, Brixton Art Gallery, Rochdale Art Gallery and the Tara Arts Centre, to name but a few.

Sutapa's work addresses important issues for Black women and women everywhere, and by using myths and iconography from ancient Hindu mythologies, Sutapa reworks her rich, cultural history to question Western attitudes and assumptions. Sutapa's parents are very proud of her work. They were also surprised to see the powerful way in which she was using images, derived from stories of their heritage which they'd passed on to their children.

It doesn't bother Sutapa if the kind of symbolism she uses isn't immediately apparent to her audience, *'I want people to research into my culture, as I've been doing into European and Western culture.'* She sees part of her role as an Asian woman artist, to challenge the ignorant and arrogant assumption, that is often made about Western culture, being somehow 'superior' to Eastern culture. *'All those assumptions are very serious in how they affect our lives because they become part of that institutional framework that binds all of us. I think there are different ways of challenging them – films, television, photography, for me producing artwork is what I enjoy.'*

Sutapa explained to me the idea within Hindu culture, that every woman is seen as a goddess, because the idea of gods and goddesses exist in such a strong human form. The goddess Kali for instance, is always represented with a garland of men's heads round her neck and the head of a man in one hand. The garland is symbolic of evil, and Kali was created to destroy evil. In Sutapa's painting, **Housewives with Steak Knives,** she depicts a strong, multi-armed woman, wearing a necklace of men's heads, with one arm holding a steak knife, and in the other a decapitated male head. Sutapa's aim is to bring in icons and myths and continue them into her work, past becomes present, Kali becomes 'Housewives with Steak Knives'. Hindu culture was originally matriarchal, and yet Sutapa points out, *'The only way in which we now assess Asian culture is to say, Oh aren't they oppressed, what d'you think about arranged marriages? And we have to ask, why is it that women have arranged marriages? Arranged marriages were reinforced as an idea, with the invasion of the British in the Indian sub-continent, because it was a fashionable concept which came from Victorian England. So I'm trying to bring forward these images to make people ask, where is the link?*

The Last Mango in Paris shows two women, sitting together, laughing, and talking, while they each peel a mango. The caption underneath the painting relays to us their conversation:

M: 'If you were to be re-born, and had a choice what would you come back as?'
B: 'If I were to be re-born again, I would be born an English dog, because in England they look after their dogs really well.'

Any inclination the viewer might feel to use racial stereotypes to label Asian women, are instantly swept away, by the humorous conversation they are having. *'Humour and the use of satire is intrinsic to much of my work.'* Sutapa emphasised, and she was keen to stress, that contrary to how Asians are usually portrayed by the media, as having no idea of the real world – we are in fact very much aware of our economic and political situation – why we're here, and what our relation is to the dominant social and ideological thinking i.e. British and European culture. And something which Sutapa sees as lacking, when Asian people are portrayed, is their sense of humour. By taking humour and satire to the extreme in her work, Sutapa wants a platform from which people can begin to address their own racism.

Sutapa was trying to say a lot about domesticity and the domestic life of Asian women, in 'The Last Mango in Paris'. Sutapa explained, *'Why my work is often about domestic scenes, is that although my mother has never been politically active, she's been active and not passive in the ways she's educated and raised her own children – influenced their thinking and ideas – it's a very positive influence.'* Sutapa does to a certain extent agree with feminists who attack the basic ideas behind the family network. But she went on to make the point that, *'What isn't taken into consideration is the fact that coming from a totally different cultural and historical background, the place of the family and the ties of the family, are very different within Asian cultures and also within Black communities in general, throughout Britain. And because of the social pressures, families have always existed within quite tight structures. I suppose because you need that; it's often your only way of getting support in an otherwise hostile country.'*

Focussing on the positive aspects of Asian family life in her work, I wondered why Sutapa hadn't touched on the problems. Regarding her own experience she told me, *'I've never really felt that oppressed within my family, the only place I've felt oppressed is outside the home. Of course, there are many problems within any sort of home life, within all cultures. In other words, these 'problems' are not issues that are exclusive to the Asian community. There are problems within the Asian community, but I think these things have to be dealt with, within those communities. I don't see it as important to highlight those issues in my works necessarily, because on T.V. that's all we hear* about. The only artwork I've produced that comes close to looking at those issues is **As I Stood Listened and Watched, My Feelings Were, This Women is Not For Burning,** which is about the physical and mental abuse that many women in many societies are subjected to because we live in a violent and patriarchal culture. It was making a reference to the dowry system – but not just making reference to that. For me the act of making a diptych in which the two female subjects switch roles, is also about speaking to two halves of a history of violence against South Asian women under the patriarchal laws of both Britain and India.'

So how did Sutapa deal with being a part of two distinct cultures? 'One needs to be positive and say there are things we need to deal with – I don't see being part of two cultures as a problem because they overlap and intersect. I do find it difficult in terms of wanting to know about my roots and not having access to that information and knowledge at my fingertips, because Eurocentric culture is such that it doesn't teach you anything about the Asian continent, nor the African or Australian continents for example. That's what I find a problem, but these are not intrinsic problems, rather they're created by the dominant culture and the education system in the UK which only wants to tell a particular kind of narrative about those geographies the British colonised.'

What advice then, had she, for aspiring Black women artists? 'It's really important that Black artists are able to make their links very strong, so that they can act as a kind of support mechanism for each other and for future generations. We don't necessarily need white institutions and spaces to make our work visible, we don't have to operate in those areas, but I think it's useful if we do though, because the wider the contexts and spaces in which our work is seen and experienced, the better the understanding of who we are. My own experience has been that building supportive networks with other women who are also Black, presents contexts that counter isolation and allows us to share our narratives, our experiences and our art.'

19 Sonia Boyce, 'Extracts from a conversation with Pitika Ntuli', 1986

Sonia Boyce undertook her Foundation course in Art and Design at East Ham College of Art and Technology (1979–80) before studying Fine Art at Stourbridge College in the West Midlands (1980–83). In December 1986 – January 1987 Boyce was the recipient of a solo exhibition at the AIR Gallery in London, and the catalogue for that show included extracts from a conversation between Boyce and the South African poet and sculptor Pitika Ntuli, which are reproduced here. Boyce recalls her early interest in drawing as a way of communicating with her mother, while noting that her experience of collage was both liberating and constraining. She describes the importance of feminist artists Susan Hiller and Margaret Harrison, and identifies her relationship with Lubaina Himid as 'a lifeline'. In this text Boyce also provides an insight into her mode of working: of collecting and collating images and materials that are then worked on, redrawn, arranged and refined in order to tell particular stories.

*   *   *

Two or three years old, it is difficult to remember now, I began to draw on Mama's wallpaper. Mama, a strong woman. Powerful, precise, always right. Besides, she was bigger than me. She dressed me, fed me. I didn't have adequate words to communicate with her. I began to draw pictures instead.

One of five children, I was an awkward child. Always falling over, very slow at eating my food. I remember being scared of everything, the dark, birds, dogs, mice, heights, steps, spiders, being smothered by blankets, the police, death – the ultimate, mysterious, darkness. Early memories of Lena Horne, beautiful, almost white, I wanted to be white.

Later, on the degree course the tutors were dismissive. I was black, therefore I wasn't there. I drew my feet very big on a patterned background. "I'm here, you can't wish me away". Being a black woman is a perpetual struggle to be heard and appreciated as a human being. Many thoughts and fast fleeting images ran through me. I stretched my tiny arms to enfold the world but my embrace was inadequate. I put on political arms as an extension. Ideas burned, images continued to elude me. College gave me space and taught me the meaning of defending oneself. I was almost thrown out of the course. The pressures to conform, subtle (sometimes not so subtle) force themselves from all sides – the church, the family, school, college, on and on.

My life was shaken by the foundation course. I started doing self-portraits. I needed to see myself. At home I worked on collages from Ebony Magazine. I had a secret life as a secret painter. The work was bitter. It centred on black women's fixation with hair.

After a brief holiday I returned to do something simple. They advised me to paint a still-life. I chose playing cards and envelopes. I was sending secret messages to my mother, continuing a long conversation. The bridge they call my back was not broken. Secret messages to my mother were not enough. I wanted to go public. Pregnant with frustration I drew "Dancing Feet" and "Coconut" (1982). They celebrate the regaining of my political self from the cultural shock of living in a small town, one of few blacks.

To make work, to exhibit is not an act of indulgence. It is to pay homage to life, to those who influence me, to my people. When I was fourteen my art teacher, Mrs. Franklin, said "go to college". There was no question about it, no doubt. She still teaches me now, even at previews. Margaret Harrison came to our foundation course as a visiting lecturer. I was one of eighty students, inconspicuous, not at all pushy. She taught us that even rape can be a subject for our canvasses – sexual abuse, abuse of trust, abuse of power, an everyday occurrence, a highly political act. Frida Kahlo gave me so much so often. I have learnt from her canvasses. Circles of strength. Susan Hiller, another visiting artist came to our college for one day in 1983. She saw potential and gave support. She still continues to. Lubaina Himid threw me a life line offering a home base which also catapulted me into the limelight, something I cannot handle. I have a problem with my success.

My art, my life is rushed. Too busy beyond work. My time is spent rushing from point one to point ten only to end up at point three. I don't know what I am achieving. To paint is almost a miracle. But then art is an excellent disciplinarian and addiction.

I spend most of my art working time collecting possible material for further work. Only a few reach the stage where they are worked on. They are always in a state of readiness. Collections of wallpaper designs, patterns and material, they tell stories. I start with an image in my head. As I begin to draw, the image changes, becomes modified, focussed. There is a lot of censorship in my painting at a conscious level. Sometimes dreams help. What I suppress by day forces itself onto my consciousness by night, stubbornly painting itself on my canvas.

Sometimes it is frightening to discuss work. Your work paints, sculpts or writes you in turn revealing your silent subconscious fears, likes, dislikes. In life we take too much for granted.

An art director comes into my home to look at my pictures. "Is this how you see Christians?" After confusing his beliefs, I lost the chance to exhibit. He acted on his beliefs. I stood by mine. I respect the right of people to hold beliefs but I do not necessarily respect the beliefs. I also have the right to oppose those views. Contradictions within the Christian church reverberate within families. My brother is a Jehovah's Witness; my mother, a regular Christian. "You don't believe in blood transfusions?" she asks my brother. My brother quotes chapter and verse from the Holy Book to justify his beliefs. I am just a witness.

Hollywood, media projects, self-interests, images on television. Later, in my dreams, I see myself as a victim within a paw's grasp of King Kong. But I am safe inside the four walls of my house. The world itself enters my home. My family, compact and complex, acts, reacts and reflects. I, in turn, interpret the world outwardly in lines, tone and colour.

20 Salman Rushdie, Stuart Hall and Darcus Howe, *On Handsworth Songs*, 1987

In January 1987 a series of letters about the film *Handsworth Songs* (1986) by the Black Audio Film Collective were published in the *Guardian* newspaper. The film had been commissioned by Channel 4 and is a multi-layered experimental documentary about the causes and consequences of the civil uprisings in Britain in 1985; the title specifically refers to the riots that took place in Handsworth, Birmingham, in September that year. The letters by sociologist Stuart Hall and broadcaster and political activist Darcus Howe were written in response to an article about the film by the novelist Salman Rushdie. Together these three texts constitute an unprecedented debate between three respected figures from within the Black cultural sphere about the form and content of Black filmmaking specifically, and Black artistic endeavour more generally.

*   *   *

SALMAN RUSHDIE, 'SONGS DOESN'T KNOW THE SCORE'

(*Guardian*, 12 January 1987)

In *The Heart of a Woman*, volume four of her famous autobiography, Maya Angelou describes a meeting of the Harlem Writers' Guild, at which she read some of her work and had it torn to pieces by the group.

It taught her a tough lesson: 'If I wanted to write, I had to be willing to develop a kind of concentration found mostly in people awaiting execution. I had to learn technique and surrender my ignorance.'

It just isn't enough to be black and blue, or even black and angry. The message is plain enough in Angelou's self-portrait, in Louise Meriwether's marvellous *Daddy Was A Numbers Runner,* in Toni Morrison and Paule Marshall; if you want to tell the untold stories, if you want to give voice to the voiceless, you've got to find a language. Which goes for film as well as prose, for documentary as well as autobiography. Use the wrong language, and you're dumb and blind.

Down at the Metro cinema, in Soho, there's a new documentary starting a three-week run, *Handsworth Songs,* made by Black Audio Film Collective. The 'buzz' about the picture is good. *New Socialist* likes it, *City Limits* likes it, people are calling it multi-layered, 'original', imaginative, its makers talk of speaking in metaphors, its director John Akomfrah is getting mentioned around town as a talent to watch.

Unfortunately, it's no good, and the trouble does seem to be one of language.

Let me put it this way. If I say 'Handsworth', what do you see? Most Britons would see fire, riots, looted shops, young Rastas and helmeted cops by night. A big story; front page. Perhaps a West Side Story: Officer Krupke, armed to the teeth versus the kids with the social disease.

There's a line that *Handsworth Songs* wants us to learn. 'There are no stories in the riots,' it repeats, 'only the ghosts of other stories'. The trouble is, we aren't told the other stories. What we get is what we know from TV. Blacks as trouble; blacks as victims. Here is a Rasta dodging the police; here are the old news-clips of the folks in the fifties getting off the boat, singing calypsos about 'darling London'.

Little did they know, eh? But we don't hear about their lives, or the lives of their British-born children. We don't hear Handsworth's songs.

Why not? The film's handouts provide a clue. 'The film attempts to excavate hidden ruptures/agonies of "Race".' It 'looks at the riots as a political field coloured by the trajectories of industrial decline and structural crisis.' Oh dear. The sad thing is that while the film-makers are trying to excavate ruptures and work out how trajectories can colour fields, they let us hear so little of the much richer language of their subjects.

When Home Secretary Hurd visits Handsworth looking bemused, just after the riots, a black voice is heard to say: 'The higher monkey climb, the more he will expose.' If only more of this sort of wit and freshness could have found its way into the film. But the makers are too busy 're-positioning the convergence of "Race" and "Criminality",' describing a living world in the dead language of race industry professionals. I don't know Handsworth very well, but I do know it's bursting with tales worth telling. Take a look at Derek Bishton and John Reardon's 1984 photo-and-text essay, *Home Front*. There are Vietnamese boat people in Handsworth, where Father Peter Diem, a refugee himself, runs a pastoral centre to which they come for comfort.

There's an Asian businessman in Handsworth who made his pile by employing his fellow-Asians in sweat-shops to make, of all things, the Harrington jackets beloved by the skinheads who were also, as it happened, fond of bashing the odd Paki.

Here are two old British soldiers. One, name of Shri Dalip Singh, sits stiffly in his army tunic, sporting his Africa Star with pride; the other, a certain Jagat Singh, is a broken old gent who has been arrested for drunkenness on these streets over 300 times. Some nights they catch him trying to direct the traffic.

It's a religious place, Handsworth. What was once a Methodist chapel is now one of many Sikh gurdwaras. Here is the Good News Asian Church, and there you can see Rasta groundations, a mosque, Pentecostal halls, and Hindu Jain and Buddhist places of worship. Many of Handsworth's songs are hymns of praise. But there's reggae, too, there are Toasters at blues dances, there are Punjabi *ghazals* and Two Tone bands.

These days, the kids in Handsworth like to dance the Wobble. And some of its denizens dream of distant 'liberations', nurturing, for example, the dark fantasy of Khalistan.

It's important, I believe, to tell such stories; to say, this is England: *Allahu Akbar* from the minaret of Birmingham mosque, the Ethiopian World Federation which helps Handsworth Rastas 'return' to the land of Ras Tafari. These are English scenes now, English songs.

You won't find them or anything like them, in *Handsworth Songs*, though for some reason you will see plenty of footage about troubles in Tottenham and Brixton, which is just the sort of blurring you know the Harlem writers would have jumped on, no matter how right-on it looked.

It isn't easy for black voices to be heard. It isn't easy to get it said that the state attacks us, that the police are militarized. It isn't easy to fight back against media stereotypes. As a result, whenever somebody says what we all know, even if they say it clumsily and in jargon, there's a strong desire to cheer, just because they managed to get something said, they managed to get through.

I don't think that's much help, myself. That kind of celebration makes us lazy.

Next time, let's start telling those ghost-stories. If we know why the caged bird sings, let's listen to her song.

STUART HALL, 'SONG OF HANDSWORTH PRAISE'

(*Guardian*, 15 January 1987)
Sir, I must take issue with the way Salman Rushdie (Agenda, January 12) attacked Black Audio Film Collective and its film

Handsworth Songs, from his well-deserved but secure position in the literary firmament.

Of course, the film isn't perfect. Of course, a mere recital of the known contours of racism and oppression in the same, old, stale language does no one any good. Of course, black artists, deserve something more from us than mere celebration for having managed to say anything at all.

What I don't understand is how anyone watching the film could have missed the struggle which it represents, precisely, to find a new language. The most obvious thing to me about the film is its break with the tired style of the riot-documentary.

For example, the way documentary footage has been retimed, tinted, overprinted so as to formalise and distance it; the narrative interruptions; the highly original and unpredictable soundtrack; the 'giving voice' to new subjects; the inter-cutting with the 'ghosts of other stories.'

These new ways of telling bring *Handsworth Songs* into the line with *Passion of Remembrance* and, in a different way, *My Beautiful Laundrette*, in that distinctive wave of new work by third-generation black artists, part of whose originality is precisely that they tell the black experience as an *English* experience.

For what reason, apart from making us look in new ways, does Salman Rushdie want these 'new languages'? He seems to assume that *his* songs are not only different but better, presumably because they don't deal with all that dreary stuff about riots and the police etc. He prefers colourful stories about experience, closer to 'the richer language of their subjects.'

I fully agree that there is no one 'black experience', and that we need to confront its real diversity without forcing it into simplistic moulds. But subjects and experience don't appear out of thin air. The counterposing of 'experience' to 'politics' is a false and dangerous dichotomy.

Black Audio may have been guilty of mixing its metaphors

when it spoke of 'a political field coloured by trajectories of industrial decline and structural crisis'. But it seems to be struggling harder for a language in which to represent Handsworth as I know it than Salman's lofty, disdainful, and too-complacent 'Oh dear'.

DARCUS HOWE, 'THE LANGUAGE OF BLACK CULTURE'

(*Guardian*, 19 January 1987)
Sir, I want to take issue with Stuart Hall's attack (Letters, January 15) on Salman Rushdie's critical piece on the Black Audio collective's film, *Handsworth Songs.*

I write neither from Rushdie's 'well deserved but secure position in the literary firmament' nor from, dare I say it, Stuart Hall's equally well-deserved but secure position in the academic firmament.

I have been an activist in the black movement for over 20 years, organising and developing political, cultural and artistic thrusts which have emerged from within our black communities and continue to do so today.

For some time now my activist colleagues and I have been moaning in print about the absence of critical tradition in the field of black arts and culture. We recognise that such an absence is a point of great weakness. Without it we are left with nothing but cheer-leaders on the one hand and a string of abuses on the other.

Enter Salman Rushdie with a well-written and thoughtful piece of criticism which serves the dual function of a critique of the film itself, while at the same time laying the foundations of a critical tradition. It is most welcome.

Hall's main objection is that Rushdie misses the fact of the struggle for a new language which the film represents. Rushdie does nothing of the sort. He simply says that the attempt to shape a new language does not work, and I agree with him. In the best critical tradition, he goes on to suggest what he thinks would work. And

I am certain that the film-makers will take that on board. If they don't then we are in a sorry state indeed.

Finally, I could find not a trace of loftiness, disdain nor complacency in Rushdie's critique. His is a useful and timely intervention, a far cry from the patronising 'ten out of ten for struggling' approach.

21 Lubaina Himid, 'We Will Be', 1987

In her essay 'We Will Be', Lubaina Himid reflects on her career as an artist who is both Black and a woman. She outlines some of the constraints she and other Black women artists face with regard to making work, securing funding, exhibiting and publishing. She notes the venues and organizations that have been supportive, and those that have not. What is most evident in Himid's essay however is her generosity: through organizing exhibitions she created collaborative and supportive environments in which artists could talk, share, and develop ideas. In addition, through her writing she ensures that the activities and achievements of artists are recorded. Here she highlights the achievements of Veronica Ryan and Maud Sulter in their respective teaching and research, and goes on to discuss the work of Sonia Boyce and Claudette Johnson in detail. She also reflects on her own artistic practice, before asserting that Black women artists are 'here to stay'.

* * *

Being an artist, being black and a woman has its difficulties. These are that teaching in art schools is hardly ever possible, that our writing and criticism are rarely ever published, and that getting grants from ever-decreasing resources is miraculous. In Britain today there is not the will in art schools, in art publishing or from arts funding bodies, either to acknowledge the existence of the black woman artist or to treat her as an equal and her contribution as valid. Day-to-day economics play a major role in the lack of options and choices. Many black women live in inner city areas of the country and do not have the space for a separate studio or a studio within living accommodation. This does not make us lesser artists, but it does make us resourceful in adapting kitchens and bedrooms.

At the moment, black women artists are striking out in different directions. We have rarely thought, worked or shown as a group, but often we show in exhibitions together, for example, in *Five Black Women* at the Africa Centre and *Black Women Time Now* at the Battersea Arts Centre in 1983, in *Celebration and Demonstration* at St Mathews Meeting Place, *The Mirror Reflecting Darkly* and *The Thin Black Line* at the Institute of Contemporary Arts in 1985. We do not expect to agree with each other on form or function, and these exhibitions have proved that this is where the daring and the richness lies. We do expect a loyalty and a commitment to showing together and especially a commitment to encouraging younger women. The abolition of the metropolitan counties and all that they have done for Black Arts may sweep away some of the rungs upon which we have climbed thus far. The rungs were made from guilt and tokenism, but they have helped us to find each other and to make ourselves less invisible, at least to each other.

The best places for seeing black women's work regularly are the Brixton Gallery and the Black Art Gallery in London, while other places have made token and occasional gestures in our direction. These gestures were linked to funding and, while they were good opportunities for the artists, may never occur again without some hard arguing. In the years since 1981 there have been a fair number of exhibitions which, though not showing exclusively the work of black women, have featured them to some degree. The *Race Today* collective's *Creation for Liberation* open exhibitions, one a year since 1983, funded by either the Greater London Council or Greater London Arts or both, is one example which takes place each summer in Brixton. Black women also showed at the Black Art Gallery in Finsbury Park in the *Heroes and Heroines* exhibition and in *Heart in Exile*, its opening show. This gallery, while totally committed to showing the work of black artists, has been rather slow in accepting that women have a valid and equal contribution to make. In January 1985 a huge exhibition took place at the Festival Hall which combined the work of black crafts people and so-called 'fine' artists. It was called *New Horizons* and women featured in both sections. This was funded directly by the Greater London Council. *Into the Open* at the Mappin Art Gallery in Sheffield in 1984 showed the work of only five women, as compared to fifteen men, but each artist had the opportunity to show a good body of work – a rare thing in a mixed show.

So far the most obvious places in which to show work up and down the country have been hopelessly silent. I assume that they are waiting for black women artists to go away or give up, or to prove themselves. If so, they are out of luck. How can galleries like the Tate, the Serpentine or the Whitechapel in London, the Museum of Modern Art in Oxford, the Arnolfini in Bristol or the Third Eye Centre in Glasgow, justify their total boycott of our work? Doubtless, they can claim to have shown, in some corner of some downstairs room, the work of one black artist who happened to be a woman. But I have never noticed any work by black women artists in major survey exhibitions like the *Hayward Annual* or the *British Art Show* in 1985. Black women are committed to showing work in local and community venues, but we have every right to be seen in the so-called places of excellence too.

In art schools black women are usually separated from each other, one for every two or three years' worth of fine art students. There are then three main methods of teaching: an insistence that, as a black woman, the artist has something to be angry about and should express it; an insistence that angry or political statements are not art; a complete lack of any tuition at all. The instructions are always opposite to the artist's own mode of working. She therefore has little idea whether she is a victim of racism, of boredom, or is just a lousy artist.

In the last few years, largely through women's exhibitions and occasional forays into art schools as visiting lecturers, black women have begun to counteract this teaching and to learn from each other. Veronica Ryan, who has shown quite widely at major galleries in London as well as around the country, has been very instrumental in encouraging and teaching students while being respected as an artist by the establishment. Maud Sulter has done a great deal of research into black women's creativity in Britain, while Marlene Smith and Sutapa Biswas are coming forward as strong political artists, challenging myths and stereotypes fearlessly.

The themes in the work of black women artists cover a wide spectrum. We are making ourselves more visible by making positive images of black women, we are reclaiming history, linking national economics with colonialism and racism, with slavery, starvation and lynchings. There are some women whose work revolves around home, childhood and family, all of which are inextricably linked with racism in education, the challenging of racial stereotypes, and breaking through tokenism and sexism. These, and the broader themes of black heroes and heroines of the struggle for equality and freedom, international politics and the theft of our culture over hundreds of years show a personal/general, general/political, political/personal spiral in our work.

Sonia Boyce said of herself in 1983:

I am British born of West Indian parents. I live a schizophrenic life, between an anglicised background and a West Indian foreground; to put it another way, between 'but look at my trials nah', and 'gaw blimey'. My work tries to reconcile both of these. Most of the work has evolved from memories of 'trivial' events or milestones in my

life. The pictures attempt to be funny / ironic / sarcastic / symbolic –
public and private images.[1]

She is a storyteller. Her pieces are figurative and decorative epics
about what life has been like for Sonia Boyce, as she says, a mixture
of Gonga peas and rice and bangers and mash. She does not protest, predict or dictate, she remembers. She creates to remember
her childhood and to remind us of ours. She uses pastels, layer upon
layer of deep soft colour: rich purples, lilacs, browns, blues and
oranges. The scenes are often interiors, fabulously wall-papered
beyond the imagination of the Sanderson's catalogue. The women
seem to be dreaming and thinking, far off into the distance, both
backwards and forwards, taking in gossip, remembering times, the
odd rueful smile reflects the irony of life in Britain; the British, the
schools and the rules. This work draws the black viewer into a
conspiracy of knowing and recognition. Many of the pieces recall
incidents which have occurred often in her life and that have also
happened to other black women. There were Sundays spent in
delicate and pretty clothes unable to play, beribboned and bored.
There was the drag of being in love with the 'wrong' man. 'It was
one of the unwritten laws at school that black girls never became
too familiar with white boys. After two years with Nigel I still find
it difficult to walk down the street holding his hand.' She recalls
the joy of listening to women gossip, about abortion, separation,
adultery, travel. She has drawn the terror of dreaming about King
Kong, the film, the creature, the 'natives'. One large drawing, of a
young woman in the kitchen washing up, recalls the pandemon-
ium that can be caused by colours, head dress, and patterned cloth
when worn by black school students in Britain. Recently Sonia has
turned her attention to the church and its influence on her family
and on other black people worldwide. In this work she uses text,
images and titles 'Missionary position I' and 'Missionary position
II'. During a residency in a London school she focussed on the

theme of the portrait and of daughters and mothers. She drew her mother, surrounded by her favourite things, standing looking far from complacent and yet quite complete. Sonia's work is simple storytelling and honest revelation: rare gifts.

In two years she has provided dealers, curators and critics with much fodder. She has exhibited widely and in addition to those exhibitions mentioned above, has shown work in the Bluecoat Gallery in Liverpool, in the Riverside Studios, the Gimpel Fils gallery and the Nicola Jacobs gallery in London, the last being in a show chosen by the art critic of the *Guardian* newspaper, Waldemar Januszczak. She has shown that she can and will exhibit with anyone, anywhere, no matter who selects her work. Waldemar Januszczak, while loathing black art, has tried relentlessly to single out her work for critical praise using terms like 'sensation of intimacy', 'insight into the strain', and 'unsettled dreams'. He believes that she is wasted in showing with other black artists. He is wrong. With his help she could fall headlong into the trap of producing work for sale to and for the eyes of a privileged white minority who completely misunderstand her work, but grab it anyway. She could be in danger of becoming a much sought-after curio: the acceptable face of black art.

Claudette Johnson is more committed to sharing skills with black women than she is to producing goods, a gain for black women, a loss for dealers and buyers. She has produced some of the most dynamic images of black women over the last few years which are daring, challenging and moving. They urge the black woman viewer onwards and upwards. Their 'mistake' was that they did not intentionally communicate with the white viewer in the same way – they were not meant to. White men longed to adorn the walls of their houses with them while white women tried to prevent her from being given a grant to produce more work on the grounds that her work was not meant for them and was therefore exclusive.

What is Black Art?

In the exhibition catalogue for *The Thin Black Line* she says:

The black women in my drawings are monoliths. Larger than life versions of women, invisible to white eyes and naked to our own. They are women who have been close to me all my life with different stories. They are not objects. Every black woman who survives art college, fairy tales and a repressive society to make images of her reality – deserves the name artist.[2]

For me Claudette's drawings explore what strength means, what beauty means and what that power can do. They invite us to participate in the battle for equality, dignity and freedom of expression. They explore our sexuality and its myths and legends. In some drawings the women dare to say and do what we should all be doing every day, challenging male superiority, laughing at it, ignoring it. Some works have a stern, silent calm before the storm's fury. In another drawing in strong, dark reds and greens, there is a unity between mother and daughter; the older woman giving through experience, the younger woman giving with daring and energy. There are no words to help you with these works, there is a low humming intensity of colour, a richness of browns, sweeping arches, swirling shapes and merging meanings. There is a correct interpretation, but it is personal to the viewer and at the same time widely and loudly politically relevant.

In my own work, which ranges from wooden cut-outs to collages and paintings, I am trying to do several things, probably too many. I make images of black women because there are not enough of them. I expose the lies of the printed media because they have got away with too much for too long. And I am interested in smashing the notion that creative genius is solely in the hands of the white male. I want to change the order of things and take back the art which has been stolen. My work is satirical and sometimes vicious, uplifting and funny, depending upon your health, your wealth, your colour or gender. I use found materials, cloth, cardboard, paper and drawing pins, but have been seduced recently by acrylics while painting a mobile mural on wooden panels for Notting Hill. I am interested in the colour possibilities of paint but am repelled by its pretensions to magic.

In the past I made some wooden cut-out pieces of white male nudes with three foot long penises. I was trying to laugh at them, to sneer, and to jibe, to expose them as liars and cheats, but I have since decided that they are best left well alone, ignored. There are too few visual images of black women – we are not all nurses or Tina Turner. I want to destroy the stereotypes that television, the newspapers and advertisements are constantly feeding us – when they acknowledge that we exist at all. I am only interested in painting black women as independent, strong-thinking people. I try not to be naive and over-optimistic, we are not going to be able to run off into the sunset together, not without a bit of a fight.

I believe we should not be fooled by fashionable funding and token gestures, but we must take advantage of them. I have spent much time in organising exhibitions as well as showing in them: *Five Black Women* at the Africa Centre, *Black Women Time Now* at the Battersea Arts Centre, and most recently *The Thin Black Line* at the Institute of Contemporary Arts in London. I also co-selected *Into the Open*, an exhibition at the Mappin Art Gallery in Sheffield. Showing work in these and other exhibitions has given me the courage to go on making things. For this I have had to rely on other black artists and curators. White dealers, critics and curators, whether male or female, are not in the least interested in my work, with one or two exceptions.[3] I am not either sad or exotic enough for funding bodies and galleries: frankly, this pleases me.

The artists I have mentioned here are all concerned with the politics and realities of being Black Women. We can debate about how and why we differ in our creative expression of these realities. Our methods vary individually from satire to storytelling, from timely vengeance to careful analysis, from calls to arms to the smashing of stereotypes. We are claiming what is ours and making ourselves visible. We are a few of the hundreds of creative black women in Britain. We are here to stay.

NOTES

1 Sonia Boyce, statement in *Five Black Women* exhibition, The Africa Centre, London, September 1983.

2 Claudette Johnson, statement in *The Thin Black Line* exhibition catalogue, Institute of Contemporary Arts, London, November 1985.

3 The critic and writer Sarah Kent has been consistently supportive of my work for some years.

22 Keith Piper, 'Black Art: A Statement', 1987

As an art student at Lanchester Polytechnic, Coventry (1979), Trent Polytechnic, Nottingham (1980–83), and the Royal College of Art, London (1984–6), Keith Piper was a member of the Blk Art Group, and participated in exhibitions such as *Black Art An' Done* (1981) and *The Pan-African Connection* (1983). Like Eddie Chambers and Donald Rodney, Piper made urgent and often visceral works that addressed the experience of being young, male and Black in 1980s Britain. His work regularly referenced British colonial history and the transatlantic trade of enslaved African people, as well as the hopes and dreams of the *Windrush* generation of Caribbean migrants who arrived in Britain during the late 1940s and 1950s. In this statement, written in 1987, Piper reflects on the changing definition of 'Black art' and his own relationship with didactic approaches to art making. He acknowledges the limitations of his earlier position based in an aggressive revolutionary rhetoric and recognizes the significant contributions made by Black women artists to debates regarding the form and function of Black creativity. Nonetheless, he reminds readers to stay alert to the current political climate and identifies the dangers posed by the 'New Right', which seeks to shape history according to its own agenda.

* * *

My father used to say:

> Take me back to those days of old,
> When Black art was hot and not cold.

Personally, I do not believe in the concept of a 'golden age'. This is either some past historical space (a subject of nostalgia), or some utopian era at which we will inevitably arrive through the development and consolidation of our activities.

History shows us that the Arts, or more specifically in this case 'Fine Art', unlike (the) Sciences, holds too antagonistic a view of itself to effectively build upon what has gone before. Preceding events are more often than not reacted against, denigrated as passé, or parodied as kitsch. Because of this art changes rather than advances.

These changes, however, can be seen as significant in that they reflect the shifting aspirations, anxieties and preoccupations of the period, displaying how these factors play upon the production of art communities in general, and individual artists in particular. Therefore, within the study of art histories, or the history of any particular artist's production, it becomes essential to link this with the cultural, political and social currents which inform that production.

Bearing this framework in mind, it is possible to characterise the past five years of the Black Art movement in this country in terms of the passage from the sense of being an aspirant body of consensus on the verge of consolidation, to the recognition of a panoply of varying ideas occupying a loosely defined space called 'Black Art'.

The debate around the question 'What is Black Art?' has been largely superseded in recent years by a tacit but widely held acknowledgment of the movement as a 'broad church'. Many of us will argue that this state of affairs has arisen out of the failure of those of us who in the early Eighties argued for a confrontational and didactic function for Black Art, to successfully press our case home. Some of us would bemoan the fact that in 1987 Black Art sits more comfortably than ever before on the whitewashed walls of the art's mainstream. That far from the mainstream having to alter its elitist eurocentric conception of the world in order to accommodate the work of Black Artists, it is the work of Black Artists which has changed to accommodate the tastes and sensitivities of the mainstream. In short, some of us would argue that Black Art, like Brixton, is undergoing a process of 'gentrification'.

Personally, I would not endorse quite so pessimistic a point of view. A cursory glance at the work, in particular of the latest wave of young Black Artists, will reveal that the 'broad church' is in fact standing upon a fundamental bed-rock of consensus. For instance, I believe that it is widely acknowledged by Black Artists that we are engaged in the task of accumulating signs and evidences, fragments of the materials, both physical and informational, which describe our context(s) as Black people. It is out of these fragments, or more specifically those fragments which we choose to utilise as our raw material, that we formulate both the content of our statements, and the mode of address through which that content is articulated.

Not long ago somebody pointed out that you don't hear the world 'Revolution' any more, not even in Black Art. Certainly, the arrogant sense of historical mission which characterised much of the work produced in the mid to late Seventies, Linton Kwesi Johnson sensed that 'a brand new breed of Blacks has now emerged, leading on the rough scene . . .', has lost its appeal; partly through a greater sensitivity to the contributions made by our parents. It was a recognition that the agenda of Black struggle in this country did not open at Notting Hill in 1976, but has been and is an ongoing process as old as the Black presence (in Britain) itself. It was also a recognition of the limitations inherent in the type of aggressive rhetoric reminiscent of those points in the mid-Sixties American politics at which Black radicalism and machismo appeared to become synonymous. In this respect, it is important to acknowledge the success with which Black women artists in recent years have rewritten and resensitised the debate around the nature of the utterance employed before and its grounding in the politics of gender.

My own work since the early Eighties has consciously struggled to retain its identification with the didactic wing of the Black Arts movement. This lies in a still unresolved desire to see Black Art prove itself a functional and socially necessary activity. Within an overview of this epoch, recognising the myriad of needs of individuals and communities suffering the worst effects of this deep winter of Thatcherism, I believe that it has become more essential than ever before for Visual Art to take up a consciousness raising role. In an era in which the 'New Right' more than ever before has a keen vested interest in reshaping global histories in its own image, Black Art must set about the task with added vigour of realigning the shattered fragments of our histories before they are dispersed forever.

23 Mumtaz Karimjee, 'Black and Asian: Definitions and Redefinitions', 1987

Mumtaz Karimjee is a self-taught, independent photographer. In addition to creating a body of photographic work that explores the representation of Asian women, the lived experience of South Asian people in Britain, and her own lesbian identity, Karimjee made significant contributions as an arts administrator, curator and writer to the critical debates regarding Black art during the 1980s. Karimjee completed her BA Hons in Modern Languages (Chinese and German) at the Polytechnic of Central London in 1982, having spent time studying in China – at Beijing University (1978–9) and then Nanjing University (1980–81). She started taking photographs whilst in China, and some of these were included in the exhibition, *Black Women Time Now* curated by Lubaina Himid at the Battersea Arts Centre in 1983. In this text, Karimjee considers the terms 'Black' and 'Asian' in relation to her own identity and the ways in which they may be used inclusively and exclusively according to different contexts and settings. Karimjee's text was originally published in *Mukti*, a grassroots feminist magazine produced by a collective of women of South Asian heritage in Britain.

*　*　*

I am a photographer whose work has concentrated on exhibitions dealing with issues representation, mainly of women who

I consider to be Black and Asian. In the summer of 1985 certain events made me seriously question the use of the terms Black and Asian, particularly in relation to my own identity. At that time my work was included in what I had thought was a Black Women's Arts Festival, but found that in that particular context I was not considered Black, only Asian. At the same time the organisers of an Asian Arts Festival considered my work – photographic essays on China – unsuitable for inclusion because although I was Asian, it was felt my work was not really Asian, but Chinese. As a result I felt excluded and marginalised. In both situations the organisers were categorising me in ways I found difficult to accept. The following piece is my response, and through writing it I was able to clarify, for myself at least, my own position as a Black and Asian woman. In the final analysis I feel that it is this racist society and its hostility to my and the existence of all Black people which forces us to constantly question who we are, where we belong and why. It never allows us the security to just sit back and be simply who we are without justifying our existence.

I, a British woman of Indian origin, an Asian woman, and part of the Black community and Black struggle in this country. I also identify myself with the Third World and Third World struggles. Just as my struggle here in this country is part of the Black struggle which includes the struggles of all the various groups in the Black community, so on an even wider scale, the Black struggle in this country is part of the struggle of all Third World peoples.

There are differences between the different groups which make up the Black community in Britain, and I believe it is only possible to become a positive force in the community as a whole if first of all I accept and claim for myself my own specific identity. To do this is not to deny or negate my place in the Black community, but rather of say, I, a British woman of Indian origin, am part of the Black struggle and join in that struggle with all the strength and creative force that comes out of being who I am. For me to create that strength and force – and I must consciously create it because it does not magically appear – I must know who I am and where I come from, ie I must know my origins and they must be an integral part of me. I must be able to stand up and say who I am in such a way that it will be clearly understood everywhere.

The Black community in Britain is not monolithic, and while I consider myself part of the Black community, there are clearly occasions when the word Black does not include me – sometimes it means only African / Caribbean, at other times it includes those of us of Asian, ie South Asian, origin, but excludes others. For me, Black is a political term, which I use to explain my political position, not to explain my racial origins. I feel and continue to feel that I am Black in the context of the struggle of all non-white non-indigenous communities in this country regardless of their skin colour. If the word Black is to be used in any other way, if certain groups are to be excluded for other reasons then the term Black must be redefined.

What about the word Asian? Why do I call myself a Black British woman of Indian origin and not simply an Asian woman? The word Asian has, I feel, been misused and come to mean something that it isn't. Yes, just as I am Black, I am also Asian, but so too are the Chinese, Malaysians, Japanese and all the other peoples of Asia. How can I claim the term Asian for myself only when I come from only a very small part of Asia? I know that in this country Asian means from the Indian sub-continent or South Asia, so why not South Asian instead of taking over the whole continent of Asia and excluding others who are also Asian?

Finally, why do I insist I am of Indian origin and not simply Indian? Because my particular herstory includes not only India, but also Africa and Britain. I am part of the Asian community in Britain which encompasses all Asians, not just South Asians, and this Asian community is part of the Black community in Britain.

24 Samena Rana, 'Disability and Photography', 1987

During her short career, Samena Rana (1958–92) created a compelling body of photographic works that utilized archival family images alongside photographs composed in her studio. Rana came to the UK from Pakistan aged twelve to receive medical treatment after an accident. She spent her adult life in a wheelchair, and her work addressed not only her geographic and cultural displacement but also her disability. Her essay 'Disability and Photography' was first published in *Polareyes: A Journal by and about Black Women working in Photography* in 1987 and outlines some of the challenges that she faced as a disabled artist. In particular, she recounts how, when she enrolled on a photography course at the Sir John Cass School of Art (now part of London Metropolitan University) she found that the darkroom facilities were inaccessible to wheelchair users. In 1985 Rana initiated a campaign for the creation of an accessible darkroom at Camerawork, London, and later, as a member of that gallery's management committee, she fought to improve opportunities for disabled artists.

*　*　*

Disability is about values, and as we live in a society where the emphasis is on being visually 'perfect' a person with any kind of handicap is therefore a person who is not 'perfect', whether it's in looks, colour, ability which may be physical or mental, a hidden one, or an apparent one, is heavily discriminated against.

I am an Asian disabled woman, photographer and a teacher. Some people would say I'm in a position to be able to relate to all of these minority groups. Yes, I think I can, but what has had the most affect on my life is the disability aspect.

I wanted to write this article to try to illustrate some of the problems I have come across; especially whenever I have tried to do anything which has challenged existing attitudes. I hope that some people will benefit from my experiences, and that their awareness, it does not matter how small and practical, can make a big difference to someone's independence.

I started doing photography about five years ago when I enrolled at Sir John Cass School of Arts to do a part-time photography course. I was told that I would be a fire hazard, because the class appropriate for my level was on the second floor and I had to use the lift to get there and in the event of fire I would not be able to use the lift. There was no other way of getting down. After a lot of persuasion and heated arguments I managed to convince the Principal that I did not mind being carried down the stairs if there was a fire. The darkroom there was totally inaccessible; the lecturers however were very supportive, but I found it very frustrating to have to sit and watch other people doing their developing and printing, so I left and approached Camerawork to modify a darkroom. That was the beginning of a very big and drawn out process of finding an accessible darkroom and someone who could modify cameras.

Photography has always meant a lot to me as I like to capture certain moments which possibly would never occur again, because a certain combination of factors may not gather again in the same manner. I love people and colours, and photos are a way of sharing and saying so much, which words would not be able to express.

A year and a half ago I actually started to do my own developing and printing of black and white photos. This was at the Battersea Arts Centre where S.H.A.P.E. had started a darkroom which was accessible. What bliss! Even though finding the transport to get there was extremely difficult.

About a month ago Camerawork finished their darkroom as well. That is brilliant; so now I don't have to make the long journey to Battersea anymore. I can actually spend my time and energy on doing the work instead of finding access and persuading people that it's a good idea to invest in a darkroom which can be used by people with disabilities.

Being a little bit more positive I can see that attitudes are changing and that things; the Dial-a-Ride service is an example, are getting better. There are people who argue whether it should be 'Disabled People' or 'People with Disabilities' or whether 'helpers' should be 'facilitators' or 'arms and legs' or whatever. I personally don't care, because to me, disability is not a game of words but a way of life, which is full of physical limitations, and mental and emotional barriers which create the loss of opportunities to participate in the community on an equal level. These frustrations are created by society's ignorance and the absurd attitudes which exist towards disabled people, whether they be partly or totally blind, or deaf, or who are in some way physically impaired. Also those who are mentally ill or mentally handicapped or whose speech is impaired, and who have hidden or apparent handicaps resulting from epilepsy or ageing.

It would be encouraging to see more practical constructive improvements made in the field of the Arts, especially in Visual Arts. This would enable more disabled people to make their own initiatives, instead of endless meetings and conferences held on their behalf by able-bodied people, when disabled people can't get there because of the lack of adequate transport.

25 Allan deSouza, 'Portrait of the Artist as a Dirty Young Man', 1987

Artist and writer Al-An deSouza, who went under the name Allan deSouza until 2022, principally worked in photography and photocopy art during the 1980s. They participated in the exhibition *Unrecorded Truths*, curated by Lubaina Himid at The Elbow Room, London, in 1986, and were a co-editor of *Bazaar: South Asian Arts Magazine*, established in 1987. deSouza's *Portrait of the Artist as a Dirty Young Man* was originally published in issue 3 of *Bazaar* and was later reprinted in the book *Ecstatic Antibodies: Resisting the AIDS Mythology* edited by Tessa Boffin and Sunil Gupta (1990). In 1988 deSouza participated in the exhibition, *Against the Clause*, an exhibition of photocopy art championing defiance against Section 28 of the newly passed Local Government Act which banned the 'promotion' of homosexuality in publicly funded organizations such as schools and art galleries. In their prose-poem, reproduced here, deSouza confronts the ways in which British colonialists and Christian missionaries engaged in 'civilizing' missions in Africa and Asia during the nineteenth century. They conclude their text by addressing common perceptions of homosexuality as being akin to a virus, and the ways in which AIDS was widely presented by those in power as a Black disease and a consequence of uncivilized perversity. deSouza argues however that it is colonialism and its legacies – poverty, continued exploitation and racism – that pose the greatest threats; readers are encouraged to push back.

*   *   *

Following the assumptions
God is good; is white; male; heterosexual;

the prescription:
Cleanliness is next to godliness.

It follows that the cleanest, i.e. those closest to god, are the natural regulators (Lords and Masters) of His world.
So . . . .

'Take up the White Man's burden
Send forth the best ye breed
Go blind your sons to exile
To serve your captives' need.'[1]

'If it were assumed that the Africans were racially inferior, and yet spiritually equal and capable of receiving the Christian message, the moral duty of the superior race was clear. It was to take up the "white man's burden" and exercise a trust over the spiritual and material welfare of people whose racial status was equivalent to that of minors.'[2]

'the filthy personal habits of even the most highly educated classes in India – which like the degradation of Hindu women are unequalled even among the most primitive African and Australian savages . . . makes the claim for Swaraj (self-rule) seem nonsense and the will to grant it almost a crime.'[3]

And so on.
And so forth.

Let the wheel turn.

Do you need reminding of just how these Lords and Masters regulated our earth?
Will that bring to life the cries of fear and agony?
Will the cries of disbelief and anger reverberate in your head?
Will your own voice be heard?

Jallianwala Bagh
Belsen
Hiroshima
Little Big Horn
Sharpeville
Bloody Sunday
Sabra / Shatila.

. . . .

Enough.
Lest the tears overwhelm.

Enough. Let the wheel turn.

Thus it was an Imperial Duty to rescue the 'savages' from their own degeneracy and 'discipline' them when necessary; thus it was chivalrous to Sally Forth and Save The World. As long as once saved they didn't venture back to your own shores . . .

But venture back they did.

With the arrival of these 'slaves and coolies' to the Motherland (resplendent in her bountiful love and purity) the paranoia, and ideology, of *germs* reached epidemic proportions.
This paranoia, this fear of bodily invasion and pollution, was on its own too inefficient. It had to be, and had been, carefully nurtured

and systematized into an ideology – a *germphobia* – which could be used to justify programmes of slavery when 'savages' could be subjugated, and pogroms of extermination when they couldn't.

But now those same 'savages' were HERE.

At the White cliffs of Dover and the White walls of Heathrow. Whether they had been Chinese, Irish, or Jewish peoples, more recently South Asian or Afrikan-Caribbean peoples, or even most recently Bangladeshi people – the same old arguments are trotted out. The media begins its ritual gruntings, the pigs rampage onto the streets, the bleating inhabitants nod their empty heads in approval. The whole pigsty, to hide its own filth, reverses the simile and the new-coming peoples are accused of overcrowding, insanitary conditions, sexual perversions, criminal tendencies, infectious diseases, polluting the culture, society and – heaven forbid – blood! of the Majority.

It is this Majority – not in terms of numbers – but in terms of power and control, who set the agenda.
It is this Majority which sets the agenda for how i am seen and how i am defined.
Thus am i a member of an 'ethnic' minority – a minority again not in terms of numbers but in terms of (lack of) power and (lack of) control.
Yet this definition recalls to me this: that i have sisters and brothers worldwide, similarly labelled.
It recalls to me this: that we may not have it now, but the wheel turns, and where then will lie the power and control?
It recalls to me this: that what the wheel needs is pushing.

This Majority which has the power to enforce its fears of the human body into a national phobia of 'foreigners' – an obsession with racial and societal purity. Thus are 'foreigners' seen as a viral infection of the national body. The purity of the 'British culture' is seen to be 'swamped', and like a disease these alien bodies must be limited and controlled. Immigration and Integration.

According to that (in)famous Lord and Master Roy Hattersley, you can't have one without the other. Without immigration control, without integration, the excess of foreign bodies causes infection. Thus in Southall, South Asian children had to be 'bussed' to other schools so that they could be safely 'absorbed'.

Thus, (Moral) Majority parents in Dewsbury didn't want their kids infected with the germ of alien habits. Always the innocent who suffer . . .

Thus, honorary Lord and Master Margaret Thatcher, wishes to clean up the 'inner-cities' – breeding grounds of all that is foreign and diseased. As does North America, within and without its borders. As did Lord and Master Adolf Hitler with the Warsaw ghetto, to exterminate the 'vermin'.

Enough. Let the wheel turn

The idea that groups or individuals carry disease with them and can infect an 'innocent' population extends into the realm of sexuality. 'Disease' in this case means more than physical symptoms, it means also the infection of moral values.

To the Majority, the only legitimate sexual expression is within the institution of heterosexual Marriage. Without Marriage (and its retainers of pornography and prostitution) society as they know it would cease to exist; or if it did then it was criminalised out of existence.

So, the British in India introduced laws regulating marriage and land ownership, ostensibly to benefit women and the poor. In practice, they worked otherwise. Witness: the Nayar matrilineal system in South India had no marriage system, and women had active control over their own sexualities. Anathema to the British, the Nayar system was completely destroyed by the new laws.[4]

Similarly with homosexuality which remains largely criminalized. A minority in terms of power, lesbians and gay men are stigmatized as "dirty" – and hence diseased, sick, and criminally perverse. Witness: the raiding of gay clubs by police wearing rubber gloves.

With AIDS, the Majority wield a further weapon in their arsenal of righteousness. Current 'gay plague' hysteria ominously parallels Nazi propaganda. Then, not only were Jewish people incarcerated and exterminated; so also were socialists and communists, gypsies,[5] and homosexual men. Each group was accused of infecting the purity and stability of the Reich.

Witness: before it was burnt down in 1933 by a fascist gang, the Institute of Sexual Science (set up by Magnus Hirschfield, founder of the first gay rights movement), was described by a Berlin newspaper as an 'unparalleled breeding ground of filth and dirt'.

As such propaganda paved the way for a Lord and Master and his death camps, so the present media hysteria allows public figures to advocate such measures as 'gassing queers', and to claim their authority directly from god.

And the pigsty inhabitants shut their eyes and nod their approval. In their minds gay men are by definition guilty.

But the Majority also views homosexuality as not a sickness in itself; but merely a tumour, a result of a deadlier disease wrought by the Women's Movement: the emasculation of Masculinity, and the demise of Marriage and the Family.

In one foul breath, they serve a death sentence on lesbians and gay men, and a life sentence on women, re-imprisoned within the home.

And the bleating inhabitants continue to nod.

A convenient bonus for the Majority is the apparent origin of AIDS in Africa. To them, it further 'proves' their long-held view of Afrikan peoples as dirty and degenerate. The possibility that AIDS originated in monkeys only reinforces their belief that Afrikans cross-bre(e)d with apes.[6] From such beliefs it was only a short step to the slave trade.

It is said that there is nothing new under the sun.
So it is with the method of the Majority.
In the c17, Europe was ravaged by syphilis, another 'scourge from god'. Great claims were made to 'prove' its origins lay with the Native Americans, and brought to Europe by Columbus and his crew. For one thing, it throws an interesting light on Columbus' activities in North America.

Recent AIDS research throws into question the Africa-Haiti-USA transmission route, and adds the possibility of it being reversed, i.e. from USA to Haiti to Zaire; from Europe to other central African states.
Yet the search for an origin is also the search for a scapegoat. If we consider why AIDS has claimed so many lives in Africa and in Haiti we have to consider these countries' post-colonial relationship to the USA and Europe. The exploitation and destruction of their self-reliant economies have placed them in a position of dependence to the Imperial nations.
Enforced poverty has created the conditions for the transmission of any number of diseases.

Poverty: inadequate medical facilities; vaccination needles are shared and vaccine are often self-administered within family groups.

Poverty: blood supplies are not treated.

Poverty: the body is continually assaulted by minor infection, making it less resistant to fatal diseases and syndromes such as AIDS.[7]

Poverty: prostitution by both men and women is often the only way for them to survive;

> Defined as dirty and diseased
> For many the wheel turns
> Such that they are forced into conditions of dirt
> > disease
> >
> > poverty

For many the wheel has turned
Such that they have died from those inflicted conditions

> For those gone
> Those here
> And those to come

PUSH THE WHEEL

NOTES

1 'To wait, in heavy harness,
On fluttered folk and Wild –
Your new-caught, sullen peoples;
Half devil and half child.'
Rudyard Kipling, *The White Man's Burden* 1899.

2 Curtin, *Image of Africa*, Repro. in *Staying Power, The History of Black People in Britain*, Peter Fryer, Pluto Press, 1984.

Allan deSouza, 'Portrait of the Artist as a Dirty Young Man', 1987

3 *New Statesman and Nation*, 1927. Repro. p. 31 in *Daughters of Independence –
Gender, Caste and Class in India*, Joanna Liddle, Rama Joshi. Zed Books, 1986.

4 p. 28, *Daughters of Independence*

5 Stigmatized as 'dirty' – hence diseased, uneducated, criminal; it is still
legally tolerated and socially accepted to discriminate with such notices as
"NO TRAVELLERS".

6 *Staying Power*, Ibid (2).

7 Witness: 1985 figures for life expectancy in Sierra Leone: men, 30.6; women,
33.5 years. Repro. *New Internationalist*, no. 175.

also see: 1) *Sex and Germs, The Politics of AIDS*
          Cindy Patton, South End Press, 1985.
     2) *AIDS and the New Puritanism*
       Dennis Altman, Pluto Press, 1986.
     3) *Ayahs, Lascars and Princes*
       Rozina Visram, Pluto Press, 1986.

26 'Rita Keegan talks to Clare Rendell', 1987

In this extended first-person narrative, artist, curator and archivist Rita Keegan provides insight into her early life in the United States and how she came to settle in London in 1980, having studied Fine Art at the San Francisco Art Institute from 1969 to 1972. She discusses her approach to art-making and the ways that she pushed the boundaries of Fine Art by working in textiles and craft materials alongside photography and digital technologies. Since the 1980s Keegan has been a pivotal figure within the Black arts community; she helped set up the Brixton Art Gallery in 1981, and in 1982 she curated the first exhibition by The Black Women Artists Collective, *Mirror Reflecting Darkly*, at that gallery. From 1985 Keegan was a member of staff at the Women Artists Slide Library (now based at Goldsmiths, University of London), where she established the Women Artists of Colour Index, an archive dedicated to recording the achievements of Black women artists.

* * *

I was born in New York. My mother is Dominican and my father Canadian, so I didn't have a typical Black American upbringing. Our attitudes and diet had more in common with an English/ Commonwealth background. At school I was always the dumb one, whereas my brother got on well. Years later he told me I was dyslexic, he had heard my parents discussing it. At the time, it meant I was always in problem classes, mixing with kids with learning difficulties or discipline problems.

None of this affected me too much because I always knew I'd be an artist. At 14 I went to an art high school in the Bronx. I tried out all sorts of techniques, then concentrated on illustration and costume design. When I left I worked in Bloomingdale's, then I studied for a Diploma and became an assistant teacher in my old school (the Prodigal Daughter returns!). There seemed no chance of going to college since I had no money and no decent grades.

In 1968 I moved to San Francisco. My brother had started a photography course at the Art Institute, so I decided to apply to the same college. I heard nothing from them, so I returned to work in New York, then travelled to Mexico. Suddenly I heard that the Institute had accepted me. I took out a loan and started looking for jobs to put myself through school. I always looked for art-related jobs like teaching or costume designing. We had to buy all our painting supplies and there was no student housing. There were a lot of wealthy students on the course, and I was always amazed by the amount of materials wasted.

Compared with English art schools, there was far less snobbery about fine v. applied art. I concentrated on painting but I also studied crafts like printmaking and ceramics. About one third of the teachers were women – a higher proportion than in an average English college. The photographer Imogen Cunningham taught us, also Mary O'Neill, the Black woman painter. But there was no women's movement in art yet, no books on women's art. The ideal woman was still barefoot and pregnant – and possibly weaving . . .

A lot was happening in the late 1960s, and San Francisco seemed the place to be. There was the War in Vietnam, Black Power, the Visionary Painters, the Hippies, the Happenings, Zap comics, the newly opened Vorpel Gallery. I remember we marched into the Dean's office demanding Third World Scholarships. He granted them. I can't imagine the authorities listening to students nowadays.

My main bad memory of college was at my graduation in 1972. I was almost named Student of the Year, but they gave it to a man because they decided that for his career's sake he needed it more! This was my introduction to women's issues.

On leaving college, I taught painting for a year at the charity-funded medical centre, Hospitality House. This was a drop-in centre for junkies, prostitutes, runaways etc. in what they called the Tenderloin district of San Francisco. In 1973, I travelled to the West Indies and on to Europe. I had my passport stolen in Vienna and I got stuck in London on a temporary passport that had expired. It was easier to make money in England than in the States and the rents were lower, but it was very hard being an illegal alien who couldn't leave the country.

When I managed to return to America I went to live in Hollywood. I made space for a large studio in my flat, and I found work in set designing and upholstery. But Hollywood was not a very exciting place to be. The only culture there was yoghourt . . . (They say things have improved now). I went travelling again to Amsterdam, and in 1979 I was back in England.

I like London as a city. It combines the best of Los Angeles and New York. It has the village atmosphere of New York without the hysteria. It has the fast pace of Los Angeles but is a lot more accessible and not so dominated by cars. I feel London adapts to you, and not vice versa. I have been in London now for eight years: I have no strength to leave, I am getting older and it will be more difficult to find a job in the States.

Also, my work is beginning to be shown over here. The people I've met have affected my work. I have begun to do more mixed media pieces, and they've had a better reception over here than in the States. Nevertheless, the elitism of paint in this country makes me angry. I have more opportunities to show my paintings than

my sculpture or textiles, and I think my move to mixed media is
a conscious retaliation.

Meeting the Zamani Soweto Sisters was an inspiration to me.
I made a textile piece for their exhibition in Brixton Art Gallery
in June 1986. My interest in textiles is a natural development from
my sewing. I have always made my own clothes, and the history
of clothes is important to me. Dress reform has been crucial for
women: the increasing freedom of women's dress has had effects
on women's minds!

Getting involved with the Brixton Art Gallery gave purpose to
my early years in England. When I worked with Françoise Dupré,
Teri Bullen and lots of other women on the first *Women's Work*
exhibition in November 1983, I began to read and to explore wom-
en's writing in a way I hadn't done since I left college. I enjoyed the
feedback that comes from working with other women, and realised that many of us have similar histories. I also realised that documentation is crucial. If you don't document yourself, nobody else
is going to. A photocopied sheet is better than nothing. The work
of the Women Artists Slide Library in documenting women's art
is so important for future generations of women.

As a volunteer in Brixton Gallery, I developed skills in hanging
work and dealing with the press – and I learnt about women in the
art world. I have never exhibited a lot. The formalities, the need for
an agent, has put me off. I prefer to paint instead, and to make art
in the community. But community art is a very time-consuming
and low priority activity in Britain. The negotiations with British
Rail to establish Brixton Art Gallery and to protect its future, as
well as attracting funding, demands a lot of dedication, and such
an operation needs many workers to sustain it.

The lack of interest in community art in Britain arises from the
fact that art is not viewed as a necessity. America has a strong art-
buying culture. Corporations can claim tax relief and the approach
is less elitist: whatever is there is theirs.

My involvement with Brixton Gallery in this discouraging climate began to drain my energies, and now I need to concentrate on my own work for a time.

Many of my paintings are self-portraits. It's not for egocentric reasons, it's simply that I am an available subject. I play a lot of different roles in my life and my appearance changes, but I am the same. I like to play with my own personal costuming. Different pieces of jewellery provoke memories, and in one painting I wear a dress of cotton made in Africa, produced in Germany and designed for the African market. Symbolism is important to me: in one of my works there are cracks across my face, as if to show that while you can be strong and do many things it doesn't mean they leave no traces.

Another reason why I concentrate on self-portraits is that I find the artist and model relationship offensive. It is using another person as your expression. In making a self-portrait, I have given myself permission. A lot of Black women are doing this now. What else do we have? We have no property, no money, no bodies of our own. We have to work from ourselves. And speaking from my own experience, it is not as easy for a large Black woman to celebrate herself!

In my textile work, I have begun to realise the importance of presentation and high standards of production. It helps in breaking down resistance to the medium and making it more accessible. In the *Love, Sex and Romance* show at Brixton Gallery in October 1985, the works by Roxane Permar, Wendy Latham and myself that were singled out by reviewers were all in frames. It is as if people can only deal with certain messages.

I hope that in the future I can combine an involvement in community art with my own work. It is easy to criticise organisations and their work but much harder to become involved, to do things, to be critical where necessary, but to be supportive.

27 Sutapa Biswas and Marlene Smith, 'Black Women Artists', 1988

In their essay *Black Women Artists*, Sutapa Biswas and Marlene Smith issue a call for nuanced and scholarly writing on the work of Black women artists. They are critical of the ways in which white feminist and left-wing male writers fail to adequately engage with and discuss artworks by Black practitioners. They pointedly state: 'Little is written and therefore little is known.' It is notable that throughout the 1980s, sympathetic, critical engagement with the work of Black artists by established art critics and art historians was rare. As this article describes, it was mainly left to artists to write about the work of their peers. Here Biswas and Smith not only call for the development of a critical cultural and art historical framework within which the formal and aesthetic language of artistic productions by Black women artists can be situated and interpreted, but they also offer an example of how to undertake that task. Rather than focus on issues relating to the artists' ethnicity, they instead focus their discussion and interpretation on the work of art itself. They discuss two very different artworks, Zarina Bhimji's *She Loved to Breathe – Pure Silence* (1987) and Sonia Boyce's *Missionary Position II* (1985), through close attention to their materials, modes of creation or construction, and the iconographic meaning of the objects and figures depicted. Prophetically, they identify Bhimji's *She Loved to Breathe – Pure Silence*, now in the

V&A Collection, London, and Boyce's *Missionary Position II*, now in the Tate Collection, as 'icons in the making'.

*   *   *

WILL THE ART CRITIC PLEASE STEP FORWARD

Black women's struggles for political change have led to an increased involvement in several fields, amongst them education, media, local government, health, and the arts.

The role that the arts play within the context of wider political and social change has been significant. However, Black women's contribution to the arts in that context has never been recognized, and within this debate the particular concerns and work of Black women are given next to no space at all. Little is written and therefore little is known.

Many Black artists in Britain site themselves within a Black art movement, attempting to challenge art world Eurocentricism. The significant increase in the number of exhibitions by Black artists indicates that this movement has had an impact. Whilst it is encouraging to see a number of Black women artists exhibiting, organising, speaking and writing about art, the dynamics of the movement and its relationship to the establishment is problematic on a number of fronts. Progress has been difficult to quantify.

Access is still an important issue. Very few Black women have access to the means to produce and exhibit. For those that take on formal art education, the experience of being isolated within the institution is demoralising. There are only a few galleries that are committed to showing Black art. Mainstream galleries have until recently remained closed to work by Black artists. When they do show our work, it is often the tokenistic gesture of their equal opportunities policy. Additionally the audiences these venues court and attract is limited to the white middle class. For those Black artists that seek to intervene in that arena and to challenge the system's view of 'us', 'them' and history, there is a consistent battle against the marginalisation of our ideas as well as our practice.

These are just some of the issues facing us. As Black women and visual artists much of our energies are diffused because we have to work simultaneously on many different fronts. We must make our images, organise exhibitions, be art critics, historians, administrators, and speakers. We must be the watchdogs of art establishment bureaucracies; sitting as individuals on various panels, as a means of ensuring that Black people are not overlooked. The list is endless.

In this article we start from a premise that our movement needs a more developed infrastructure to sustain it and aid its growth. We are concerned specifically with the need for more written material. This call for alternative art histories and criticisms is not new. The vital function that critics can and should play in developing the ideas has been recognised by Black artists for some time. We attempt here to identify some of the factors that operate to undermine the development of Black art criticism; a language with which we can discuss the meanings of Black art. By presenting our own attempts to read the work of Zarina Bhimji and Sonia Boyce, we hope to give Black women artists space and encourage the discussion of all our work.

WATCHING THEM WATCHING US

Within the context of current art criticism, the nineteenth century view of Black people as 'other' is still dominant. On the right, mainstream art has failed to acknowledge the work of Black artists. The left on the other hand has framed us within an anthropological context. This point is taken up by Rasheed Araeen in his article *From Primitivism to Ethnic Art*.[1] In either case the Black artist is removed from the immediate culture in which they are actively engaged and placed into a construction of 'otherness'.

These notions are still being used to define and fix the positions of non-European peoples in such a way that they are deprived of their active and critical functions within contemporary culture. In other words, because the dominant culture has defined Black people as aliens, we are always positioned *outside of* rather than on equal terms.

The effects of this notion on art criticism can be observed in the interview between art critic John Roberts in conversation with the artist Sonia Boyce.[2] His frame of reference is informed not only by this nineteenth century view, but through the application of what might be defined as a dominant mainstream 'common sense' notion of *what Black people are about*.[3] In his interview there is little reference to the images themselves, and John Roberts falls into other 'common sense' stereotypes about Black people.[4] He states that the cultural roots of Black kids are located 'predominantly in music and dance'.[5]

The problem is not that the critic should wish to discuss music as an influence on her work, but that in his preoccupation, John Roberts overlooks Sonia's statement, as a visual artist, that Mexican painter Frida Kahlo was the most critical influence on her at the time.

Similarly, feminist art critics have evaded issues of race. For example, recent texts which have sought to address the issues of race and gender have been inadequate. In *Framing Feminism, Art and The Women's Movement 1970–85*,[6] Black women's work is dealt with as an adjunct to the main thesis. Conversely in *The Struggle for Black Art*,[7] the issues of gender are not dealt with.

This is not to imply that by simply naming Black women artists these texts would improve. Their problem lies beyond the ability to list Black women's exhibitions or reproduce their images. Rather there is a case to make that critical theories for reading their art need to be revised to make the issues of both race and gender central and connected.

There is a failure to recognise the full significance of the developing discourses on race / gender and cultural production. As Paul Gilroy points out in his book *There Ain't no Black in the Union Jack*,[8] Black people are not in the process of losing or abandoning their identities. We are witnessing in Britain and internationally a synthesis of different cultural inputs that ultimately makes us question the idea of identity as fixed and absolute.

BLACK ARTS & AUTHENTICITY – A CALL FOR MORE WRITING

In calling for more writing about Black women's work it is also necessary to discuss the problems that Black art activists, as writers, face in a context of near invisibility. The lack of published material on the history of Black art in this country causes problems which can only be remedied when lengthy research is carried out and published. Currently 'overviews' can only be misinformed and therefore are, in turn, misinforming.[9]

The establishment, as it does with Black communities and other interest groups, has a tendency to attempt to identify particular individuals as the authenticating voices. The community leader thus becomes the authentic voice, charged with identifying the problems and priorities of the community. We are not concerned here with questions of sincerity, since the result can lead to a spectacle of individuals vying for the position as the Black vanguard.

This increases the tendency for writers to address, as for example, Maud Sulter does in her review of Sonia Boyce's work,[10] not the work itself but the *authenticity* of the artist. Conscious of the way in which a token representation of Black art can be appropriated and aware that marginalised individuals alone do not represent a forceful challenge to the mainstream, critics are diverted into assessing the artists credibility without reference to the images. There is no attempt to develop a framework through which the viewer or the reader can engage with the language of the images in formal, conceptual and aesthetic terms.

It is important now more than ever that Black women intervene constructively and consistently within this debate. And we can only reiterate how important we feel it is to develop an infrastructure within which the actual work by Black women is discussed.

ICONS IN THE MAKING

It would be contradictory to call for a discussion of Black women's art and yet fail to begin addressing this ourselves. Below we discuss two specific works by **Zarina Bhimji** and **Sonia Boyce**. While both works resist the notion of a fixed identity, they reflect common political realities and aspirations.

She Loved to Breathe – Pure Silence (1987) – Zarina Bhimji

Zarina, (born Uganda 1963) is an artist who mainly explores the use of photography within her work. She uses both image and text which are of equal importance.

The piece *She Loved To Breath – Pure Silence* is a kind of installation of images centrally positioned within a space.

The piece comprises sheets of perspex hung delicately from the ceiling, and beneath which are sprinkled intense red- and orange-coloured spices. Between the sheets of perspex are mounted many images which are put together so that the panels can be read from both sides. This way of displaying the piece is important since it breaks with the normal conventions of showing photographic images flatly positioned against a wall. Because the images are centrally suspended, the viewer is forced to walk around the piece, actively engaging in it.

In her work, technical decisions that have gone into making the piece are very important and work hand in hand with the aesthetic considerations. The development process of the photographic images she includes, for example, are carefully made to lend a particular feel. The photograph shown here, has been processed on bromide paper to give contrast and depth to the image. The photograph has also been tinted in a light pink – which noticeably contrasts the colours of the spices. Her work is also unusual in that the words she uses have been printed on muslin.

Zarina explores the use of metaphors in both her images and text which are important to the meaning of the work as a whole.

For example, in the image shown, Zarina has chosen slippers as a cultural signifier, but also as a metaphor for an Asian woman. The bird and slippers are also metaphors used to signify migration.

She Loved To Breath – Pure Silence is about the experience of migration. It not only raises issues in and around migration – that of forced movement, identity, status, nationality, but also explores its personal and traumatic effects.

The juxtaposition of the dead (or sleeping) bird, and the empty slippers has both an inviting/sensuous and jarring/disturbing effect. There is a sense of mourning in the picture, and a sense of loss. The dead(?) bird and empty slippers are icons and metaphors used to express feelings in the aftermath of a traumatic experience. The pain and anguish are echoed by the lines in Zarina's text:

'The anger turned inward where could it go except to make pain? It flowed into me with her milk.'

Zarina deals with questions of silence, and the international pain and feelings of displacement. The politics of silence and its implications within the lives of black women is strongly indicated in the title of the piece and throughout the text.

The use of a passport image is a pointed reference to the status of Black women in terms of Home Office Legislation. Rubber gloves are also presented within a frame making an understated reference to virginity tests, violation of black women's bodies (as carried out by law). Her images accentuate the vulnerability of their status by the fact that they are suspended from the ceiling. The piece reflects issues of nationality and identity, but somehow resists notions of a fixed identity.

Because of Zarina Bhimji's careful consideration and construction of the piece, the work goes beyond the boundaries of the immediate image and text. *She Loved to Breathe – Pure Silence* is an example of the considered techniques Black women are exploring in writing about our own lives, whilst simultaneously resisting fixed definitions.

Missionary Position II (1985) – Sonia Boyce

Sonia (born in east London in 1962) is an artist whose work mainly incorporates the use of pastel and charcoal on paper, though more recently she has also worked with photographic images and screen-printing. Sonia's reasons for using pastel on paper are related to the fact that historically, pastels have been a medium in which many women artists have worked.

Missionary Position II is a narrative piece that explores the area of Christianity and religion and the complex relationship of Black women in both.

The image consists of two Black women set within a domestic interior. They are both central to the piece of work. Before we look further at the work, it is important to point out that in much of Sonia's work, home is a point of focus. It signifies a place where the identity of a Black person is freely expressed. In this piece however, Sonia sites a subtle disruption to that space.

In *Missionary Position II* there seems to be a certain polarity between the two women portrayed. The woman to our right reaches out to the woman on the left. Her eyes and mouth are open as if in dialogue. The woman she reaches out toward, however, seems to almost resist the other's presence. Her eyes and her mouth are shut, her eyebrows raised, and her hands clasped as if in prayer. It is as if her dialogue is with god.

Sonia uses certain signifiers to highlight this distance between the two women. On the top left- and right-hand corners of the drawing, we see the lower half of two decorative peacocks faced in opposite directions as if in confrontation. The viewer is given a sense of uneasiness because we are not able to see the peacocks as a whole.

The regimented patterns on the wallpaper give a sense of austerity to the atmosphere of the interior. This austerity is also emphasized by the contrasting pattern and rich texture of the carpet. The awkwardness of the atmosphere is further enhanced by the fact that although there is a sofa behind the women, they occupy the floor. One feels a certain sense of unease also in the enclosed small space of the interior.

Sonia is critical of the notion that religion and politics can be separated from each other. The text reads:

'They say keep politics out of religion And religion out of politics – but when were they ever separate.'

The decisions we made in writing this have been personal ones. We have by no means presented the reader with an in-depth or full account on the complexities of work by Black women artists. Instead, we have been selective and have tried to concentrate on what have been for us some key areas.

The ideas presented draw on a range of discussions. We would like to see these discussions in print. In sharing our thoughts, we hope that it might stimulate discussion outside the confines of the art establishment.

NOTES

1. Rasheed Araeen, 'From Primitivism to Ethnic Arts', *Third Text* 1 (Autumn 1987), pp. 6–25.

2. John Roberts, 'Interview with Sonia Boyce', *Third Text*' 1 (Autumn 1987), pp. 55–64.

3. Ibid.

4. Errol Lawrence, 'Just Plain Common Sense: The "roots" of racism' in Centre for Contemporary Cultural Studies, *The Empire Strikes Back: Race and Racism in 70's Britain* (Routledge: London, 1982), pp. 47–94.

5. John Roberts, ibid.

6. Rozsika Parker and Griselda Pollock (eds), *Framing Feminism – Art and the Women's Movement 1970–85* (London: Pandora, 1987).

7. Kwesi Owusu, *The Struggle For Black Art: What Can We Consider Better Than Freedom?* (London: Comedia, 1986).

8. Paul Gilroy, *There Ain't No Black in the Union Jack: The Cultural Politics of Race and Nation* (London: Hutchinson Press, 1987), p. 155.

9. In 2022, Biswas noted that further discussion of the cross-references between the works being made by Black British artists of this period was, and continues to be, required. (Conversation with the editor, 11 May 2022.)

10. Maud Sulter, 'Sonia Boyce', *Spare Rib* 175 (February 1987).

28 Ingrid Pollard, 'Reel to Reel: Explorations around Black Women in Film', 1988

Ingrid Pollard is a photographer and media artist. She exhibited three knitted jumpers in the show *Black Women Time Now* at the Battersea Arts Centre in 1983, and in 1986 her documentary photographs were exhibited in *The Thin Black Line* at the ICA, London, and *Reflections on the Black Experience* at Brixton Art Gallery. During the mid-1980s Pollard worked at Lenthall Road Workshops Collective in Hackney, East London, and established a collaborative working relationship with artist and poet Maud Sulter; their articles were published in magazines including *ArtRage* and *Spare Rib*. In 1987 Pollard completed her series *Pastoral Interludes* (V&A Collection), which addresses the presence of Black people in the English countryside; the series was first exhibited in a group show of the photography collective D-Max, of which Pollard was a member. The D-Max exhibition toured the Ikon Gallery, Birmingham, the Watershed, Bristol, The Photographers' Gallery, London, and elsewhere in 1987–8. Pollard had started her undergraduate studies in Film and Video at the London College of Printing in 1985, and in this article, published in a special issue of the journal *Feminist Art News*, edited by Sulter and Lubaina Himid, she reflects on the representation of Black women in all aspects of the film, television and music industries. She notes a symbiotic relationship between the stereotypical images of Black women presented on screen and those white professionals who work *behind* the camera. Pollard identifies an urgent need for a greater diversity of images of Black women that are made and controlled by Black women film-makers and producers.

*   *   *

I would like this article to present some ideas considered by one Black woman film student/graduate in her quest for the image of Black women in film/cinema.

On telling people I studied film at college they usually say, 'You're going to make films?' a little incredulously. I am left with the same question myself. I am both excited at the prospect of being involved in filmmaking – a medium with the power to reach people globally. In the local Odeon, or in a completely different culture, perhaps, in a 3rd world nation, in a local 'cinema', the picture is the same for the mass viewing. The darkened room, the upturned eager faces splashed with flickering light. People meeting each other, with the only similarity being we have both watched old episodes of the 'Lucille Ball I love Lucy Show' or 'Superman' films. While T.V. has the intimacy to reach right into the home of the viewer, the filmmaker has the potential to create their own version of the world.

But the industry is a microcosm of the society I live in. Look at most credits on television programmes. Producers, directors, technicians, skilled crew members are usually men – while researchers, continuity, make up, etc. and the legions of assistants too, are usually women. Money is scarce, so competition for production costs is high. Profits and ratings are of paramount importance so the end products, from major film studios, can be conservative: sticking to predictable styles, plots and big star name as a drawing point. Only, occasionally will they be shocked by the success of an independent or low budget film such as 'She's gotta have it' (Spike Lee 1986), or 'La Bamba' (1987 Luis Valdez), before rushing off to consume that product and repeat the style. The industry is racist in both its treatment of performers, and the production team.

I sit and wonder whether this is a safe choice. Is this industry a place to explore my own Black woman's creativity? I look at the current view of Black women both behind the camera, in the many areas of production and crew, and the action *in front* of the camera. The image of Black women before the camera affecting the view of Black women behind the camera. If Black women continue to be seen only as servile sexual beings *in front* of the camera, not capable of controlling their lives or being assertive, by the creators of those images, it stands to reason this same sentiment will be echoed in the expectations of the Black women production members and crew.

Our current view of Black women on screen contains the old stereotypes, coming out of the expansive days of colonialism; rarefied and honed through the early Hollywood studio system. The servants and maids, prostitutes, still present in 'Mona Lisa' (Neil Jordan 1985). The sexy, erotic performer taken on successfully by Grace Jones and Tina Turner. The victims and criminals, evident in television series like 'Hill Street Blues' – while our place in pornography remains secure. Reminding us that any positive change in images of women continues to be undermined by the fact these degrading images are commonly available. Just as any intervention by Black independent film makers is undermined by the B B C being able to put on 'Gone with the Wind' as peak weekend viewing. If I look to images of Black women in the music industry, as an arena in which Black women are allowed to be successful, which uses film and video promos as a selling point, I see a similar limited range of ways for Black women to be. These images are dominated by glamour and sophistication. The Whitneys and Sades have their sexuality, beauty, and glamour pushed forward at the expense of their music. Even when we do hear that Janet Jackson is in 'Control', this image is another stereotype of Black women. If we continue to only see Whitney giggling and laughing in videos and publicity, our expectation of her political consciousness will remain low. What is put forward in these image of these Black women can limit the audience's expectations of them.

If we look towards alternatives to these images, both in cinema and music, many of these are still clothed in the early stereotyped characters simply refined for 1980's consumption. The Black performing spectacle, such as the opera singer in the film 'Diva' (1981 Jean-Jacques Beineix). A seemingly positive image . . . but the singer is aloof, a goddess to be put on a pedestal, anything but human. Nola Darling in 'She's Gotta Have It' (Spike Lee 1986) offers us once again the Black woman as a symbol of sexuality. In the same theme, the sexually sophisticated nature of Grace Jones' image is apparently a complicated association of ideas filtered through the earlier influence of Jean Paul Goude. His white male images show her as cut-up, manipulated, reassembled as required. Sold to us in an objectified fetishised way. Photographed in a cage implying her animalistic nature and rampant sexuality. (1982 Jean-Paul Goude; 'Jungle Fever')

In contrast the sexuality of Whoopi Goldberg seems to be played down, right down to her androgenous names; Terri in 'Jumping Jack Flash' (1986 Penny Marshall) and Berni in 'Burglar'. (1987 Hugh Wilson). She talks and fights her way out of trouble, her sexuality and race played down, only appearing as the butt of a joke. Both Jones and Goldberg have images so manufactured, so packaged, as to give clues to their sexualities, yet the end product tenders them no real sexual power.

As a Black woman I am witness to a range of ways Black women can be, but this reality is not borne out in their representations present in the media. There is a gap which is partly due to many producers, writers, directors, having a limited view of Black people. The issue of 'Race' is often the only reason for casting Black people in films, thus the 'real' story, centre stage remains for the 'white stars'. This practice is evident in the current spate of films about whites in Africa such as 'Out of Africa' (1985 Sydney Pollock) 'Kitchen Toto' (1987 Harry Hook) and 'Cry Freedom' (1987 Richard Attenborough). Here the struggles of previously colonised nations are used as a backdrop for romance or adventure reflecting back the white characters at least twice their natural size.

Alternatively, the fact of race is ignored; Black characters tokenised. Race is skin deep. As in 'She Must Be Seeing Things' (1987 Sheila McLaughlin). The film has themes of jealousy, fantasies, sado-masochistic power struggles, within a relationship between two women: one Black, one White. The issue of race is never brought up in the film; the relationship between power/race, jealousy/race, sex/race does not enter the discourse. If white filmmakers want to imperialise the issue of race they must be prepared to make interventions on the issue not in just a simplistic, 'problem related/unrelated' way, but also looking at (facing up to?) the uniqueness that mutual differences can bring to the creative act. Neither would I expect all films by Black filmmakers to have to be about race – this is too limiting. Black characters should be seen in a range of roles. The discussion of the actual creation of positive images/roles is beyond the scope of this article, however it is obvious that the inclusion of Black people in all levels of production will affect the portrayals of Black people which we currently see.

I know that I am not alone in being hungry for images of Black women, heroines, everyday ordinary Black women. I also have to face the uneasy pleasure I take in certain images of Grace Jones. She struts across the stage, she owns the space, or so it seems. It *is* good to see Whoopi be assertive in her films, not relying on a man to get her out of trouble. And I am glad that Janet Jackson can sing about being in 'Control' and produces some of her own music. But I feel my pleasure is a by-product to the intended audience which is young, white and male.

This prospective filmmaker is left with positive thoughts for the future in this industry. I would like to contribute to new directions in the production of new images of Black women in the media. Yet I keep in mind that some films produced by Black independent filmmakers, on both sides of the Atlantic, receive a lot of critical attention from a Black audience hungry for these images. And in turn these new films are readily consumed by the dominant culture which is stale with its own redundant images. The replacement of these reactionary images can only come from looking into ourselves to an image which we know is real.

29 Maud Sulter, 'Call and Response', 1988

In what might be regarded as a manifesto, the Scottish-Ghanaian poet and visual artist Maud Sulter discusses the ways in which Black women have been dismissed and diminished within the art world, and in wider society. Writing in the journal *Feminist Art News (FAN)*, she despairs that so many strong and powerful Black female voices have fallen silent in the wake of persistent denigration and psychologically damaging attacks. She points to the ways in which the prioritization of the individual within capitalist societies, manifested in the figure of the lone (white, male) artist-genius, has created dysfunctional societies that render Black women invisible. Finding solace and solidarity with other Black women, Sulter asserts the importance of fostering collective, collaborative and supportive feminist spaces. She advocates sharing skills, writing about, exhibiting and recording the work of others to ensure that the histories of Black women's creativity are not forgotten. Throughout her text, Sulter draws on the work of Black lesbian poets and activists Audre Lorde, Cheryl Clarke and Michelle Cliff to assert a Black female identity that is rooted in an awareness of personal erotic desire as the wellspring for creativity and revolutionary change.

* * *

'As a black woman I believe that if the women's movement is to survive it must not only intellectualise about change but be up-front to confront the status quo. As feminists we must look at identity and its adoption more closely. Feminist identity has hardly been discussed at all; we must do so now as we enter a critical time for the women's movement as for many other movements.'

From Cultural Abuse in Babylon, FAN Vol I Issue 9

It is five years since I wrote those words. Thumbing through that issue, I see the listing for *5 Black Women at the Africa Centre*. So it was around that time that I started to meet other women who defined themselves as Black artists (I myself could only see myself as creative in a literary sense with art a sort of secret activity). To see those words placed in parentheses brings a slight ironic smile to my lips. Of course to be able to see oneself at all in this society is quite an achievement. It brings to mind the first three lines from Cheryl Clarke's poem *We Are Everywhere,*

We are everywhere and white people still do not see us.
They force us from sidewalks.
Mistake us for men.[1]

Those were heady days, meeting all those women of African and Asian descent. Seeing the diversity of the work, its themes, its media, its messages. It seemed like connections could be made across different political spheres, nationally and internationally. We could name ourselves artists within our glorious traditions and continue to contribute to the advancement of our communities. Art would have a relevance as it had in the past. Its very function would be to communicate; hopes and fears; dreams and realities.

It is nineteen eighty eight and I have lost my voice but not the will to create. Some days I fear that I've become like a black swan, that the voice may only return for that final song, a requiem for a life now passing. Perhaps that is where the problem lies. In passing. Not long after *Black Woman Time Now* at Battersea Arts

Centre I took a trip to Amsterdam. There was a Black dance event happening in the centre of town so I bought a ticket and went along. While we waited for the first bell, I gazed around the bar hoping to see some Black people to whom I could chat and make some contacts around town. Sure enough there were some there and so as we made our way to our seats I resolved to say 'Hi!' at the interval. Well, not only was luck on my side but the Great Black Muse too, because there at the bar stood, instantly recognisable, a fine Zami whom it transpired was also a playwright, and in whose company were more of the same. To cut a long and inspiring story short, by the end of the performance we had made plans to visit an anti-racist event in Rotterdam that weekend. In time those women would become my friends, confidants, lovers even. So then there were more contacts with other writers, artists, performers and life looked rosy, if a little in a haze.

That haze was a sort of smokescreen around the issue of sexuality. I knew that several of the finest most radical artists back in London were lesbians but I also knew that much went unspoken. I sensed a danger there, a danger that pulled me back from the brink of desire; the desire to know myself truly, and it took time to resolve the need to confront the danger head on. Audre Lorde's crucial essay *Uses of the Erotic as Power* was discussed by some of us and incorporated into our philosophies and practices as feminist artists.[2] Her call and response can make the feartest woman strong. So I also began putting Black women artists' work on walls and was even asked to exhibit my work in shows such as *The Thin Black Line*. So there we were confronting the establishment head on, illuminating their marginalisation of us for all to see. Some of the brothers, they got so mad at us for making a statement about ourselves that they are still trying to get even. It seems we should not have taken the space to do with it what we wanted to with cameras, paintbrushes, plaster. And it seems to me that is where the rot started to set in. This Blackwomensartthing was getting serious. Without funding, without support we were making things happen for ourselves. In the face of divisive reviews. Indiscreet talk behind our backs. Did we care? It seemed not. That is until some of that Zami energy got put on hold for ourselves. Then things started to change. Vilification in print became the norm. Voices we needed to hear were silent, some of which are absent from this magazine because they feel no longer able to share their creativity for fear of physical and psychological attack. Good strong Black voices, across a spectrum of sexuality, class and politics and I am angry. And I am sad. Why should we accept the role of surrogate mother to all artists? Ours are *not* pretend family relationships, this thing's for real. Perhaps it should not be surprising that what would perhaps be too easily labelled (by whom and why?) a Blackwomen's Art Movement does not exist for visual artists in Britain. As I have outlined, there are traces of a presence scattered like cowrie shells in sand. Signposts that indicate a past where we tried to transcend the labels of 'otherness' which left no place for the exploration of who we were as individuals, as family, as collectives across divisions.

How do we exist in a world where we are invisibilised as women of African descent? Where our cultures are seen as having no 'classical' root (although Greek scholars sat at the feet of Egyptians . . .)? Where our self-organising, which I often feel takes the shape of gathering at the cooking pot to sort things out, is seen as a threat to coalition. Bernice Reagon's essay in *Home Girls* on coalition politics should be on every feminist's reading list. What she says is true . . . what Malcolm X said rings true too, 'I am not a diner until you let me dine', and that just is not good enough. Across Europe in cities such as Derby, Berlin, Amsterdam, Leicester, Leeds, Blackwomen's groups are organising. And all see cultural production as a vital element in the struggle. So I wonder sometimes if this lack of communication is perhaps the price the art school trained artist pays for that three or four years spent in institutions. Where the doctrine of the Artist is Divine holds court. And where a hierarchy of practice, with Fine Art at the top and Craft at the bottom, is encouraged.

Jean Michel Basquiat is dead and so my journal continues to swell with the names of our dead Black men. I can see him as if he were in this room, captured in a stunning portrait by James Van Der Zee seated looking fine. Or speaking so eloquently in *The State of the Art*. Both examples contextualised within the context of other Black visual artists. We were born in the same year, and now he's dead. Yes, names of women who are no longer with us are there too, their passing too soon in coming. Ironic then that in this country psychoanalytic poseurs get grants to produce full colour pictures of 'dead' Black women. So is there a future for the Black Artist in this hostile world, or are we too readily submitting our creativity to the same will which creates 12 billion dollars on 'space travel' (war missions) and yet 'cannot' find a 'cure' (or is it an antidote?) for AIDS? Throughout the same Black Triangle where one hundred million died in slavery days, too many are dying of this epidemic of many which includes our rape, our murder, our poverty, and our criminalisation. Ben Johnson crossing that line indexed that he was number one . . . twenty years after I sat in front of a flickering black and white tv in a tenement in Glasgow and saw two clenched black gloved hands salute made me feel *brave*. So perhaps there is a message there, a sign. In two short decades the collective power of the hand becomes the selective urge to be no. 1 in the rush for the fast buck.

What is art to me? To you? To the women in Kumasi? The command to not explore these questions is a criminal act. So the test seems to be, can we hit this wall of opposition at such a high velocity and live? Is life enough?

Being written out of history can happen to you. There is no safety in collusion with those who want to oppress our art and suppress our voices. They will turn their weapons on you, and who will be there to help you if your contemporaries no longer exist? Who makes Black women's work visible if not other Black women? This magazine has been carved out of the contributors' own resources. We have worked for too long to be denied space in feminist journals just because today it seems fashionable to be black feminist artists. Why is this so, when it is so unfashionable elsewhere; who's co-opting whom? What I would like to know is what does it mean to each individual who so names herself? After all, if theirs is the real 'authenticity', as dated today as postmodernism will be tomorrow, that 'coming out' is their responsibility. Who bothers to take our work seriously, why the desire for a purely self referential laudation from white pseudointellectuals over our equals? No-one will document our future but ourselves. Entering the danger zone, of not making opportunities for each other, is self defeating. We must take each task in turn. Putting on shows, making the work, documenting our experiences. If we don't take turns, the circle will no longer be open but closed in upon itself until it is no bigger than a full stop.

Since the 1960's Blackwomen have been engaged in discourses about the politics of sexuality and creativity around contemporary art practice. Most of the texts available to us in Britain have been written by Blacksistas from the US. Perhaps the most influential have been Audre Lorde's *Uses of the Erotic as Power* and Michelle Cliff's *Object into Subject: Some thoughts on the work of Black Women Artists*.[3] These writings have helped develop our ideas around issues of Blackwomen's representation and position in a white heterosexist male dominated world. In terms of an international perspective there must be more exchange. We must not 'come from somewhere else' and step on other activists toes by not recognising what has gone before in order to create a climate where that very thing can happen. There are very many important texts which should be available to be read, published, distributed and this can only be truly successful if there is more exchanging of information and a sharing of skills and resources. Forging a Black identity built on our African diaspora helps challenge the hegemonic multi-cultural 'thang' which denies most resolutely our heritages in their multiplicity and diversities. Then we can continue to forge together with all other women of colour a challenge that will turn this world around. Not forgetting that simultaneously, if not indeed first, we need to sit by that calabash and get down to some serious business in building on that foundation that has been created for us. No longer being afraid of our erotic, and the source of our creativity we can go forward to a passionate future. As Blackwomen, as friends.

NOTES

1. From Cheryl Clarke, *Living as a Lesbian: Poetry* (New York, 1986), p. 59.

2. Audre Lorde, 'The Uses of the Erotic: The Erotic as Power', in *Sister Outsider: Essays and Speeches* (Trumansberg, NY, 1984), pp. 53–9.

3. Michelle Cliff, 'Object into Subject: Some Thoughts on the Work of Black Women Artists', *Heresies* 15 (4:3) (1982), pp. 34–40.

30 'Allan deSouza interviews Shaheen Merali', 1988

First published in issue 6 of *Bazaar: South Asian Arts Magazine*, in this interview artist and curator Shaheen Merali discusses his work and career with fellow artist Allan deSouza. During the late 1980s, Merali worked principally in batik, a labour-intensive and pre-modern craft technique of dyeing fabric, developed in sites across Asia and dating back to the fifth century. The method applies hot wax to fabrics, rendering those areas dye-resistant; multiple wax applications and dyes can be used to produce highly intricate designs. Merali sought to break down the hierarchies between craft and fine art, and in this interview he expresses his belief that art should be open and accessible to everyone. deSouza perceptively discusses Merali's anti-colonial imagery and together they reflect on how form and content can work together to make powerful and challenging statements.

*   *   *

I met Shaheen Merali at the One Spirit Gallery in Haringey which he runs with partner Khadijah Frischaur. Finishing off a batik workshop with a group of young Black people with disabilities, he flitted from one person to another, a suggestion here, a word of encouragement there. Brilliantly coloured batiks in the making were hung up to dry, materials cleared away, everyone escorted to the bus-stop, and Shaheen was back to show me the batik that he had been working on.

A wild swirling mass of colours held in check by starkly drawn figures. The image is obviously set in India during the Raj. At the very centre is a cannon aimed away from the viewer into the colour-lashed landscape. Strapped to the mouth of the cannon is an Indian man who we can see is about to be horrifically executed. A white civilian woman is preparing to fire the cannon under orders from a British soldier. In one corner is another Indian man; emaciated, and obviously suffering.

ALLAN: Shaheen, can you tell me why this particular scenario, and why is it a woman firing the cannon?

SHAHEEN: The incident is compiled from a variety of historical evidence. It's also about the role of British women in India. The British were there as a class – not just the men, the women were there too. The men formed the upper levels of power and mostly gave the orders, but the women also took an active as well as sup-portive role. White women cannot pretend that imperialism was nothing to do with them. It's not something that can be swept away and for us to work together, we have to acknowledge these things.

ALLAN: I've always seen your work as being about strength and survival. So many of your portraits, including those of your own family, are of people who have faced obstacles and over-come them: people who are survivors. Yet in this work, Indian people seem once again to be cast as victims with no way out.

SHAHEEN: I'm dealing with a situation which actually used to happen. Certain things have to be documented – the destruction of the land as well as the extermination of the people. And it is still continuing. How many British and US multi-nationals are operating in India under the guise of aid, but are poisoning the environment?

ALLAN: Or off-loading products which wouldn't pass the health and safety standards here?

SHAHEEN: Exactly. But also, this is not an isolated piece of work. It's the first in a series, and each piece depicts a different area of struggle. The second image shows a group of women, each with a different craft. Behind them is another woman with a rifle who is protecting their space. It was these crafts, these 'home-industries' that formed the basis or the possibility of economic independence. So I'm not saying that we are or will remain victims; but colonialism has shaped our view of ourselves so we take an inferior position. In the art world, for example, we are still not free from the need for approval from the white establishment.

ALLAN: Right. Now that's a perspective which I know informs a lot of your organising work, and I want to come to that later. But first I want to turn to a more personal history. This image is not just an historical account, the emotion in it is of a very personal nature. Can you tell me a little about your own background?

SHAHEEN: My family are originally from Rajula in Gujarat. They went to what was then Tanganyika to work on the railways where my parents were born. While working in factories and on the railways my father trained himself in accountancy so he could better support the extended family. In 1970, the family moved to England, again forced by economic and political reasons to migrate. My father however was not allowed in as he was a 'British protected' citizen and did not have full citizenship. So it was just my mother looking after the five children without any support. She would work in a factory making light bulbs, look after us, and campaign to get my father into the country. There was no law centre, no organised campaign – she had to do everything herself. I remember once when we were living in Barnet, and Margaret Thatcher was the local

194

MP; my mother and I were banging on the doors of the Town Hall
trying to get in to see her, so she would do something for my father.

ALLAN: And we're still banging at the doors, except it's no longer
just at the Town Hall . . .

SHAHEEN: Exactly. The strain took its toll on my mother. She
developed cancer and was also put on a repeat prescription of anti-
depressants, so whenever she went to the doctor she was simply
given more drugs to which she became addicted. Eventually my
father was allowed in to the country, but they only had a short
time together – my mother died six months later.

ALLAN: Without dismissing the importance of these events, to
yourself and your family, it feels like I'm listening to a history of
a whole generation: each family would add different details, but
the pattern would be the same for so many. So, to build on that
history, let me come to your own experience and development as
an artist. For me, one of the strengths of your work is that is contains so much of this history.

SHAHEEN: Before my mother died, art for me was about making
doodles. When she died I became more conscious of the feelings
of separation and death affecting us, and about our situation in
England. Art became a way of expressing emotions and reflecting real situations. I stopped looking at Da Vinci and Van Gogh as
role models and began to look at my own life. Later there was a
certain amount of pressure to follow a 'solid' career –

ALLAN: Uh, huh . . .

SHAHEEN: – So after 'A' levels, I began a social administration
course. After a year I decided I had to follow what I wanted to

do and paid for myself to get through a foundation Art course. After three rejections – at one interview they asked me why I drew Black people as if there could be no conceivable reason for it – I began a Fine Art degree course at Gwent. During my second year I went to India and returned with a lot of work – films, photographs and drawings. Back at college they told me they didn't want 'Indian postcards', they wanted English sculptures. So I moved from the sculpture department to Ceramics and carried on working there right through college without tuition or proper assessments.

ALLAN: It sounds so familiar. Despite their facade of liberalness, art schools are one of the major preventatives to any kind of change.

SHAHEEN: Right. Anyway, so after college, I returned to London. I was introduced to batik by Dividar Kumar, a friend from India, and soon after met Carl Clark. Carl and I have worked together since. Carl took a lot of inspiration from India, and I wanted to do some work about being born in Africa. So we would mix work, using both African and South Asian references. It was like we were trying to break a mould of a . . . a . . .

ALLAN: – a kind of nationalism?

SHAHEEN: – almost, yes. We needed to show that we could work from another culture. We had to recognise differences between cultures, but at the same time overcome any divisions.

ALLAN: Yes, so often we are forced into one of two extremes – either a rigid 'ethnicity' where we all separate off into our respective 'cultures', or a facade of unity where there is no recognition or support of difference. Earlier we mentioned the need to overcome a sense of inferiority, and the need to be independent. These, and the struggle for unity form the basis for a lot of your organising work. How does the gallery fit into this?

SHAHEEN: Anywhere, but especially here in Haringey, there is a real lack of art exhibition spaces where work is also being produced. Tell me, where can you go to see an exhibition and not only watch, but learn the skills and techniques necessary to produce that work? We are trying to demystify the art process; we start with something small and grow from there to give an opportunity to those who never get a chance.

I made a choice of using media which are not European, which are not used in art schools. There is a hierarchy of skills which means that certain other skills are neglected. When you conform to that hierarchy you lose track of where you are coming from. A visual vocabulary is an essential part of our identities. European media – TV etc – overpower and take away a personal vocabulary. It's like art schools, they try to exchange your own vocabulary for theirs.

ALLAN: In a way this hierarchy, this imposition of values, this controlling of individual perceptions, deprives us of a sense of self; it prevents us becoming truly independent. Is this where workshops can be effective?

SHAHEEN: Right. One reason for doing workshops is to be in touch with people who haven't become part of the art world. Everyone has their own skills, and a right to participate in the available media, in order to develop their skills. We try to build people up, to promote themselves – not just in protest, but as positive activity. In the batik workshops, people come over a six-week period and learn the skills and techniques. They are then prepared to set up on their own. We work mainly with local artists and unemployed people, and also, like today, we run a series of workshops with Black people with disabilities.

ALLAN: And exhibitions. What kind of work do you show?

SHAHEEN: Well, we're always on the look-out for new artists. We show work mainly by artists of African and Asian descent. We've also shown Cypriot artists and an exhibition of Australian and anti-bicentennial posters. We always try to incorporate other things into an exhibition – workshops, talks, performances – so it becomes a complete event.

ALLAN: Shaheen, thank you. I'm afraid we've run out of time. There is so much more we can talk about, which needs to be talked about. Maybe next time, eh, we'll think about a book?!

31 Gilane Tawadros, 'Other Britains, Other Britons', 1988

Curator and writer Gilane Tawadros starts her essay on Black photographers in Britain with a quote by celebrated Marxist historian, C. L. R. James, in which he argues that, 'The black man or woman who is born here and grows up here has something special to contribute to Western civilization'. Tawadros then proceeds to discuss how a new generation of Black British photographers have challenged and problematized the way that 'Britishness' and 'Blackness' have been regarded as mutually exclusive categories. She argues that David Lewis, David A. Bailey and Ingrid Pollard, who were members of the photographic collective D-Max, alongside Zarina Bhimji and Mitra Tabrizian, each challenge myopic versions of British history which would seek to downplay or ignore the destructive and traumatic consequences of colonialism. Tawadros discusses how these artists respectively address such varied issues as the prolonged enslavement of African people by the British; the position of the Black family within British society; the constructed nature of the idealised the English countryside; the experiences of newly arrived South Asian women in Britain; and how identities and our place in society are determined according to complex sets of relations and predetermined constructs. She suggests that by including these artists and their work within the purview of Britishness we can build a more accurate picture of the nation.

*　*　*

What is Black Art?

Those people who are in Western civilization, who have grown up in it but yet are not completely a part (made to feel and themselves feeling that they are outside) have a unique insight into their society . . . The black man or woman who is born here and grows up here has something special to contribute to Western civilization. He or she will participate in it, see it from birth, but will never be quite completely in it. What such persons have to say, therefore, will give a new vision, a deeper and stronger insight into both Western civilization and the black people in it.

C. L. R. James, Ten. 8, 1984

The new vision that characterizes the work of the young Black photographers (using the term to cover not only people of Afro-Caribbean descent but also Asians and people of Middle Eastern origins) in this volume derives from a critical reassessment of the construction of racial difference and identity in contemporary Britain. In recent years, a new generation of Black artists, born or brought up in Britain, have begun to articulate the necessity of bringing their art from the margins into the central cultural arena. The work of many of these photographers takes the form of constructed narratives which weave together threads of history, culture, personal experience, and sociopolitical realities into a tapestry whose central themes are issues of race and representation.

On a technical level the phrase "D-Max" – the name adopted by a group of Black photographers established in Britain in 1987 – refers to the maximum density of which a given emulsion is capable; on a symbolic level, the name alludes to the photographers' awareness of the aesthetic and political plurality of Blackness in British society. Since the mid 1950s, when settlers from the West Indies and the Indian subcontinent first arrived in Britain in significant numbers, notions of "Blackness" and "Britishness" as fixed and mutually exclusive categories have been called into question. Blackness has come to be seen by artists and photographers alike as a social and political construction modified by gradations of class, gender, and generation, rather than an unchanging essence or cultural absolute. At the same time the concept of "Britishness" as a single, abiding national identity is seen to contradict the reality of contemporary Britain as a multicultural society with diverse histories, religions, and traditions.

David Lewis, one of the core members of the D-Max group, addresses these issues in his image entitled *The Flag of Our Ancestors* (1985). A Black man, his head barely perceptible within the frame of the image, turns toward a Union Jack standing at his side, while against his back he holds a frame containing a pair of prison-style mug shots. The flag of the title is an ironic reference to the Union Jack and to the idea of a "United Kingdom," with a common political and cultural heritage. The Black man or woman who is born or brought up in Britain experiences the ambivalence of having, on the one hand, a British national identity, and on the other, an ancestry whose history has often been one of enslavement and criminalization under British imperial rule. Nonetheless, the history of Britain and the history of Black people are not separate; instead, as Stuart Hall observed in *Ten.8* magazine in 1984, "Slavery, colonization, and colonialism locked us all into a common, unequal, and uneven history." Furthermore, the frame-within-a-frame in Lewis's picture reminds us of the contradictory nature of representation: on one level, representation in the form of forensic photography is a device used by the state to classify and record what it defines as "criminal," in this case the Black man; on another level, photography is the expressive tool by which the Black photographer can deconstruct levels of racial and national imagery.

In his series *Family Album* (1987), David A. Bailey, another member of the D-Max group, explores several modes of representation, each of which vies for authenticity. Against the background of a "Made in England" clock and a montage of snapshots, a family album is displaced by a Black magazine which in turn is displaced by the screaming headlines of a tabloid newspaper. As the clock ticks on, marking the shifting historical context, the changing assemblages of images address the contradictions between private and public representations of race. The series progresses from innocence to experience as we move from snapshots recording serene personal episodes of family life, to an artificial image of Black family life on the cover of *Ebony* magazine, and finally to the vindictive headlines of the tabloids.

In her *Pastoral Interludes* series Ingrid Pollard – one of two women to exhibit with D-Max initially – explores the conflict between the personal and the political through the very different genre of landscape photography. As a Black woman, Pollard articulates in her images of the Lake District several levels of alienation and Otherness. The Lake District, which in many ways epitomizes the "authentic" British countryside, confirms the status of the Black woman as an outsider. These photographic landscapes recall with irony the tradition of eighteenth-century British landscape painting, which sought to establish the countryside as the natural domain of the British middle classes, as well as the Romantic "Lake Country Poets," for whom the English countryside provided a metaphor of individual freedom and transcendence. But it is from precisely that landscape that Pollard, doubly Other as both Black and female, is excluded. By confronting this idealized Britain with the reality of the Black experience, these images challenge the social and political framework within which such concepts as "naturalness" and "Otherness" are constructed.

While Zarina Bhimji is not associated with the D-Max group, her work shares their interest in exploring personal identity within the context of cultural identity and representation. *She Loved to Breathe – Pure Silence* (1987) is an installation in which intense red and orange coloured spices are sprinkled on the floor in front of large panels hanging from the ceiling; the panels, which include photographs and texts, can be read from either side. One panel in the series represents a dead bird and a pair of embroidered slippers. The slippers can be read as a metaphor for an Asian woman, but both the slippers and the bird can also signify migration. Indeed, the experience of migration in all its aspects – flight, identity, social status, nationality – acts as a central metaphorical axis of the installation.

The use of a Home Office visa stamp in one of the final images of the series is a clear reference to the degraded status of Black women (and men) under British law, as well as to the successive pieces of discriminatory legislation that have increasingly limited the rights of entry and citizenship of Black people. But in the face of such bureaucratic and legal harassment, the mounds of brightly coloured spices that appear beneath the images attest to the quality and distinctiveness of Asian culture, which resists the oppressive stamp of uniformity that British society and law attempt to impose upon it.

Among all these images, the work of Mitra Tabrizian most explicitly takes the form of constructed narratives. The triptychs in her series *The Blues* enact dramas whose settings and lighting are reminiscent of aspects of film noir. Like movies posters which depict a tense but leading moment, the images invite us to project a story onto the still photograph. These fabricated scenes underline the way in which both words and images construct our identities in everyday life: black is defined in opposition to white; man is constructed in opposition to woman. The images within each triptych undercut these seemingly clearcut distinctions: a Black man appears in a white mask, while a white man's face, reflected in a car mirror, is echoed by the image of a Black man's face in the car's headlights. By compounding and complicating these simplistic but familiar oppositions, these photographs challenge the ways in which culture and society position us and construct our identities.

Black art and politics do not occupy separate spheres. Together, the diverse images here begin to chart the cultural and political terrain in which racial difference and identity are constructed, and represent the first stage of a kind of photographic inventory of the sort described by the Italian writer and activist Antonio Gramsci:

> The starting point of critical elaboration is the consciousness of what one really is, and is 'knowing thyself' as a product of the historical process to date, which has deposited in you an infinity of traces, without leaving an inventory; therefore it is imperative at the outset to compile such an inventory.

32 Rotimi Fani-Kayode, 'Traces of Ecstasy', 1988

In his photographic practice Rotimi Fani-Kayode produced 'imaginative interpretations of life'. He rejected reportage or documentary street photography in favour of sensuous, seductive and complex portraits of nude or semi-nude Black men which addressed themes of Blackness, masculinity, homosexual desire, rage and ancestral spirituality. Fani-Kayode was born in Nigeria to a prominent political Yoruba family and, following the military coup of 1966, he and his family moved to Britain as political exiles. He undertook an MFA in Fine Arts & Photography at the Pratt Institute in New York, and returned to the UK in 1983. Settling in London, he became a member of the Brixton Artists Collective and exhibited at the Brixton Art Gallery, before becoming a founding member and inaugural chair of Autograph – the Association of Black Photographers (now Autograph ABP). In this essay, published in the photography magazine *Ten.8* in 1988, Fani-Kayode addresses his approach to image making and discusses the ways in which his work is informed by colonial histories, Yoruba spirituality and cosmology, the Christian church's suppression of homosexuality, and contemporary homophobia in Britain.

*   *   *

It has been my destiny to end up as an artist with a sexual taste for other young men. As a result of this, a certain distance has necessarily developed between myself and my origins. The distance is even greater as a result of my having left Africa as a refugee over 20 years ago.

On three counts I am an outsider: in matters of sexuality; in terms of geographical and cultural dislocation; and in the sense of not having become the sort of respectably married professional my parents might have hoped for.

Such a position gives me a feeling of having very little to lose. It produces a sense of personal freedom from the hegemony of convention. For one who has managed to hang on to his own creativity through the crises of adolescence and in spite of the pressures to conform, it has a liberating effect. It opens up areas of creative enquiry which might otherwise have remained forbidden.

At the same time, traces of the former values remain, making it possible to take new readings on to them from an unusual vantage point. The results are bound to be disorientating.

In African traditional art, the mask does not represent a material reality: rather, the artist strives to approach a spiritual reality in it through images suggested by human and animal forms. I think photography can aspire to the same imaginative interpretations of life.

My reality is not the same as that which is often presented to us in Western photographs. As an African working in a western medium, I try to bring out the spiritual dimension in my pictures so that concepts of 'reality' become ambiguous and are opened to reinterpretation. This requires what Yoruba priests and artists call a 'technique of ecstasy'.

Both aesthetically and ethically, I seek to translate my rage and my desire into new images which will undermine conventional perceptions and which may reveal hidden worlds. Many of the images are seen as sexually explicit – or more precisely, homosexually explicit. I make my pictures homosexual on purpose. Black men from the Third World have not previously revealed either to their own peoples or to the West a certain shocking fact: they can desire each other.

Some Western photographers have shown that they can desire Black males (albeit rather neurotically). But the exploitative mythologising of Black virility on behalf of the homosexual bourgeoisie is ultimately no different from the vulgar objectification of Africa which we know at one extreme from the work of Leni Riefenstahl and, at the other from the 'victim' images which appear constantly in the media. It is now time for us to reappropriate such images and to transform them ritualistically into images of our own creation. For me, this involves an imaginative investigation of Blackness, maleness and sexuality, rather than more straightforward reportage.

However, this is more easily said than done. Working in a Western context, the African artist inevitably encounters racism. And since I have concentrated much of my work on male eroticism, I have also had homophobic reactions to it, both from the white and Black communities. Although this is disappointing on a purely human level, perhaps it also produces a kind of essential conflict through which to struggle to new visions. It is a conflict, however, between unequal partners and is, in that sense, one in which I remain at a disadvantage.

For this reason, I have been active in various groups which are organised around issues of race and sexuality. For the individual, such joint activity can provide confidence and insight. For artists, it can transform and extend one's Westernised ideas – for instance, that art is a product of individual inspiration or that it must conform to certain aesthetic principles of taste, style and content. It can also have the very concrete effect of providing the means for otherwise isolated and powerless artists to show their work and to insist on being taken seriously.

An awareness of history has been of fundamental importance in the development of my creativity. The history of Africa and of the Black race has been constantly distorted. Even in Africa, my education was given in English in Christian schools, as though the language and culture of my own people, the Yoruba, were inadequate or in some way unsuitable for the healthy development of young minds. In exploring Yoruba history and civilisation, I have rediscovered and revalidated areas of my experience and understanding of the world. I see parallels now between my own work and that of the Osogbo artists in Yorubaland who themselves have resisted the cultural subversions of neo-colonialism and who celebrate the rich, secret world of our ancestors.

It remains true, however, that the great Yoruba civilisations of the past, like so many other non-European cultures, are still consigned by the West to the museums of "primitive" art and culture.

The Yoruba cosmology, comparable in its complexities and subtleties to Greek and Oriental philosophical myth, is treated as no more than a bizarre superstition which, as if by miracle, happened to inspire the creation of some of the most sensitive and delicate artefacts in the history of art.

Modern Yoruba art (amongst which I situate my own contributions) may now sometimes fetch high prices in the galleries of New York and Paris. It is prized for its exotic appeal. Similarly, the modern versions of Yoruba beliefs carried by the slaves to the New World have become, in their carnival form, tourist attractions. In Brazil, Haiti and other parts of the Caribbean, the earth reverberates with old Yoruba rhythms which are now much appreciated by those jaded Western ears which are still sensitive enough to catch the spirit of the old rites. In other words, the Europeans, faced with the dogged survival of alien cultures, and as mercantile as ever they were in the days of the Trade, are now trying to sell our culture as a consumer product. I am inevitably caught up in this.

Another aspect of history – that of sexuality – has also affected me deeply. Official history has always denied the validity of erotic relationships and experiences between members of the same sex.

As in the fields of politics and economics, the historians of social and sexual relations have been readily assisted in their fabrications by the Church. But in spite of all attempts by Church and state to suppress homosexuality, it is clear that enriching sexual relationships between members of the same sex have always existed. They are part of the human condition, even if the concept of sexual identity is a more recent notion.

There is a grim chapter of European history which was not drummed into me at school. I only discovered much later that the Nazis had developed the most extreme form of homophobia to have existed in modern times, and attempted to exterminate homosexuals in the concentration camps. It came not so much as a surprise but as yet another example of the long-standing European tradition of the violent suppression of otherness. It touches me just as closely as the knowledge that millions of my ancestors were killed or enslaved in order to ensure European political, economic and cultural hegemony of the world.

I see in the current attitudes of the British Government towards Black people, women, homosexuals – in short, anyone who represents otherness – a move back in the direction of the fascistic values which for a brief period in the 60s and 70s ceased to dominate our lives. For this reason I feel it is essential to resist all attempts that discourage the expression of one's identity. In my case, my identity has been constructed from my own sense of otherness, whether cultural, racial or sexual. The three aspects are not separate within me. Photography is the tool by which I feel most confident in expressing myself. It is photography, therefore – Black, African, homosexual photography – which I must use not just as an instrument, but as a weapon if I am to resist attacks on my integrity and, indeed, my existence on my own terms.

It is no surprise to find that one's work is shunned or actively discouraged by the Establishment. The homosexual bourgeoisie has been more supportive – not because it is especially noted for its championing of Black artists, but because Black ass sells almost as well as Black dick. As a result of homosexual interest, I have had various portfolios printed in the gay press, and in February a book of nudes will be published by GMP. Also, there has been some attention given to my erotic work by the sort of straight galleries which receive funding from more progressive local authorities.

But in the main, both galleries and press have felt safer with my 'ethnic' work. Occasionally they will take on board some of the less-overtly threatening and outrageous pictures – in the classic liberal tradition. But Black is still only beautiful as long as it keeps within white frames of reference.

I have been more disconcerted by the response to my work from certain sections of the self-proclaimed avant-garde, however. At the recent MiSFiTS exhibition at Oval House (which happened to coincide with the unveiling of a plaque to commemorate the birth there of Lord Montgomery of Alamein) I was asked, along with other artists, to remove my work in case it attracted unfavourable publicity for Oval House. We refused, naturally. Unfortunately, the press were too busy paying homage to Monty so the national reputation of Oval House was saved, and we were denied some free publicity. It is perhaps gratifying that the inadequacies of Oval House's Equal Opportunities Policy have since been recognised by many of its erstwhile supporters. But given the new Government ruling against local authority funding for any form of 'promotion' of homosexuality, I assume that, in any case, community organisations will no longer be allowed to show my work.

As for Africa itself, if I ever managed to get an exhibition in say Lagos, I suspect riots would break out. I would certainly be charged with being a purveyor of corrupt and decadent Western values.

However, sometimes I think that if I took my work into the rural areas, where life is still vigorously in touch with itself and its roots, the reception might be more constructive. Perhaps they would recognise my smallpox Gods, my transexual priests, my images of desirable Black men in a state of sexual frenzy, or the tranquillity of communion with the spirit world. Perhaps they have far less fear of encountering the darkest of Africa's dark secrets by which some of us seek to gain access to the soul.

33 Coco Fusco, 'An Interview with Martina Attille and Isaac Julien of Sankofa', 1988

Black independent film-making in Britain generated considerable controversy during the 1980s as young film-makers and producers sought to create new modes of visual representation that mixed mainstream and avant-garde styles. Film-makers Martina Attille (now known as Judah Attille), Maureen Blackwood, Robert Crusz, Isaac Julien and Nadine Marsh-Edwards founded Sankofa Film and Video Collective in 1983, and collectively challenged the narrow and reductive representation of Black people as either 'victims' or 'problems' in mainstream cinema and documentary film. Instead they presented complex and layered reflections on the lived realities, histories and dreams of Black people. Sankofa operated as a workshop: committed to a model of 'integrated practice' in which collective film-making was undertaken alongside the provision of training and education programmes and audience outreach. It was argued that this workshop model enabled Black film-makers to specifically engage with issues that were of concern to Black audiences and develop a Black visual aesthetic. In this interview with Cuban-American artist and curator Coco Fusco, Sankofa members Attille and Julien discuss the origins of the group; the ways in which their work exists within and against established (white) filmic conventions; and the influence of political philosopher Frantz Fanon (1926–61) and critical theorist Homi Bhabha (b. 1949), amongst others, on their work. During the interview three of Sankofa's most important films are discussed at length: *Territories* (1985), *Passion of Remembrance* (1986) and *Dreaming Rivers* (1988).

* * *

COCO FUSCO: What was happening in the independent film sector when you formed as a group? What made you come together to form a workshop?

ISAAC JULIEN: We wanted to challenge the fairly Eurocentric positions of white independents making films about Black people. In 1984 we organized a discussion series called "Power and Control." One of the issues in the series concerned the power to appropriate. What was being asked at the time, and what continues to be asked, is whether Third Cinema[1] can be produced by white filmmakers. The kind of questions that we tried to propose had to do with power, i.e., Black people's relationship to the media technology and where they were placed in them.

COCO FUSCO: What was different about your situation, comparing it to that of the first generation of Black filmmakers in Britain?

ISAAC JULIEN There's a gap between the first Black films that were made in the 1960's by Lionel Ngakane and Lloyd Reckord,[2] and our work. There had not been a full development of Black film culture until the development of the workshops. Other filmmakers appeared such as Menelik Shabazz and Horace Ové, but they were working as individuals. There was no Black film organization making institutional demands. It was precisely because we went to university and because of the 1981 riots, that we could then pull together and make an intervention into the media. The Workshop Declaration was designed without our participation but we saw it as a very important space where we could develop several things at once.

MARTINA ATTILLE: The programs of study we chose at university were critical of cultural forms and their production. When we began to work as filmmakers we were compelled not only to make films but also to make an intervention into film theory and critique it. We did not only want to address mass communications but also education – everything that threatens to take away the autonomy that we have to define ourselves. For Black people there are very few spaces where you can actually define your own activity and define and control the quality of your life.

Film became available to us because Channel 4 came on the scene. That was a moment in which we had an entry point into media. There have been other Black people in television, but they were on the periphery, working on short term contracts, trying to negotiate membership into the union. The workshop movement offered a certain amount of security just to develop ideas, to make interventions that were broader than just television or just cinema or individual programs. The workshops were built around the idea of continuity of work. That's what we wanted.

COCO FUSCO: What prompted you to make *Territories* (1985) at the time that you did and in the way that you did?

ISAAC JULIEN: In retrospect, I was tired of the realist debate, the populism versus modernism debate, which was focused on fairly conventional documentaries. In looking at several of those documentaries in the very limited Black film history that existed in Britain at that time I noted that there were several films about carnival, because it was the biggest event. At the same moment I was reading "The Other Question" by Homi Bhabha which appeared in *Screen*[3] in 1983. In a way those two things synthesized. I saw many films about Blacks made by Black and white filmmakers which didn't really grapple with the question of exotica in that representation. There wasn't a politics of representation in those documentaries.

Territories was a film about the politics of representation which included the Black subject. Within the arena that included the Black subject carnival was a very pivotal point. (I wasn't familiar with the writing of Mikhail Bakhtin[4] at the time, but in retrospect I can see the way they are directly related.) Carnival was the space where, for a day, disorder was allowed. That is what is so interesting about carnival: there were so many different eruptions around sexuality, around smoking "ganja," around the way that area was policed. Those different tensions were all placed in that space.

COCO FUSCO: What were the cultural questions that were relevant for you to deal with in *Territories*?

ISAAC JULIEN: Questions of the diaspora, questions of policing. The significance of the sound systems in the carnival. In other words, what does Blackness mean to a Black culture? That was the main question. What does it mean for us? There are many films about racism and anti-racism, but what do these signs mean for us? In the second part of the film there are montages of the two Black men dancing with each other, which you see a lot in carnival, but you wouldn't necessarily interpret it as something that would be called a homosexual relationship. I wanted to explore those questions, anchor the debates in that space, in a Black space. I can look back on it now and I can see how I was trying to break with the realist debate and do something else. I can see now how the format I chose also had its limitations, but it was important for me at the time to try to do something like that. I saw *Territories* as a film essay around civil disorder and semiological questions for Black people.

COCO FUSCO: Do any of those issues carry over to *Passion of Remembrance* (1986)?

MARTINA ATTILLE: *Passion of Remembrance* (1986) started as a project called "Systems of Control." The reality of the way Black communities are policed is still very much a part of our experience and it is part of our concern. When we started doing the research, however, we looked away from the traditional areas – such as metropolitan policing – focusing instead on the ways in which policing takes on more intimate forms within our communities and relationships.

COCO FUSCO: Why was policing an issue?

MARTINA ATTILLE: Because control is an issue. If you're engaged with a medium like film, you're trying to communicate ideas to people. And those ideas inevitably come from your experience of the world. We as filmmakers had control over the images we created. But there was a sense of accountability imposed on us by our community to produce certain types of images. In a way we anticipated that. We had had screenings and discussions called "Power and Control," and we heard audiences ask for positive images. There needed then to be a critique around what positive images were.

ISAAC JULIEN: At the same time we were sick of seeing images of Black people involved in civil disorder, because of the riots.

MARTINA ATTILLE: The cliche of Black person as victim of police brutality was a quite sensational way of looking at Black experience. I think there are many more subtleties to it than that.

With *Passion* we took things to point zero: the family, the man and the woman. Those were metaphors we used to talk about our experience in Britain at the time. We quite deliberately chose

216

to look at the intimacies of our relationships to each other. And we also wanted to open up certain ways – we're not only talking about Black people, we're talking about British society as well. When you set up a company like Sankofa it is important to have a profile, to gather interest in your work. So we chose to work on a feature length fiction, rather than documentary, in part as an attempt to expand our potential audience. Working within that medium we wanted to create a narrative rich in imagery. Some people say it was quite literary.

ISAAC JULIEN: Or eclectic.

MARTINA ATTILLE: We quite deliberately used two geographic spaces. One is the urban landscape, the cityscape with the Baptiste family placed in it. Maggie Baptiste is looking at England. She's looking at archive footage, looking to history for some sense of what has gone on before and what's going to come in the future. She's looking at English streets cast with long shadows of previous struggles and protest. At the same time she and her friends look for release of the tension on those same streets, in the cheap glitter of their clothes and the cheap glitter of the West End. The urban landscape, that claustrophobic landscape, that was our experience. There is no time to sit down and explain to people how you're feeling or what's going on in your mind, or that you're worried about the future. It's jobs or no jobs. You dance, kiss, and run.

With the open landscape, on the other hand, we wanted to evoke a dreamscape. A place of deliverance, of redemption. A place where there's nothing to get in the way of intimate contact. The man and the woman in the landscape don't touch each other because there is so much between them that hasn't been resolved. There is so much bitterness and frustration. They can't even come close to each other in the end, and instead look away from each other.

COCO FUSCO: What were the most important agendas?

MARTINA ATTILLE: The legacy of the sixties is important. The Black movement has a particular style which historically has been male dominated. As the woman in the landscape says, you can't hide behind the fist forever. Although the fist was a crucially important rallying symbol we must look behind the sign to see what it stands for.

ISAAC JULIEN: It has to stand for much more now. Its agenda has to broaden. Other men have found the Black fist to be something that doesn't include them. Nor did the symbol originally include questions of sexuality and gender. Those questions informed *Passion* to a great extent. Many Black male directors continue to make films about policing and racism because those are the areas in which they feel most directly affected.

MARTINA ATTILLE: We're not just making films to entertain, to get people to relax. We're trying to make some intervention, or take up and respond to our environment. If we sit down as three Black women and a Black man, whose parents come from the West Indies, or whatever, we do so with certain cultural and political positions and priorities. *Passion* is a fiction film but it is very much a document of the time we came together as four young Black people. It embodied that coming together as a relatively young media organization on the media scene. The media scene here is extremely competitive – not just among Black people, but as a whole. So *Passion* represents all the tensions of those things. The man and the woman in the landscape could easily be the old guard versus the new guard; the static old guard man, and the young, volatile woman with a new sense of politics, full of resentment and frustration. *Passion* comes out of a time when there didn't seem to be that much dialogue between different sections of our community. The leaders weren't as obvious as they had been in the past and *Passion* was suggesting that it was about time that we talked.

ISAAC JULIEN: I don't think *Passion* was only about the politics of us coming together though. It was also about what had come before. Extensive research was done on Black political organizations in the '60s and the '70s. We did an enormous amount of research on policing. Altogether this work informed the characters. They were archetypes.

COCO FUSCO: Can we discuss the way in which the legacy of Black American radicalism from the '60s and '70s informed the film? What is your relationship to this? Why turn to it, as opposed to, let's say, African nationalist revolutionary texts from the '50s and '60s? Obviously, we're not talking about a film history informing your films, we're talking about a political history and a written history informing your films.

ISAAC JULIEN: There was a Black Power movement in Britain that borrowed many of its signs and symbols from America. We do borrow from other cultures within the diaspora, but we are specifically talking about a Black British experience – and we have to be very careful not to substitute an American experience for a Black British experience.

MARTINA ATTILLE: The similarities between the American and British experience are in the politics of the diaspora really. It's not like an African nationalism directed back to the homeland, back to the source. We wanted to follow the journey back in stages. The experience of migration, of coming to England, and of people being taken to America – of having to assert your identity within a foreign environment – was quite important. In some parts of

Africa we're still talking about colonial relationships, about the involvement of outside forces occupying those territories. People have migrated here following the resources, following their own resources. And then they have to assert their right to be part of society in the same way that Black Americans had to do. There are differences between our and their experiences, different experiences within the economy – slavery in that country – whereas the West Indian experience was one of colonialism and coming over here – leaving, to some extent voluntarily, though in reality people didn't always have the choice.

ISAAC JULIEN: In relation to your question of borrowing or talking about influences from the Black American experience – in borrowing those things, we were also prioritizing issues such as British national identity. We did not naively try to transplant a Black American experience onto the Black British experience. It was very important to us to talk about our experience in the diaspora, and the specificity of that Black experience.

We always thought that *Passion* would be very interesting for American audiences. Not very many people had recognized Britain as being either Black, or mixed-race, or Asian. They didn't recognize all those other identities in Britishness.

MARTINA ATTILLE: In the male speaker there's the popular rhetoric of that movement that echoed out into other territories. But at the same time there's the character Maggie who is our vehicle for looking specifically at England. Our eye through the Baptiste family is very firmly on the British experience. Whereas the landscape represents a more international concern, something that is transatlantic, something more universal.

COCO FUSCO: We've talked about philosophical, theoretical and literary influences. What about visual? Much of the criticism concerning your work claims that the arguments are Black and the film style is Euro-American, i.e. white avant-garde. I don't believe that that is really the issue, nor is it the way that your approach need be characterized. What are the dynamics that you seek to evoke on a visual plane?

ISAAC JULIEN: The white avant-garde can't help but try to seize upon *Passion* and claim it as borrowing from The Grammar, from their film grammars. I've never seen, for example, *Riddles of the Sphinx*[5]. I've never seen many of these films. As much as I like Laura Mulvey and her essay "Visual Pleasure and Narrative Cinema,"[6] which is very important, her pleasure is not the same as the kind of pleasure that we're talking about and articulating. There's a difference. And I think that in a sense, when you talk about the avant-garde as it were, it's very easy to try to compare the way *Passion* is made with white avant-garde filmmakers. That's not to say there aren't influences. There are some avant-garde filmmakers, such as Ken McMullen and Sally Potter, whose work I am interested in. But if I were going to cite direct influences, I would look to Haile Gerima and Charles Burnett.

MARTINA ATTILLE: And Med Hondo's work.

ISAAC JULIEN: There is still to be developed a vocabulary of Black film criticism that can start to talk about our work.

COCO FUSCO: Some Black cultural critics have argued that "authentic" Black cultural tradition is found in preaching and other oral, performative discourses. In thinking about culture and colonization, it has historically been the case that visual culture is the first to be dominated, and is extremely difficult to develop as a sphere of resistance. How do you relate these issues to your own situation as, in a sense, visual artists?

ISAAC JULIEN: *Territories* was an attempt to deal with the question of what Black representation means for Black people. That was its first question. As far as I'm concerned the avant-garde is dead. *Territories* and *Passion of Remembrance* are not about the things that were going on in the white avant-garde. We're not interested in just breaking rules and conventions. Which is not to say that there isn't a cultural and political world that informs the white avant-garde of the '70s, because there is. But I think that it's too easy to reduce cultural endeavor to a formal exercise.

COCO FUSCO: How do you respond to the argument that these issues were hashed out in the '70s, because in a sense, sexism, racism and colonialism are the same problematic being recast over and over again on different terms?

MARTINA ATTILLE: Each of these moments – the prioritizing of race, of sexuality, etc. – has almost been like an academic exercise, an intellectual exercise in which we explore in more depth what the crisis in each of those areas is. But I don't think that it really happens like that in real life. One's experiences of these states is more relational, shifting in relation to who you are talking to, where you're standing, what country you're in. The frustration I feel with the way our work is put into established categories is that although we were educated with those theories, we also resisted them. We had no choice but to resist because there wasn't really a place for us. We hadn't actually shaped that theory. We had to study Eurocentric traditions in our own absence. One of the reasons that Sankofa formed was to explore the gaps in the theory and also the gaps in the visual representation. We, as Black media producers, have self-conscious political priorities which we bring to that. Our work isn't just informed by established traditions that existed before us. We also sought to transform the established theories. The work that is being produced by groups like Sankofa is a few steps ahead of the language of critique that could actually make sense of the work.

COCO FUSCO: Could you say more about the problem of a lag in critical language?

MARTINA ATTILLE: A workshop movement develops in England, and then an established white film critic can say something to the effect that Black groups came along on the tail end of that movement. Now, we came into the movement knowing what the inadequacies were, realizing the ways in which Black film was marginalized. Nonetheless, the workshops offered the chance to have some autonomy over what we created. In addition to this, there were certain experiences – certain histories that hadn't really been talked about in the British context – which we could begin to talk about.

In forming as Black groups, we identified our specificity in terms of race and other issues of interest such as gender and sexuality. On the other hand, in terms of critics and film theory – the voice of authority – the subjectivity of the voice is never clearly identified. It's asexual, classless, raceless. Until you can get to the point where the theory can identify its own cultural and political priorities then it's going to be out of step with the work, which is very self conscious, very specific about what it's trying to do.

ISAAC JULIEN: The Black cultural theories that are being developed at this particular moment are largely limited to the historical traditions which Black people have been participating in and developing and shaping. These traditions have influenced the twentieth century to such an extent that one has to talk about vernacular culture and the relationship between those cultural practices and the Black intellectual.

On the other hand, when we talk about the visual we must address the psychoanalytic, which also has its limitations. It's only very recently that any work has begun which tries to look at Franz Fanon's writings and derive a theory of Black representation, and which confronts the pleasure of the visual. Psychoanalytic discourse has been the most successful intervention in developing a critique of the visual dimension of cinema in its attention to fantasy and memory, to spectatorship, gender and sexuality. What we are now developing is a discourse about the Black subject and the visual plane.

MARTINA ATTILLE: Once we had the responsibility of Black representation or Black images, we found out that there's no space for fiction allowed. Even if you say that you're making a fiction film, people still want to know who those characters are. They want them to add some sort of credibility to their own lives. There still exists a desire for identification among Black audiences. As a filmmaker you try to create a fiction in which there is enough distance for you to read what the film is saying as a whole. Still, the grip of realism remains very tight in terms of a Black audience.

ISAAC JULIEN: One of the phenomena you can trace in the diaspora is that Black subjects are never really in the visual plane. We want to explore what happens to Black subjectivity when it sees white images. We know that 40% of American film audiences are Black, and they see many kinds of films. There don't have to be Black images all the time, but then we know from the psychoanalytical work done on Black subjectivity that in our psyches there is a massive dilemma taking place. It affects you in every moment as a Black person. You don't see yourself.

MARTINA ATTILLE: You think you're white.

ISAAC JULIEN: How do you start to grapple with these sorts of questions? Well, these are questions that we are starting to grapple with. We do need psychoanalysis.

COCO FUSCO: Is it psychoanalysis precisely or a more reflexive position towards representation?

ISAAC JULIEN: You must realize that linguistic, literary, and in some cases theoretical arenas of representation, are not talking about representation, as it were, in the visual text. We must develop a contestation as we theorize how our work functions visually. Filmmakers such as Haile Gerima have compared their work to experimentation in jazz and bebop. You can look to Langston Hughes' poems, like "Montage of a Dream Deferred."[7] He uses the word montage, which is very interesting to me, in order to talk about Black urban experiences. I would say that *Passion* is a montage. In *Passion* we're asking questions about the state of British culture. There are no whites in the film – but why shouldn't white people go to see films about Black culture and Black people the same way that Black people go to see films about white culture and white subjects?

The crisis around race is not just a theoretical one, it's a crisis at all levels. It's very obvious what informs it in the age of Reaganism and Thatcherism. When you walk in New York streets and you see the number of Black people on the streets begging something tells you that there is something wrong about the system. If you go to the Dia Art Foundation for a lecture on issues relating to colonialism and there are no Black people in that room, but there's one Black person giving the lecture, you think to yourself, well there's something wrong. In London this hasn't happened as much. I was really surprised by the cultural apartheid in New York. Issues such as Nicaragua, first world involvement in the third world, and the invasion of Grenada – these are questions that we cannot not talk about. And these are key sites of representation. And this is precisely what is being signalled when people like Jean Baudrillard[8] talk about the end. It's about certain kinds of worlds coming to an end. We can see that one of the biggest problems in the discourse of postmodernism is that it doesn't talk about the Black subject. Nor does it address colonial discourse.

COCO FUSCO: There is some discussion in third world cultural debates about postmodernism in that context as a kind of appropriation or reinterpretation of the strategies that are associated with postmodernism in the first world. The formal relativism implied by postmodernist discourse might have specific resonances for those who have been in a situation of subjugation, in terms of a visual vocabulary. It has been argued that this can have a kind of emancipatory potential, because it makes anything available without any guilt attached. It can be seen as the theoretical recognition of a situation in which the cultural producer is constantly bombarded by images coming from all over the place all the time. There is an extremely problematic history to be dealt with here. Historically speaking, when third world artists borrow from the first world it has been called colonialism, but when the modernists borrowed from Africa, for example, it was an enrichment of the vocabulary of the fine arts.

ISAAC JULIEN: Can there be a return to an enrichment of the white avant-garde in its Eurocentric vein, or is it truly dead? At moments of crisis it does turn to other things to revitalize it. There are positions from which we can debate these arguments. This time the old arguments are not going to work. Our entry into postmodernism is predicated on being used as an alibi for the West, for white critical discourse. And I think that that is very important in relation to all the different struggles that are being waged at this time, by other Black peoples. Theorizing our own experiences around modernity is very important.

MARTINA ATTILLE: If anything, Black representation must confront modernity, and question whether our understanding of modernity embraces Black experiences. Black people's experience of capitalism hasn't really been dealt with enough. For us to leap to the postmodern would be to overlook the unfinished business of modernity: the way that Black people have travelled, in search of resources, in search of better lives; how they shaped new societies, new cultures, new vocabularies, and new accents within the modern world. There are great gaps in documenting that experience from a Black perspective.

We must be sure that when we talk about race, the white subject doesn't slip out the back door, and leave the Blacks to sort this out among themselves. It's as if whiteness doesn't find a place within the discourse around race until you actually get white subjectivity to declare its interest, to actually explore its colonialist past, its fascination and its fetishes.

ISAAC JULIEN: It fears and desires and pleasures.

MARTINA ATTILLE: Unless you get people to discuss race in terms of what is invested in Blackness, and what is invested in whiteness, what is denied by both, then you're always going to get the subject of race being the subject of Blackness.

COCO FUSCO: You just talked about how the race question is not just a Black question. How can you relate that to the question of whether or not there is a Black aesthetic?

MARTINA ATTILLE: I think that if aesthetic is determined by your relationship to power, then yes, there is a difference. It results in a difference in one's perception of the world. But we are part of an environment which is Black and white. It seems to me that to construct a notion of a Black aesthetic allows you to leave another aesthetic untouched, unchallenged. It's never clearly labelled as such, but it's a white aesthetic. We have to adjust ourselves in relation to that aesthetic. When people talk about Black aesthetics and go on a search for one, I see a kind of reductionism in the assumption that we the Black people must be doing something else outside and separate from our total environment. There are many aesthetics, not just one. There are many experiences, many economies to work with. I resist actually trying to form a Black aesthetic that doesn't take into account the diversity and range of our experience.

ISAAC JULIEN: Because of modernity, I think our interception there can be called upon to make things more interesting. Where does Black experience fit in? In a sense *Passion* and Black Audio's *Handsworth Songs* are trying to grapple with these issues.

To talk about diasporic culture is to talk about the process of modernity and your relationship to it as a Black subject. In a sense, I am not a postcolonial subject, I'm sorry.

MARTINA ATTILLE: If I am a postcolonial subject, then so are the white people. This is the aftermath. We're still reaching for things. Our colonial history isn't that far away. We're still going through that process. Colonialist attitudes are still quite strong in our society.

ISAAC JULIEN: Especially when you start talking about the nation. People talk about multiracial culture, but what about multiracial nations?

COCO FUSCO: Can we talk about *Dreaming Rivers* a bit?

MARTINA ATTILLE: *Dreaming Rivers* (1988) started off as a project about representation of Black women, following a discussion series we had organized called "Black Women and Representation." I wanted to talk about images of Black women in film. And what audiences were meant to see or read from images of Black women. In researching it and talking to artists such as Sonia Boyce, Simone Alexander, and Marlene Smith – I began to feel that the original conception was to talk about the images, but that the moment would be best used by trying to make an image, to tell a story through the images, to express a mood, a feeling. Discussions with Sonia Boyce (who became the film's set designer) were quite crucial – her practice as a visual artist for me captures some of the intimacies of Black life in this country without being apologetic, without relying on theory. Her point of view, her family, the textures, and even the smells and tastes of that experience. I wanted to capture something as unapologetic and as there and as real as those pictures, those paintings. And so, with *Dreaming Rivers*, although the issues were there – in those images – they are less dependent on the spoken word, and more dependent on the knowledge of the recent history of visual representation produced by Black women artists in the U.K. The film is therefore about continuity and transformation.

Dreaming Rivers is about Miss T., a Black, dark skinned woman from the Caribbean. A colonial subject relocated physically, but psychically connected to that past homeland. She is caught between both directions really, leaving the Caribbean to come to England – for dreams, for hope, for love. And then not realizing some of those ambitions, she is caught in the stormy sea, in the Atlantic, on the way back to a place of security, past happiness of youth. Miss T. is a subject in the process of migration, in the midst of the journey. And the imagery for that is like death, which promises new life. The journey hasn't ended – it's represented by her children, who have to lay her down. They represent differences – one person split into three – which fractures into even more again. I wanted to deal with the postcolonial situation and the experience of migration. I would date one point of our modernity from the stage of migration, and the complex processes by which we constantly interact with and change our environment with our histories.

Sankofa: mythical bird which signifies the act of looking into the past to prepare for the future.

NOTES

1. Third Cinema is a cinematic term originally proposed by Argentine film-makers Fernando Solanas and Octavio Getino in their 1969 essay, "Towards A Third Cinema." In contrast to the commercially-oriented "first cinema" of Hollywood, and auteurist endeavors – which fall into their "second cinema" category – they posited a third cinema of liberation, a politically engaged, militant cinematic practice integral to decolonization, and unassimilatable to any dominant political system.

2. Lionel Ngakane made *Jemimah and Johnny* in 1963, and Lloyd Reckord made *Ten Bob in Winter* in 1959.

3. Homi K. Bhabha, "The Other Question – The Stereotype and Colonial Discourse," *Screen* 24, no. 6 (November-December 1983), pp. 18-36.

4. Mikhail Bakhtin, Soviet literary theorist of the early revolutionary period, is the author of *The Dialogic Imagination*. His studies of the novel present notions of literature and language in modernity as stratified, fragmented subunits of constant flux and in constant conflict with one another.

5. *Riddles of the Sphinx* is a film by Peter Wollen and Laura Mulvey.

6. Laura Mulvey, "Visual Pleasure and Narrative Cinema," *Screen* 16, no. 3 (Autumn 1975), pp. 6-18.

7. "Montage of a Dream Deferred" is an extended work, divided into 87 sections, depicting Black urban experiences. Formally, the structure of the work is influenced by bebop and jazz. The poem can be found in *Selected Poems of Langston Hughes* (London: Pluto Press Limited, 1959), pp. 221-272.

8. French philosopher Jean Baudrillard's books include *The Mirror of Production*, *The System of Objects*, *For A Critique of the Political Economy of the Sign*, *On Seduction*, and *Simulacras and Simulation*.

34 Rasheed Araeen and Eddie Chambers, 'Black Art: A Discussion', 1988

The following text is an abridged version of a much longer and wide-ranging discussion between artists Rasheed Araeen and Eddie Chambers first published in the journal *Third Text*. Araeen and Chambers discuss definitions of the term 'Black Art' in light of their own curatorial practices, and although they are largely sympathetic to the other's position, they nonetheless profess nuanced disagreements. Araeen starts the conversation by proposing that Chambers' definition of who could create 'Black Art', and what the content or subject of 'Black Art' is, had changed since the early 1980s from a pan-African, highly political and confrontational position, to one that could include the work of Asian artists and address a wide range of subjects, broadly defined as the 'Black experience'. Araeen and Chambers discuss the differences between their respective exhibitions staged in 1988, *The Essential Black Art* (Chisenhale Gallery, London, and touring), and *Black Art: Plotting the Course* (Gallery Oldham and touring). While Araeen's exhibition took a relatively narrow position that 'Black Art' specifically engaged with politics, Chambers' exhibition suggested that it need not be restricted to protest art but could reflect a variety of lived experiences; they discuss paintings by Errol Lloyd and Shanti Thomas in this broader context. In relation to Chambers' work with the photographic collective D-Max (whose members included David A. Bailey, Marc Boothe, Godfrey Brown, Gilbert John, David Lewis and Ingrid Pollard), Araeen raises the question of whether a 'Black aesthetic' exists: might an audience recognize an artwork as having been made by a Black artist because of a particular aesthetic (look or form), regardless of the content of the image? The conversation concludes with a brief discussion on the future of 'Black Art'.

*   *   *

RASHEED ARAEEN: Eddie, to begin with, thanks for coming over to have a chat together about various issues vis-a-vis black art. One of the reasons why I wanted to talk to you was the fact that you were perhaps the first person in Britain to use the term 'black art' in a definitive manner, in 1981, and since then you have been writing to explain what is black art. Your position has been consistent with your practice as a politically committed radical black artist.

It would be useful to start this conversation with your own definition of black art, but it would not be fair to ask you to clarify your position now. Perhaps I should start by explaining what I understand your position has been; and then you may respond to it.

Your perception of black art was within the political struggle of black people, here in Britain as well as abroad, which in the beginning was confined within the context of what you called Pan-African Connection. This was perhaps because you were committed to the Pan-African struggle, and you worked with people who were of only African origin. But later you began to include Asians in your definition of 'black', while maintaining a radical political position.

It seems that your position has now become broad and eclectic, which is clear from the recent show you have curated, BLACK ART: PLOTTING THE COURSE.[1] Am I right in my observation that your position has changed, so much so that you can now put together all black artists irrespective of the nature of their work?

EDDIE CHAMBERS: I think, to a certain degree, yes. Between 1981 and 1985 I was involved with other artists who were of Afro-Caribbean origin, but later I began to work with Asian artists as well. But I'm not sure if my definition of black art has changed. What has happened is that I have become aware of other definitions, and I now respect other positions as well. You have to take on board other peoples' realities, you know, other peoples' perceptions even when they are different from your own. I realised that there were other definitions of Black art which did not correspond to my own early definition, and there was no question of a confrontation of ideologies or positions. I'm now quite happy with this change, working with all artists of both Asian and Afro-Caribbean origin.

RASHEED ARAEEN: This takes us back to the early definition of 'black art', which was located historically as a movement vis-a-vis black struggle. How would you define black art now within the present context?

EDDIE CHAMBERS: I would define Black art as art produced by black people largely and specially for the black audience, and which, in terms of its content, addresses black experience. It deals with in its totality the history of slavery, imperialism and racism, which affects the position of black people here in the West as well as other parts of the world – in the Americas, and in Africa itself. The function of Black art, as I saw it a few years ago, was to confront the white establishment for its racism, as much as to address the black community in its struggle for human equality. I think Black art has still that role to play.

RASHEED ARAEEN: You have raised some important issues here, and one of them is the relationship between the black artist and the community. I agree with you that one of the functions of black art is to raise consciousness among the black community, but I don't see why it should limit itself to addressing black audiences only.

EDDIE CHAMBERS: The issue here is one of priorities, and I think the priority for the black artist is to address black people. Until we are in a position to talk to each other about our collective experiences, about our specific problems, I don't think we can jump the gun, or whatever, and begin to address the whole society. Having said that I'm aware that this creates problems in relation to gallery spaces or outlets which are run by white people, and thus you enter into a situation which perhaps is full of contradictions. I suppose if you are realistic and you are concerned with the black community, you need venues which are located within and recognised by our own community. I'm aware of all these problems, but we cannot escape our responsibility to the community.

RASHEED ARAEEN: One of the concerns of black people in general, and the black artist in particular has been to struggle against marginalisation. But if we are going to put black art in a specific category with specific and limited functions, don't you think we are ourselves marginalising the role and function of the black artist in this society?

EDDIE CHAMBERS: No, I don't think so. Black art is about something specific and is different from art practice in general. It is difficult to compare it with anything else or to put it in a wider context, because its basic function is communication with black audiences. The issue of marginalisation is something else. It is a different issue, and it should not be confused with the priority of Black art to build a bridge between the individual black artist and the community.

RASHEED ARAEEN: But that is only one function of so-called black art, and I don't understand why you keep on insisting on that function. Why can't it rise above that function and also address the whole society? You cannot reduce art to only one specific function.

EDDIE CHAMBERS: Well, I think, that's probably where we differ in our views.

RASHEED ARAEEN: If we perceive black art only in those terms, there is a danger of its being separated from the main body of this society. If black artists are going to address only the black community and white artists address white society, it seems to me to be a recipe for a cultural bantustan.

EDDIE CHAMBERS: I don't think so. The struggle to build a bridge between black artists and the black community is not an exclusive struggle. It does not exist at the expense of other things. I do recognise the validity of the struggle vis-a-vis white institutions. My own approach now, which may be pragmatic, in curating exhibitions is to place Black art in white gallery spaces. There is a kind of duality to the whole situation, but unfortunately there is no correlation between the two. It may be dangerous to generalise, but the fact remains that the black community is not interested in what goes on in the mainstream galleries.

RASHEED ARAEEN: Even then, I don't think it is a contradiction for black artists to seek access to these spaces, which to me are not necessarily white spaces. The institutions of this country must belong to all the people, and if they are dominated by whites only then it is the right of black artists to demand their share of the pie.

EDDIE CHAMBERS: I don't want to appear as if I'm dogmatic or pedantic, but I do think it's important to stress that art institutions in this country are very *white*, and it's not incidental that they are *white*. I do accept the argument that we should have access to the mainstream gallery spaces, but I don't underestimate the fact that they are white spaces because the whole structure is white.

RASHEED ARAEEN: Are you then suggesting that we should have alternative institutions or organisations which are run by black people themselves?

EDDIE CHAMBERS: No, no, not necessarily, because it can be argued that the Black alternatives do not necessarily alter the situation. I have never asked for separate gallery spaces. In the past I did support the existence of some black galleries, but not any more. They did serve some useful purpose in terms of showing young Black artists who would have not otherwise been exposed, but that did not automatically lead to an improvement in the general situation. I'm critical of white institutions, but that does not mean that I'm in favour of separate Black organisations.

RASHEED ARAEEN: To get back to the definition of black art, do you make a distinction between what you call 'Black art' and art produced by black artists in general?

EDDIE CHAMBERS: Definitely. I think the difference is fundamental. Not every Black artist produces Black art, and I used to castigate those artists who showed no interest in it. Now I don't.

RASHEED ARAEEN: So you recognise that there are black artists who are not part of the black art movement, and their work should be looked at in accordance with the nature of the work.

EDDIE CHAMBERS: Definitely.

RASHEED ARAEEN: So, that makes the definition of black art different from the category in which every artist of AfroAsian origin is put in together by the general public as well as by the establishment – particularly by the funding bodies. However, it's still difficult to distinguish what is black art and what is not.

EDDIE CHAMBERS: Don't you think the difference is obvious?

RASHEED ARAEEN: Theoretically, yes. In some cases the difference is obvious, particularly when the rhetoric of black struggle is explicitly expressed. But there are also artists who claim to be producing black art but it is not clear from their work.

EDDIE CHAMBERS: Then it is a misuse of the term.

RASHEED ARAEEN: No, I don't think so. It's not just the question of 'a misuse of the term', but there are reasons which are complex and which make the young generation of black artists identify with black art. It seems that it also makes it easier for them to have access to some gallery spaces.

EDDIE CHAMBERS: I don't think that's necessarily the case.

RASHEED ARAEEN: Let me put it differently. Maybe it's not correct to say that it makes it easier for them to find certain venues. But we cannot deny the fact that the black artist does have a sense of insecurity in this society, to say the least, and the identification with black art can make things easier, particularly when most of the funding is available under the category of 'black art'. This is particularly true for the young generation of black artists. It's not a question of opportunism, but there are very few choices available.

EDDIE CHAMBERS: That may be so. But it can also be argued that the opposite is true. In fact, if you are ambitious you must keep away from the idea of Black art; and this is clear from the fact that those Black artists who have been successful in recent years do not like the term. If you look at their work, you would know why.

RASHEED ARAEEN: I'm not saying they should. It must be up to the artists themselves to contextualise their work, and we should respect their position and look at their work within that context. But we must, at the same time, recognise that there exists a general perception which puts all the artists of AfroAsian origin within the same category: if you are a black artist then you produce black art. The objective of the show *The Essential Black Art*[2] was to clarify this confusion. I distinguish black art on ideological and political grounds, but that does not mean that I believe in propaganda art. Political issues must be incorporated within the articulation or expression of other things which make the work of art a work of art, and this goes for those works which express anti-racist or anti-imperialist positions.

You know that there were nasty reviews of the show, which included a review by a black writer who accused me of misrepresenting black art because I had emphasised the fact that the basic context of black art was political. It emerged as part of black and Third World movements, and its specific formation (which is historical) should not be confused with other things. That's why we need a clarity about what we mean by black art; and if we take a broad or eclectic view of it we might also fall into the trap in which every black artist is thrown in the name of diversity and difference.

My real worry here is that your own position is moving towards a broader concept of black art in which it would be very difficult to distinguish between black art as a specific historical formation and the general category recognised and promoted by the establishment. In the catalogue essay of the show *Black Art: Plotting the Course*, which you recently selected and curated, you have taken this position. What is the nature of the shift here?

EDDIE CHAMBERS: What I tried to do in this exhibition was to go beyond what I thought to be the limitation of *The Essential Black Art*. My main objection to your view is that it was limited in terms of historical period, and you make no connection with Black Arts movement in America which to me is very important. I have argued that there is a definite link between what happened in America and subsequently in Britain, and the connection goes back to the Harlem Renaissance of the '20s.

RASHEED ARAEEN: [. . .] At the moment I want to stay with the issue of what you now consider to be black art. I'm particularly concerned with some of the works you have included in your exhibition, such as of Gurminder Sikand, John Lyons, Errol Lloyd, Shanti Thomas . . ., which present a problem for me. How am I to consider them as examples of black art?

I'm not saying that they are not good works of art. It's not the issue here. These works give no indication of what you yourself would consider to be black art. When I look at *The Domino Players* by Errol Lloyd or *The Rotimaker* by Shanti Thomas, for example, what I see is the theme or subject of the way of life of African or Asian people. This is something which could have been painted by any artist, and there is a history of such themes being painted by white artists. How do you justify these works as black art?

What is Black Art?

EDDIE CHAMBERS: Firstly, I should make it clear that much of the premise on which *Black Art: Plotting the Course* exists, centres around the notion that there is a wider constituency of artists whose practice criss-crosses the ideology of Black art. The artists you have mentioned are not necessarily the artists one would associate with Black art movement, but there are specific works by them with which I would have no problems in classifying as Black art.

RASHEED ARAEEN: Let us look at *The Rotimaker* by Shanti Thomas. It shows an Indian woman kneading dough before breadmaking. You have yourself often implied, if not asserted, that black art is the expression of a particular experience what we call black experience – an experience of black people living in a racist society or subjected to imperial domination. I don't see how the Indian way of breadmaking has anything to do with racism or imperialism.

EDDIE CHAMBERS: What you say is true. But that is not what *The Rotimaker* is about. I would argue that this painting is an expression of certain aspects of black experience. I should also make it clear here that Black art is not only about protest against racism or imperialism, but it can also be reflective of our existence as black people.

RASHEED ARAEEN: *Roti*-making has been done in the Indian subcontinent, as well as in the Middle East, from time immemorial, and it has very little to do with the experience of Western colonialism.

EDDIE CHAMBERS: You can say that apparently it has nothing to do with racism or imperialism. But I think it does have a lot to do with sustenance: who feeds and sustains the family, particularly in adverse circumstances? What Shanti Thomas is trying to say is that Indian woman is the provider, a fact which is often overlooked.

RASHEED ARAEEN: I agree that the role of the woman in the sustenance of the family in our parts of the world is extremely important. But I still don't see how this role has anything to do with black experience, even if we see it as a metaphor. My feeling is that you consider every activity or experience of peoples living in their own countries in Africa, Asia or the Caribbean, as black experience.

EDDIE CHAMBERS: Yes, definitely.

RASHEED ARAEEN: But I have come across people even from Africa who on arrival in England were surprised that we here call ourselves black people; because their experience of living in their own countries had not been the same as we have in this country. How can we sitting here, define their experiences?

EDDIE CHAMBERS: Yes, but, who can deny the brutality of life of majority of people in Africa, Asia and the Caribbean.

RASHEED ARAEEN: Nobody is denying that . . .

EDDIE CHAMBERS: That is exactly what the black experience is about.

RASHEED ARAEEN: That may be so, if you are implying that the social condition of people in these parts of the world is the result of imperialism. Even then there are human experiences or social activities which are not formed by these conditions – and the Indian way of breadmaking is an example. This distinction is important if we are to understand the specificity of what we call black experience.

EDDIE CHAMBERS: Of course, I wouldn't disagree with you there.

RASHEED ARAEEN: We have our own traditions still surviving in Asia and Africa, and even in many other parts of the world where AfroAsian people live, and these traditions have very little to do with the experience of imperialism. These traditions exist today in music + dance, literature, painting, sculpture, etc. and they cannot be defined in the socio-historical context of black experience, which is of course global but with peculiarities specific to black peoples living in the Western Metropolis, unless these traditional art forms have undergone transformations resulting from this context.

EDDIE CHAMBERS: My position is based on the premise that whatever Black peoples do, wherever they are, is important. And it's important to see this in the overall context of the experience of black peoples. Let us take the example of the painting *The Domino Players* by Errol Lloyd. It is about how West Indian men socialise among themselves; how they play domino; what domino means to them vis-a-vis the Caribbean experience. And the Caribbean experience is an important part of Black experience.

RASHEED ARAEEN: So, in other words, a painting about white people playing darts in a pub would be an example of white art.

EDDIE CHAMBERS: Well, if it's painted by a white artist, I suppose it had to be.

RASHEED ARAEEN: Why couldn't it be painted by a black artist? And if it was painted by a black artist would it become black art?

EDDIE CHAMBERS: Well, if it was really painted by a Black artist, I would approach it differently expecting to find things there which would indicate more than just white people playing darts in the pub. I think the various works you have mentioned here are not just illustrations of some black themes or activity. They contain more than the objects or images you see.

RASHEED ARAEEN: I find it very difficult to accept that, because whatever way you look at these works they do not convince me of having anything to do with black experience.

EDDIE CHAMBERS: The assessment of these works as Black art was curatorial, and had nothing to do with the artists. I do not believe that these artists necessarily produce Black art, but the works I had selected do touch on the issues of Black experience.

[. . .]

RASHEED ARAEEN: [. . .] The ambition to create black aesthetics is of course laudable, and I'm very interested in the idea of a new visual language with its own distinguishable features. But I'm still not clear what it is. I know what it is in relation to Jazz, but when I look at those contemporary art works which claim to be concerned with black aesthetics, I don't find anything there which would convince me of its presence or development. Perhaps I'm showing an impatience, because what we are talking about may take a long time to develop. But if we can't look for the results now, we should at least have some theoretical clarity.

Could we therefore discuss some of the works from D-MAX exhibition which you initiated, and although you disassociated yourself from its final showing at the Photographers Gallery, London, you did write a lengthy introduction in which you outlined its objectives:

In terms of aesthetics, our second objective is to contribute to the development of something which could be referred to as a Black aesthetics in British photography. Here, the use of the word 'Black' does not particularly refer to the content of the photographs. After all, it could be argued that anthropological and sociological photographers such as John Reardon and Derek Bishton have, in their coffee-table effort 'Home Front', produced a form of 'Black' photography. Instead, the word Black refers to the photographers themselves, rather than images of Black people. In Britain at the moment, there is a sizeable number of Black photographers, but nothing exists that can visibly be identified as being a collectively-created Black aesthetic. One of the most positive aspects of this project is that it attempts to make these photographers more aware – creatively aware – of each other's existence.[3]

This is a confusing stuff, particularly when you say that the word 'Black' does not refer to the content of the photographs. My understanding had been that these photographs had been selected and legitimised as 'Black photography' not only because they were taken by black photographers but also their contents were about black life or experience. It is common sense to say that in the end we will have to look at the work, whatever it is meant to be about, or says.

EDDIE CHAMBERS: First thing to say here is that we should allow some scepticism about the notion of Black aesthetics, because there aren't any obvious examples that can be seen to clearly embody Black aesthetics. And I think that's where the problem lies. I admit that Black artists and photographers have not yet been able to move away from the dominant aesthetics. What I was therefore trying to do in the introductory essay was to outline an alternative programme. I thought that the first step towards this would be to gather Black photographers together, in order to generate regular discussions between them as well as to show them in the public venues. The first concern was how to deal with the negative or stereotype images of Black people in dominant photography, and that's what the D-MAX group has been doing.

I think a photographer like Vanley Burke, who uses the same camera, same lenses, same chemicals and paper, as white photographers, produces something which is very different, and some of the photographers in D-MAX exhibition were looking for similar results.

RASHEED ARAEEN: We don't have Burke's photographs here, but let us look at the work of Marc Boothe whom you admire. Here is a photograph of a New York street with a young black boy in the foreground. Looking at this photograph, how do we know that it has been taken by a black photographer? You would perhaps accuse me of de-contextualising the work not only in terms of isolating one work from the whole body of the artist's work as well as ignoring those questions which need to be taken into consideration while reading any work of art. But from the point of representation, is it possible to ignore the question I have asked? What I'm suggesting here is that this photograph could have been taken by a white photographer, because there is a tradition of photography in which black people have been used as a subject. And I don't accept the general notion that black people have always been represented negatively or as stereotypes within this tradition.

EDDIE CHAMBERS: I think that there is some misunderstanding about what I was getting at in my essay. Obviously, it would be simplistic – and even stupid – to say that images of black people taken by white photographers would always be negative. You would remember that I was critical of the exhibition *Black Experience* organised in 1986 by the GLC, because most of the photographs in the exhibition were based on Black themes.

RASHEED ARAEEN: But there were some good photographs . . .

EDDIE CHAMBERS: Yes, there were a few. But a large number of them were not positive at all. So it's not the case of saying that Black photographers necessarily create positive images of Black people. The issue is really very complex.

RASHEED ARAEEN: But you have stressed the point that these photographs have been taken by black photographers, and your aim was to show them together, so that their work could be discussed publicly. Of course black photographers or artists must have a chance to show their work. But, in the end, we will have to look at the work itself in terms of what it says or represents, and only on this basis can we evaluate the work specifically and critically. Of course, the question of authorship is central to the evaluation and legitimisation of works of art in our contemporary culture, and it's only in the case of white authorship that it's position is guaranteed, both socially and historically. It's the invisibility of black historical subject that we are forced to construct our visibility as part of the process of making things. If we are making specific claims on the basis of black authorship then it seems that it has to be inscribed in the work. And that's perhaps the reason why the work of David A. Bailey and Ingrid Pollard looks interesting. However, this is not the end of the story, and the complex issue of black aesthetics remains unresolved.

What worries me, personally, is that we are making claims on a basis which does not yet exist; and we would perhaps end up promoting mediocre works – which is not an unusual situation in the black arts scene today. And to tell you the truth, I was very disappointed by the D-MAX exhibition. It's time we pay some attention to the question of quality.

EDDIE CHAMBERS: Perhaps you don't know that we had serious differences within the group, and not all the photographers agreed with my idea of Black aesthetics. What in fact I wanted to do was to give some political direction, but not all of them were interested in it.

[. . .]

RASHEED ARAEEN: What is then the future of black art? I'm particularly interested in this question because you have recently curated a show called *Black Art: Plotting the Course*; that means you are indicating some future. There is also another exhibition called *Black Art: Future Directions* which is going to open in two weeks time.[4] So what are these future directions?

EDDIE CHAMBERS: I don't think that Black art is like fashion, whereby you have new colours for new seasons, changing form from one year to another. So I'm dubious about all these new directions. What I tried to do with my own show was to show some black artists together whose work was inspired by the Black art movement and whose work I personally found interesting. But as far as the future of Black art, I don't think it's very healthy – I mean ideologically.

RASHEED ARAEEN: Why do you think that the future of Black art is so bleak? Is it because black art as a radical movement is no longer there? Or is it because the term 'black art' has become a broad category which is being used by everybody irrespective of the nature of the work?

EDDIE CHAMBERS: Even if that is true, and Black art has been diluted and lost its direction, that should not indicate the end of its radical movement. Black art could still be a powerful force.

RASHEED ARAEEN: You mean to say that even when the term 'black art' has been appropriated by the establishment, and is being used as a category, black art movement could still maintain its earlier dynamic . . .

EDDIE CHAMBERS: Yes.

RASHEED ARAEEN: But why has it lost its earlier momentum?

EDDIE CHAMBERS: I don't really know. It has been encountering hard times, and somehow it fell to the ground.

RASHEED ARAEEN: I'm very surprised that you should say that. The exhibition you have curated is still around and is travelling. You must be optimistic, otherwise you would have not been involved in this exhibition.

EDDIE CHAMBERS: There are still Black artists whose work I admire, and in whose work I have hope. The only way I could have shown their work was in a large context with other artists. The fact that their work might not otherwise have been shown, is not very encouraging. And it's difficult to say what the future is, because the situation is no longer in our own hands. Yesterday you said that Black art was very popular. I don't think that's the case . . .

RASHEED ARAEEN: I'm sorry to interrupt you, Eddie, but it was you who said that black art was fashionable.

EDDIE CHAMBERS: No, no. I was only talking in reference to Black artists; Black art as a politicised form of expression is very unpopular amongst Black artists.

RASHEED ARAEEN: I would agree with you there, given the nasty reactions we had in the past . . .

EDDIE CHAMBERS: But I'm not talking about its being unpopular among the white audience or critics. I'm not really bothered by them. I'm only concerned with Black practitioners themselves. There are very few artists who would seriously accept the political framework of Black art and would also accept this framework for their own practice.

RASHEED ARAEEN: You mean there is a lack of political commitment.

EDDIE CHAMBERS: Yes. There is a lot of ambition for getting into the galleries, but there is no political commitment as far as the work is concerned.

RASHEED ARAEEN: But, Eddie, we must recognise that art is a profession. It has an economic base. The only outlet available to the artist, whether you are white or black, is through the established structures. If you say that black art is something which is meant for and addresses only the black community, while the black community has no economic power to support its artists, then the black artist is lost.

EDDIE CHAMBERS: I do appreciate what you are saying. But what I'm saying is different: there are a lot of Black artists whose only concern is to gain access to the white gallery space, which is a legitimate struggle but they are not concerned with the issues involved in it. There are many Black artists who will tell you about their experiences of racism while dealing with the galleries, but they will do nothing about it as far as their work is concerned. The struggle to gain access to the galleries has superseded the struggle to create art forms which relate to the experience of Black people.

RASHEED ARAEEN: I don't think we are talking about different things. My own view about black art movement is that it has lost its earlier momentum because it had no support from the black community itself. I'm not saying that the black community did not show any interest, but to show an interest only is different from supporting its artists economically. The black community does not have economic power to support its artists. I maybe repeating myself here, but I think it's important to emphasise. The only alternative, then, is to turn to the established system, whether one likes it or not, and to make demands within it. It has contradictions, particularly when one is engaged in a radical practice, but that's the way things are. I'm not suggesting that we should give in to the market forces, but it's an issue which we cannot ignore.

EDDIE CHAMBERS: There are a number of problems with that analysis, and I can't agree with that fully. I would have liked to go into it again, but I must go now . . .

NOTES

1 *Black Art: Plotting the Course*; Oldham Art Gallery, Oldham, Oct–Dec 1988; Wolverhampton Art Gallery, Wolverhampton, Dec–Jan 1988/89; Bluecoat Gallery, Liverpool, Feb–March 1989.

2 *The Essential Black Art*, Chisenhale Gallery, London, Feb–March 1988. The catalogue is available from Kala Press.

3 Eddie Chambers, introduction to the original catalogue for *D-Max* exhibition whose first showing took place at Ikon Gallery Birmingham, July–August 1987.

4 Editor's note: It is likely that Araeen is discussing *Black Art: New Directions*, Stoke on Trent City Museum and Art Gallery, 18 February–27 March 1989.

35 Frank Bowling, 'Formalist Art and the Black Experience', 1988

Frank Bowling arrived in Britain from British Guiana (now Guyana) in 1953 and attended the Royal College of Art in London, graduating in 1962. During the early 1960s he developed a highly individual painting style that blurred the boundaries between figurative Pop and abstract gestural forms, and which simultaneously utilized popular visual culture and autobiographical references. In 1966 he moved to New York where his work became increasingly abstract, and as a contributing editor of *Arts Magazine* between 1969 and 1972, he engaged in the many debates regarding the form and function of Black Art in the USA. In the essay reproduced here, Bowling revisits some of the ideas he had developed in the previous decades. He notes that despite the passage of time since the 1960s, debate and disagreement regarding the definition of 'Black art' continues. Bowling takes issue with overtly political works that utilize text and collage, suggesting that they ape advertising and look best in reproduction because the artists who make them have little concern with the formal properties and qualities of the artistic media in which they work. He suggests that Black art is not simply the presentation of political statements or the representation of black figures, but rather could be shaped via formal, material concerns, where the application of paint in particular ways could be harnessed to emotively express the artist's lived experience as a Black person.

* * *

My art is Formalist and my experience that of a black artist. Beginning in 1968 with the American media exhibition 'Harlem on my Mind' at the Metropolitan Museum of Art in New York City, I became fully aware that there have been many short and long statements and much discussion about the nature of Black Art. As defined during the late '60s, the declared positions of many black American artists perpetually left with me a certain discouraging confusion. Perhaps this was inevitable because of a not realised yet urgent yearning. But is Black Art realisable? Black Art seems to have gained little clarity, although the debate still rages.

The chilling notion dawned on me reading and rereading utterances by black artists and writers on art, particularly those who related themselves to the 'street', that the talking took place as they sat on the coffin of unspent possibilities. Twenty years ago it was also said that black artists doing Black Art were not making paintings or sculpture, just Black Art. They were unwilling, unable, even afraid to deal with 'dwellings': floor, walls, etc., but this is not the issue now.

Black Art, as an ideal, is very much with us. Any age alert to evolutionary or revolutionary forces that stretch possibilities, brings with it painful scholarship bracing in a wind-of-change challenge.

For me the positive thing to come through twenty-odd years and into the present situation is the demand and published assertions for a criticism to accommodate, to explicate veritably, black experience; this is a call for new structures of criticism! It is obvious that the artists, polemicists and others have moved into the mainstream and deserve praise.

As a concept, Black Art has to be contingent with aesthetic

concerns and, as such, is involved necessarily with notions of quality. There is little evidence of any singular significance, save the laudable call to arms. Nothing in this body of work has been signally original or surprising.

There are plenty of precedents for the social artist who is radically committed and involved with the living world, to be found in the work of all those artists in the history of awkward genre and realistic allegorical painting, and in whose pieces what was revealed was actually a certain conservative clinging to well-tried, now creaking, now worn-out (but not necessarily no longer valid) pictorial devices.

Most of the figuration of these social artists could be put to better use in spot advertising and graphic design. This is evidenced by the fact that most of this work appears better, more explicit and certainly accomplished, in reproduction. And the reason is that the material qualities of paint and collage in the pieces themselves do not engage one. The media reproduction process neutralises things, reduces everything to a bald graphic message totally devoid of touch or material nuance. This stuff is more about information that is underlined by the comparative distinction afforded it through its reproduction in catalogues, magazines and newspapers, counselling political awareness and the ethno-cultural choices that one must make as a black in the frontline of modern Western society.

Specific 'Black Experience' puts all out of focus and into question. Extremely literal in the worst sense, these works are designed to deny the awesome subtlety of black experience, indeed experience of any sort. At any rate, that experience doesn't show up in the handling.

The temptation is to label this work 'bad', but to use the once-derogatory term 'Bad Art' as a tag for the products of these art endeavours, has to be resisted, for few of the pieces displayed in officially organised exhibitions or dealer galleries articulate the modernist violence of black life. The question remains, bad as compared to what? Alas, we still haven't discovered any secret cache of instructions provided by the African ancestors in their distinctive 'written' style; and since this is the case, I suggest, we can't disprove 'racist lies' about black impotence. Present evidence, the recent summoning of art, i.e. painting and sculpture, to verify the existence of Black Art, does prove on one hand recalcitrant and awfully tricky, from much of what goes under that banner; on the other hand, is criticism then powerless?

The answer here is an unqualified No! What we can do and it's already happening (the on-going discussions) is to question past assumptions from the positive deductions of our experience, black experience, especially in the black Western diaspora. The trouble with eliciting from painting and sculpture a redefinition of art (with the express intention of *defining* Black Art) is that it is rather like pulling strong teeth without anaesthetic. I would suggest two ways. One, as I stated, through our experience: concrete equivalents which extend themselves through determinants, measurements, yardsticks in art. Or, total rejection of the immediate black experience, which would involve a boat trip back on the Garveyan precedent; that might, that does, imply all kinds of potential discoveries. The treasure hunt! Back to Africa!

As a Formalist, my endeavour to come to terms with the pressures of admitted black experience led me far afield. One might say I put out to sea with some books! In the summer 1964 issue of *Art and Literature* I found the English philosopher Richard Wollheim's essay 'On Expression and Expressionism' a discussion of Marion Milner's book *On Not Being Able to Paint*. "At one point Wittgenstein asks if we can imagine ourselves using one phrase and meaning another by it (e.g. saying 'It's cold here' meaning 'It's warm here') . . . our explanation would probably take the form of alleging that as we say the word cold out loud, we say warm to ourselves; (not even that I venture!) or that we treat our utterance as though it were a slip of the tongue . . ." (page 178). My travels across the continental United States taught me to believe that every dweller in the black ghetto (community?), from Junkie to Jack-of-all-trades, *knows* about those changes. Thaat! *That* is their life style. Yes. My hypothesis is that the people on the streets (the oft re-flashed 'guy off the street') are tuned in to Wittgenstein as revealed through Wollheim in *Art and Literature* or (more pertinently) the other way round. They too, among others, are aware of the limits of language in regard to ethics, beauty, to the inward and transient pulse of being and are aware of the intensely constricting nature of language. It is only in music that the human consciousness experiences immediately the realities of meaning and finds intellectual and emotional satisfaction. Music is perfectly concrete, but resists all paraphrase. While black music is real, the existence of black painting and sculpture still has to be argued.

Addressing oneself upfront or otherwise to an audience is not necessarily dealing with and reflecting the literal situation in the ghetto or community. My point, however, is that the energy is located somewhere in the subtlety of 'experience'; shared experience, trapped in the web of skeins and layers of material being worked. And this is why literalness, although precise in every measurable dimension, fails to express: fails, that is, at 'expression'. Wollheim further (same page) says ". . . we might find here a suggestion as to how the present question about the limits of expression is to be answered. For it might seem that a man can express y-ness by x-ing, only if x-ing stands to y-ness in a relation which is, or analogous to, that of meaning . . ." Experience has no literal meaning, only 'subtle', meaning idiosyncratic, personal, etc. Though it accommodates literalness, this is only part of the whole story. Literal shape for instance has no meaning, it's just shape, but it can in one sense stand (has stood, does stand) for painting through being 'depicted' (painted). I-was-aiming-at often turns out not to be I-did-so or I accomplished after literal action; except in the limited sense. Blackness is therefore no more expressed, in the literal sense, by painting a black face than by a black line, for it is the depiction of a face or a line that we are witnessing; hence, the experience that a painting 'carries' through literal and depicted shape is generally a painting experience (time, colour surface/area, perimetric demarcation points, etc.).

The black experience must therefore be operating on a different, more subtle level, or not at all. But there is a missing link. If we may turn again to Wollheim's essay, on page 190 "... I now want to suggest an association between ... two aspects of expression in art: the existence of a physiognomic link between emotion that is expressed and the expression of it, and the privileged character of the spectator's verdict. Now on the face of it ... the spectator will be expected to recognise this link but his verdict has no special authority to it: for his opinion is relevant only in so far as it is true of the link ..."

Wollheim goes on to note: "Given a man cannot express his feelings in a painting simply by standing in front of the canvas with these feelings and then trying to put them into the painting, what is the difference between the man who is in this position and the man who has rules to aid him ..." Wollheim splits this questions into two parts but, for our purpose, let us skip his observation that "... whether there is any specific kind of painting that unmistakably shows signs of having been painted to a rule: or whether since any kind of painting can be brought under a rule, we must take the painter's word for the fact that he was following a rule. In which case what is left of 'spectator supremacy' ..." And go on to conclude, with Wollheim, an admission of the difficulty. Nevertheless I cannot accept the inclusive, saying "This one wasn't rule-directed, therefore it isn't supposed to be good art." For quality is always discernible and successful expression is the ultimately revealed aspect; the distinctive character of the work, rule-directed or otherwise. The trouble with rules is that in a situation like trying to define

Black Art, the confusion is deepened by the politically polarised stands taken about what are the rules to follow. That 'experience' forges the content of works is an assertion that we will have to leave for now. But Black Art or the pretence of it is now a cult and cultists tend to put exaltation in place of thought. Ethnic and minority rights are now a cult and the beauty is that the white right-thinking world is chanting a political anthem rather than a hymn to art and culture. Politics change with elections and even with generations. Art and culture endures.

The point I have been trying to make is that depiction of black faces and black hands does not make Black Art; what does, though, lies in the formal expression by individual black artists of the black experience; alongside all other major art.

36 Lesley Sanderson, 'Artist's Statement', 1989

Lesley Sanderson completed her BA in Fine Art at Sheffield Polytechnic in 1984. Her work was subsequently included in *New Contemporaries* at the ICA, London, in 1986, and the exhibition *Black Art: Plotting the Course* (1988), curated by Eddie Chambers and staged at Oldham Art Gallery, and then touring to Liverpool and Wolverhampton. In her work from the mid to late 1980s, Sanderson sought to confront derogatory racist stereotypes through a series of powerful self-portraits. Tackling head-on a history of Orientalist images that presented South-East Asian women as exotic and passive, in paintings such as *Self-Portrait as a Chinky* (1984), Sanderson confronts and defies her (white) audiences. This short artist's statement was reproduced in the catalogue accompanying *Along the Lines of Resistance: An exhibition of contemporary feminist art* (1988), curated by Sutapa Biswas, Sarah Edge and Claire Slattery, which toured from the Cooper Gallery, Barnsley, to Rochdale Art Gallery. The show included Sanderson's painting *Time for a Change* (1988), in which she challenges audiences to compare a painting of Saw Ohn Nyun, Princess of Burma, created in the 1930s by Gerald Festus Kelly (1879–1972), with her own naked body.

*　*　*

My drawings and paintings aim to be direct and easily read. They use the self-portrait as a vehicle to confront the stereotype, to voice an opinion on racism, generally, personally and from the viewpoint of a woman. I would hope that they aren't seen as narcissistic and introverted.

I consciously work in a very straightforward, realistic way so that the image and its content aren't obscured.

"Self-portrait as a chinky" was the start in a line of work that explores racism and challenges traditions of representation. The gesture with the fingers is one that everyone is familiar with and that needs no explaining. The symbol on the face is the British Movement sign. The painting attempts to "expose a society that institutionalises its racism, celebrates its dominance."[1]

"Time for a change" is an attempt to represent the non-white woman in a more contemporary way rather than in the traditional and more familiar representation of a 'native' woman. It tries to provide an alternative to National Geographic-type media representation of 'ethnic' women being exotic and submissive. The expression and look of the unclothed figure on the left challenges the audience looking at her, making the act of looking a two-way activity. The gaze of the person depicted is always important in my work.

NOTE

1. Pete Clark, "Lesley Sanderson", *A Reputation amongst Artists*, exhibition pamphlet, Graves Art Gallery, Sheffield, 5 March – 10 April 1988.

37 Adeola Solanke, 'Donald Rodney', 1989

Donald Rodney's solo exhibition *Crisis* was staged at Chisenhale Gallery, London, January–February 1989, and later toured to the Graves Gallery, Sheffield. In this review published in the respected arts magazine *Art Monthly*, critic and playwright Adeola Solanke discusses the way in which Rodney used X-rays metaphorically to comment on the 'health' or rather, sickness, of British society. In his exhibition Rodney presented a series of oil pastel drawings made on X-rays, and installed CCTV cameras and monitors, to present Britain as a corrupt police state. In works such as *The House that Jack Built* (1987), Rodney presented the home under attack, linking contemporary events, including the attacks on Cherry Groce and Cynthia Jarrett in 1985, to the treatment of enslaved African people traded by British imperialists. Simultaneously, throughout his exhibition Rodney also referenced the work of modernist artists Pablo Picasso, Frida Kahlo and Francis Bacon, positioning his work within and against established histories of art.

* * *

Recognise that rib-cage? It could well be yours. Twenty-seven year-old artist Donald Rodney's one-man show, 'Crisis', at London's Chisenhale Gallery, presents images of ailing Britain made from X-rays.

He buys them (mainly chest X-rays) for £1 per kilo from hardup hospitals. They offer the perfect medium with which to express his public concern for the health of the nation. His choice of material is a metaphor in itself, inspired both by his preoccupation with the global experiences of black people, and his private distress as a sufferer of sickle cell disease, a hereditary blood disorder that mainly affects people of Afro-Caribbean origin.

'I've been X-rayed constantly since doctors found out I had sickle cell anaemia when I was two. I'm something of an expert at reading them now.'

The ten pieces in 'Crisis', all recent work produced since September 1988 when he was artist in residence at a community centre in Sheffield, offer a diagnostic reading of Britain today, with particular reference to the condition of black people. Rodney says, 'with X-rays you're looking beneath the surface to see what the structures of things really are. That's what I wanted to do: to look beneath the surface of our lives, see how we are, and how the structure of society has made us what we are'.

So how is the body politic? Taking the biblical notion of the body as a temple, one work, *The House that Jack Built*, comments on the experience of racism on the domestic front. It's a crude self-portrait with a scarecrow-like effigy perched on a white pedestal in front of a dissection of a house-front made out of X-rays.

Rodney used a surgeon's scalpel to carve out apocalyptic statements on the surface of the X-rays which, against the white chipboard on which they're mounted, glow with an eerie, blueish pallor.

'From the National Front throwing petrol bombs into people's homes, to the arbitrary police intrusions into homes like Cherry Groce's and Cynthia Jarrett's (both black women who suffered, the latter fatally, from police visits to their homes in London in 1985); to the deaths of John Shorthouse, Winston Brown and Colin Roach, all of whom died as a result of contact with the police, we are experiencing an infringement of our civil liberties and we ought to be concerned about our welfare,' Rodney argues. In the past, again due to lack of money, Rodney has used huge hospital sheets as the surface for his polemical work. Text featured more prominently then than now, which he says is a conscious attempt ('people don't have time to stand and read!') to 'pare the work down.'

His themes are more focused too. The issues raised in 'Crisis' relate to the global experience of black people through, if you like, the medium of black experience here in Britain. Instead of trying to tell the whole story, he calls up specific incidents and links them to the whole, and extends his range of comment even further by introducing iconography from diverse sources.

In *Britannia Hospital 1* – the first in a sequence of three works – a fictional hospital scene which represents Britain as a whole ('a sick society'), is constructed from four images. A photo of Cherry Groce, crippled after being shot by police officers, being wheeled out of hospital by Paul Boateng, one of Britain's four black MPs; a photo of policemen during the riots that her shooting precipitated; a photo of the rioting itself, and then the figure of the priest in Francis Bacon's *Pope Paul the Innocent*.

'The priest in the original is caught with an expression of horror on his face. I use the same colours and pose and put Cherry Groce's face on top,' Rodney explains.

The piece, which measures 8ft × 4ft, is a complicated composition. Again made up of X-rays pre-gridded so that mounting is made easier, here the surface is given a ghostlike, haunting effect by the use of neo-colour crayons and the placing of images over on top of the shadowy contours the X-rays already suggest.

The largest work in 'Crisis', called *Soweto/Guernica*, uses an even more complex visual vocabulary, offered as a response to the deliberate obscuring of the African origins of the work of eminent twentieth-century artists that many black artists confront at art school. Rodney studied Fine Art at Trent Polytechnic, and then took a postgraduate degree in Fine Art Multi-Media at the Slade.

'At art school we were constantly fed the history of modern

art, and the work of artists like Picasso. But little is said about the debt owed to African art in his work. I wanted to reclaim the image, and to re-use the history of Picasso's famous "you did" reply when he was asked who painted the atrocity depicted in *Guernica*, and invoke the West's culpability for the horrors occurring in South Africa.'

The photo of Hector Pieterson, the African schoolboy shot dead by police in the 1976 Soweto riots, is the central image. Across the top of the work a convoy of 'images taken from all over the place' travels, extending the dialogue from Soweto and Guernica to sites of other atrocities: from Broadwater Farm, the scene of the riot following the death of Cynthia Jarrett in 1985, to the industrial relations front, with the famous image of the mounted policeman galloping forward with his baton at the Orgreave strike, to the image of soldiers planting an American flag on Korean soil after a battle in the Korean war.

'I don't pursue originality,' Rodney says. 'Sometimes things just strike a chord. Whether the image is from Europe or Africa is not the issue. If a familiar image is put in an unfamiliar context, the viewer reads it in a totally different way.'

His current eclecticism, his increasingly sombre and thoughtful character, and his illness itself (he finds walking painful – which, looking on the positive side, means he's now more prolific), have lent this talented, fertile and (somehow) still jovial young artist a grimly original way to depict his insights into the pains of modern life.

38 Paul Gilroy, 'David A. Bailey: From Britain, Barbados or Both?', 1989

David A. Bailey's solo exhibition of photographs, *I'm Black, I'm Bajan and I'm British*, was staged at the Tom Allen Centre, London, in November–December 1989. The exhibition comprised a series of works that transported the figure of Bailey (and the viewer) both geographically and conceptually, from the UK and an idea of what Barbados *might* be like, to the Caribbean island, and a reckoning with the lived reality of Bajan life. The works in this exhibition asserted a shift in Bailey's approach to photography; works shown in his solo exhibition at the People's Gallery, London, in 1984, and *Unrecorded Truths*, curated by Lubaina Himid at The Elbow Room, London in 1986, were documentary images of Black people in everyday situations, whether at play or on political demonstrations. But, as cultural theorist Paul Gilroy makes clear in his text, by 1989, Bailey had turned his photographic practice on himself, in order to make a nuanced and personal body of work addressing the lived experience of being Black, Bajan and British.

*   *   *

A young man born and raised in the shadow of London's St Pancras station, embarks on a journey to Barbados, his parents' original home and his own home from home. There he discovers the real pleasures of recovering history and family intimacy. They cannot, however, conceal the deeper shock of his estrangement from the rhythm and the detail of Bajan life. What ought to have been scarcely more than a joyous readmission to the nurturing cultures of the Caribbean became instead an opportunity to explore his own necessarily compound identity. The superficial sense of familiarity produced in England by the simple fact of his Caribbean descent is not sufficient to give him guidance. It proves incapable of masking the realisation that Barbados is yet another island nation where he will have to turn the distinctive condition of being in but not of society, into a privilege.

The aftershock of belonging neither to Britain nor to Barbados radiates out from these images but David A. Bailey's photographs do more than seek to make a virtue out of the inescapable feelings of cultural homesickness and homelessness that they evoke. Read through the imagery of the beach, the billboard or the schoolyard, Barbados is neither what England thinks it is nor what Bailey would like it to be. The church, the schoolhouse and other core components of black cultural autonomy are all witnessed from an outsider's point of view.

The viewer is invited into an extended meditation on the relationship between image and context in the construction and transformation of Caribbean identity. The piece demands that you focus on the disjuncture between the order of meanings that the Caribbean has back home in England and the meanings it acquires when you have found your own resting place on the beach which constitutes its principal attribute.

The show . . . speaks for those of us who, like the photographer, recognise that our lives encompass the histories of the Caribbean and the British Empire but are not exhausted by those histories or the unlikely configurations of identity that they support. It dares the viewer to join the joyous, playful task of creating an identity which can contain the extensive cultural baggage of Britain's 'second generation Caribbean migrants'.

39 Gilane Tawadros, 'Lubaina Himid: *Freedom and Change*', 1989

In this text, writer and curator Gilane Tawadros provides a detailed interpretation of Lubaina Himid's multi-part installation, *Freedom and Change* (1984). Following a description of the work, Tawadros explains that it is a reworking of Pablo Picasso's *Two Women Running on the Beach* (1922). She then goes on to discuss Himid's artwork in relation to the histories of modernism and postmodernism, and the place of Black women artists within those frameworks of knowledge. For Tawadros, Himid's work challenges and undermines existing hierarchies of Western culture that have celebrated artists, including Picasso, for their appropriation of African art and visual culture, while simultaneously excluding the creative practices of Black people. Lubaina Himid studied Theatre Design at Wimbledon School of Art (1973–6), and undertook an MA in Cultural History at the Royal College of Art, London (1982–4). In addition to working as an artist, throughout the 1980s Himid curated numerous exhibitions, including *5 Black Women Artists* at the Africa Centre, London, in 1983 and *The Thin Black Line* at the ICA, London, in 1985. Gilane Tawadros' text is an extract from her longer essay, 'Beyond the Boundary: The work of Three Black Women Artists in Britain', first published in the radical journal *Third Text*, edited by Rasheed Araeen. Alongside Himid, Tawadros also analysed and discussed the work of Sutapa Biswas and Sonia

266

Boyce, and her essay was arguably the first academic text to rigorously engage with their artwork, and their art historical and philosophical contexts.

* * *

Two black women, their bodies clothed in a patchwork of coloured fabrics, are running across a plain of purple cloth. Ahead of them, beyond the frame of purple are four black dogs, their leads gripped in the hand of the woman who fixes us with her gaze. The heads of two white men, trapped in dense particles of sand, are left behind the running women and their dogs. Lubaina Himid's *Freedom and Change* (1984) is a re-working of Pablo Picasso's *Two Women Running on the Beach* (1922). The small neo-classical image of two white women racing across a de-populated coastline, made by the Spanish artist in the years following the cessation of the Great War, has been appropriated by Himid and transformed. Picasso's appropriations of African tribal masks and ceremonial figures and the assimilation of 'primitive' art into the work of modernist artists is challenged and reversed. While artists like Picasso absorbed the styles and forms of non-European art and translated them into the language of Western avant-gardism, Himid has visibly adapted Picasso's work to draw attention to the wider implications of the European process of gathering and re-using, a process wherein "Euro-American masters have stolen the genre, assimilated the methodology, oppressed the originators and claimed the prize".[1]

The significance of Himid's act of appropriation lies not only in the differing ramifications of gathering and re-using as a mode of creative expression but also in the sense of time which frames the work as a whole – a sense of history and a sense of the future – which stands in stark contrast to the consciousness of time articulated by the modern, avant-garde artist. There is a timeless, almost ahistorical quality to Picasso's *Two Women Running on the Beach*, evoked by the neo-classical figures who move through a deserted landscape devoid of any sense of time or place; which thus obscures the specificity of the historical and aesthetic framework in which the painting was made. Reaching away from an unseen past and stretching forward to an intangible future, these women emerge from the distinct context of post-World War One European society. Abandoning the traumatic memories of war which shook Western civilisation, they are running towards a future progressively modern and, at the same time, continuous with the classical Graeco-Roman roots of European culture. In short, Picasso's *Two Women* visualises a period of transition in the social and aesthetic history of Europe and denotes 'modernity' in so far as that has been defined as "the consciousness of an epoch that defines itself in relation to the past of antiquity in order to view itself as the result of a transition from old to new."[2] Moreover, it pictures a changed consciousness of time which emerged in the course of the nineteenth century and which, according to Jurgen Habermas, characterises the project of 'aesthetic modernity'.

Lubaina Himid's *Freedom and Change* expresses a period of transition from old to new and can be defined as 'modern' to the extent that this transition is articulated in relation to the past. There the similarity between the two works ends. For Himid asserts a very different relationship to the past and the future in her work. The past expressed by Picasso's *Two Women* is an abstract one, not fixed by historical time or place, wherein the contours of classical art are stretched quite literally to accommodate an unspecific and universalising conception of the past. By contrast, the past in Himid's work, defined by the configurations of white men's heads, is designated as a place shaped and presided over by a white male presence. The history of the West, and indeed the history of Western art, has privileged the mark of male individuals and rendered invisible or inferior the place of black peoples (particularly black women) within these histories. Himid's cardboard cut-outs of white male heads point to the privileged site accorded both to the originators of the grand narratives of Western culture and also to the declared origins of Western civilisation, in other words, the past of Graeco-Roman antiquity. The figurative remnants of the old order of Western culture which gave currency to notions of originality, origins and authenticity, have been thus consigned to the depths of the past. While their place in the present has been usurped by two black women who mediate between this past and a future defined by the contours of four black dogs.

Moving across a field of purple, these women designate a reign of freedom and change. As in Alice Walker's novel, the colour purple is emblematic, not of nationhood or national sovereignty, but of black womanhood which defies its relegation to the margins and enters the centre ground to assert its place *in* history.[3] Himid's women displace what Stuart Hall has called the "centred discourses of the West", but this does not imply that the grand narratives of Western culture are simply to be replaced by an alternative, totalising narrative. Rather, this process of displacement "entails putting in question (Western culture's) universalist character and its transcendental claims to speak for everyone, while being itself everywhere and nowhere."[4] Whereas Picasso's women race across a space which aspires to the status of the universal and the transcendental and which paradoxically remains confined within the perimeters of the frame; Himid's women significantly tread a borderline which marks the threshold between real and imagined space, between lived experiences and expressions of that experience. In opposition to the universalising tendencies of modernism, *Freedom and Change* assigns central importance to the position of difference. Himid articulates a "positive conception of the ethnicity of the margins, or the periphery . . . a recognition that we all speak from a particular place, out of a particular history, out of a particular experience, a particular culture without being contained by that position . . ."[5] The particular place from which

Himid's women assert their historical experience is the coastline, an ambivalent site which marks the frontier of slavery, colonialism and migration but which also denotes the positivity of the *diasporan* experience. Like the separate pieces of a patchwork, Himid has embroidered together a number of diverse histories and varying categories of creative expression (from drawing as a signifier of the academy traditions of Western art to patchwork as a signifier of domestic, 'feminine' craft) which contest the unequivocal order and monolithic perspective circumscribed by Picasso's earlier work. Himid weaves a web of cultural and historical meanings into the fabric of her work which derive both from the transformation of the original source and also from the assemblage of fragments which together dispute the authority of the established order (both historical and art historical) of Western culture.

What then are the implications of postmodernism for Lubaina Himid's *Freedom and Change*? Is her collage of fragments merely a "random cannibalization of all the styles of the past", as Jameson argues, and thus symptomatic of the "waning of our historicity" and our inability to fashion representations of our current experience? Can Himid's intimations of the illegitimacy of the grand narratives of the West be explained in terms of the death of the individual subject and a crisis of confidence in notions of progress and human emancipation? Or are these prescriptions for a postmodern condition themselves indicative of continuing periodic transformations in European thought? In this context, I would argue, Lubaina Himid's *Freedom and Change* does not substitute a history of aesthetic styles for 'real' history. Rather, in positioning two black women between a specific past delimited by white male individualism and a particular vision of the future defined by the vivid contours of a black presence, Himid situates black women and black women's artistic discourse firmly *within* history. Thus the avowed collapse of the grand narratives of Western culture, makes possible the articulation of black experience at the very centre of history and the history of art. The process of gathering and re-using, far from affirming the fragmentation of the black subject in the terms of postmodernity, attests to the centrality and dynamism of the diasporan experience, of diverse cultural influences and discontinuous histories in opposition to the false unities of Western thought which reach their apogee in the 'supreme fictions' of modernism.[6]

NOTES

1. Lubaina Himid, 'Fragments', *Feminist Arts News*, vol.2, no.8, Autumn 1988, p.8.

2. Jurgen Habermas, 'Modernity – An Incomplete Project', in Hal Foster (ed.), *Postmodern Culture*, London, Pluto Press, 1987, p.3.

3. I refer to Alice Walker's *The Colour Purple*, London, Women's Press, 1988.

4. Stuart Hall, 'New Ethnicities', in *ICA Documents 7: Black Film/British Cinema*, London, Institute of Contemporary Arts, 1988, p.29.

5. Ibid.

6. See Hal Foster, 'Postmodernism: A Preface', in Hal Foster (ed.), *Postmodern Culture*, op. cit., pp.ix–xvi.

40 Rasheed Araeen, Introduction to *The Other Story: Afro-Asian Artists in Post-War Britain*, 1989

Rasheed Araeen's work as an artist, curator and scholar has, to a very large extent, shaped the field of Black British Art History. After a decade of campaigning and rejections, in 1989 his exhibition *The Other Story: Afro-Asian Artists in Post-War Britain* opened at the Hayward Gallery, London. It subsequently toured to Wolverhampton Art Gallery, Manchester City Art Gallery and Cornerhouse, Manchester, during 1990, and was the first large-scale exhibition to survey the work of multiple generations of artists of African, Asian and Caribbean origin active in Britain. Araeen had first proposed the exhibition to the Hayward Gallery in 1978, and his struggle to secure institutional support, in the face of uninterested curators and institutionalized racism, is documented in his book, *Making Myself Visible* (1984). Araeen's aim for the exhibition was to demonstrate that despite their exclusions from mainstream or institutionalized histories of art, artists of colour did and continue to make significant contributions to the art and cultural life of Britain. Twenty-four artists were included in the show: Rasheed Araeen, Saleem Arif, Frank Bowling, Sonia Boyce, Eddie Chambers, Avinash Chandra, Avtarjeet Dhanjal, Uzo Egonu, Iqbal Geoffrey, Mona Hatoum, Lubaina Himid, Gavin Jantjes, Balraj Khanna, Li Yuan-chia, Donald Locke, David Medalla, Ronald Moody, Ahmed

Parvez, Ivan Peries, Keith Piper, Anwar Jalal Shemza, Kumiko Shimizu, Francis Newton Souza and Aubrey Williams. Araeen's curatorial intervention provided an unprecedented, and personal, overview of modernist artistic practice in Britain undertaken by artists of African, Asian and Caribbean heritage from the post-war period to the present day. In the Introduction to his exhibition catalogue, reproduced here, Araeen identifies the discipline of Art History as ideologically biased, intent on privileging a Western 'master narrative'. He goes on to outline the difficulties artists of colour faced in forging careers when the dominant British culture was steeped in the legacies of colonialism and had not yet come to terms with the collapse of Empire. Araeen describes how migrant artists, mainly from the 'New Commonwealth', were 'Othered' according to racial difference, and he questions whether pluralism and true equality can be achieved without actively recovering overlooked, hidden and erased histories.

*   *   *

INTRODUCTION: WHEN CHICKENS COME HOME TO ROOST

This is a unique story. It is a story that has never been told. Not because there was nobody to tell the story, but because it only existed in fragments, each fragment asserting its own autonomous existence removed from the context of collective history. It is therefore a story of those men and women who defied their 'otherness' and entered the modern space that was forbidden to them, not only to declare their historic claim on it but also to challenge the framework which defined and protected its boundaries. My attempt to tell this story, given my lack of proper expertise and insufficient discipline, aims to pay homage to this defiance. My own struggle as an avant-garde artist (in the West) has been fundamental in my realization of the issues, and without this struggle it would not have been possible for me to recognize the importance of this story. However, it is not the only story. There are many more, and I believe it is crucial, in our attempt to recover our place in history, 'to tell other stories than the official sequential or ideological ones produced by institutions of power'.[1]

My aims here are exploratory rather than critical, insofar as they are separable. However, this exploration must take into consideration the change that has taken place in the world since the last War, in particular the mass emigration of peoples from Africa, Asia and the Caribbean to the West, which not only changed the demographic map of Europe but also challenged the old social structures that had been maintained by the geographical separation of the colonizer and the colonized. This challenge was part of the process of decolonization across the world, with its specific articulation in the metropolis.

It would be a mistake to emphasize only the socio-political determinants of mass emigration and not to fully understand the actual aims of individual artists who left their countries of origin simply to fulfil their artistic ambitions abroad. We should also recognize the peculiarity of these ambitions, which are not fulfilled merely by a success in the market-place but by the artist's entry into the history of art. It is this entry that allows his or her work to be discussed seriously and to be recognized for its historical significance. What we face here is the dominant ideology of an imperial civilization for which the racial or cultural difference of the colonized constitutes Otherness. And of course the Other is part of its history as long as it stays outside the master narrative.

Would it be possible to inscribe this story within the master narrative of modern art history? Would not this have produced an unresolvable contradiction? A slap in the face of Hegelian metaphysics? Is not the history of art still being written according to the Hegelian historical framework in which only the Western subject is privileged? And is not this privilege achieved by arbitrary removal of other cultures/peoples from the dynamics of historical continuity? I should not perhaps have used the word 'arbitrary' and should be more profound in this respect, but I wish to avoid a situation in which I might be dragged into accusing Hegel of racism.

A good example is the way Hegel looks at Indian art and inferiorizes it by comparing it with Greek art. What is the point of comparison here? Is there a rational discourse which can establish any point of comparison objectively, beyond and outside the mythical historicization of the evolution of different cultures? Hegel's world-view removes India from any dynamic of history because it helps establish the supremacy of Western culture. India is therefore 'condemned to remain always outside history, static, immobile, and fixed for all eternity', because for Hegel 'The Hindo race has . . . proved itself unable to comprehend either persons or events as part of continuous history, because to any historical treatment a certain objectivity is essential.'[2]

The art historian John Ruskin, whose socialist credentials are often thrown in to support his humanism, did not hesitate to use strong words to belittle other cultures: 'The reader who has not before turned his attention to this subject may, however, at first have some difficulty in distinguishing between the noble grotesque of these great nations, and the barbarous grotesque of mere savageness, as seen in the work of the Hindoo and other Indian nations; or, more grossly still, in that . . . of the Pacific Islands.

'I can put the relation of Greek to all other art, in this function, before you, in easily compared and remembered examples . . . Here, on the right . . . is an Indian bull, colossal, elaborately carved, which you may take as a sufficient type of the bad art of all the earth. Faulty in form, dead in heart, and loaded with wealth externally. We will not ask the date of this; it may rest in the eternal obscurity of evil art, everywhere and forever. Now, beside this colossal bull, here is a bit of Daedalus-work, enlarged from a coin not bigger that a shilling: look at the two together, and you ought to know, henceforthward, what Greek art means to the end of your day.'[3]

What do we make of it? Diatribe? 'Diatribe' may be a strong word, but can we consider this an objective view? What is the basis of this 'objectivity' other than the power of his speech, which derives not so much from an intellectual argument but from his consciousness of belonging to the privileged class of the British Empire? Can a view founded on military conquests, and its justification on the racial and cultural superiority of the conqueror, have an objectivity? Is this objectivity not a camouflage to hide something which will reveal its imperial fantasies?

John Ruskin is not alone in his views, nor are they now out of fashion. Such views may not today be expressed so openly, or they may not be influential in the way they were a hundred years ago. But there still exist assumptions and attitudes which consider other cultures/peoples outside modern history. These attitudes and assumptions are so pervasive, so intransigent, that the very presence of the others in the modern world is seen with suspicion. When it comes to the question of the modernity of other people, the whole citadel of modernism begins to fall and the question is buried under its debris in the name of the new Father, postmodernism.

A World History of Art,[4] winner of the 1982 Mitchell Prize – 'the most prestigious award in the field of art history', according to its publishers – which is claimed to have represented for the first time all the cultures in the world equally, does include in it all the cultures and treat them almost equally. But this pluralism ends by the end of the nineteenth century. As we enter the twentieth century, African/Oceanic sculpture is taken up again, but only in connection with modernism, the development of various movements and styles – in particular Cubism. After that everything non-European, both peoples and cultures, disappears. The West then shines alone this century, the whole world reflected in its image.

When this book came out in 1982, almost everyone praised it, including Kenneth Clark: 'Much the best complete history of art that has ever been put together'. Indeed 'it explores', unlike Gombrich's *The Story of Art*[5] which cursorily mentions other cultures, 'every branch of the visual arts from every corner of the world throughout man's history . . . the arts of Asia, Africa, the Americas and the Pacific Islands as well as Europe are discussed chronologically . . . '[6] In spite of all its claims to represent 'arts . . . throughout man's history', it falls into an established pattern that obscures the achievement of other cultures in the twentieth century on the assumption that other peoples belong to historically receding cultures. We can fully understand the implication of this assumption if we return to Hegel, amongst others, who assumes that history is a narrative of the progress of ideas in the process of change, where the ultimate narrative is the narrative of Western civilization from which others must be excluded.

Art history is peculiar in its function as a master narrative, not only in that it is fundamental in the recognition and legitimation of Art with a capital A, but that it seems to be the only discourse (unlike the discourse of literature or science) which protects its Western territory so rigidly that we find hardly any exception to its Eurocentric rules.

We are confronted here by a discourse which is complex and ambivalent, for when the mask of its objectivity is lifted, what is revealed is not only a phoney rationalization but a structure which is mythical. It is this mythic structure that hides the contradictions of the bourgeois / imperial society by the invocation of the magical power of the modern artist (white, male, individual, heroic . . .). Its ambivalence, expressed particularly in its fascination for the Other's traditions, does not hide its reaffirmation of the centrality of the Western / white artist in the paradigm of modernism.[7]

There is perhaps no internal contradiction here. If art history is an ideological presentation of Western civilization, it would be logical for it to produce a narrative which conforms to its assumptions, functions and ambitions. My concern here is not to denounce its imperial (and/or patriarchal) ideology. It would be more fruitful to interrogate the nature of its narrative; to reveal the underlying myth which disguises those contradictions inherent in its claim of objective superiority, both historical and epistemological.

In order to explain what I mean by myth I quote from a recent article by Abigail Solomon-Godeau:

'Myth, as Roland Barthes famously defined it, is nothing more than depoliticized speech consistent with the classical definition of ideology (a falsification or mystification of actual social and economic relations). But mythic speech is not only about mystification, it is also, and more crucially, a productive discourse – a set of beliefs, attitudes, utterances, texts and artefacts that are themselves constitutive of social reality. Therefore, in examining mythic speech, it is necessary not only to describe its concrete manifestations, but also to attend to its silences, its absences, its omissions. For what is not spoken – what is unspeakable, mystified or occulted – turns always on historical as well as psychic repressions.'[8]

The smooth working of the myth had entailed the smooth working of the colonial system by which the imperial metropolis was successfully separated and insulated from the people of the colonies. But when the chickens began to come home to roost the outer shell of the myth began to crack. Francis Newton Souza, one of the pioneers of modern art in India, had this to say about his arrival in London in 1947: 'I was astonished by the grimness of Britain. Here was the country that was running, only a few years before, an empire encircling nearly three-quarters of the globe. Yet there was no joy in it. The people were grim-faced after a prolonged war. So this was the environment when I arrived in England. The empire had been lost; the Labour government was in power; half-baked ideas of socialism floated around; the Marshall Plan with its heavy dose of US aid to Europe was in operation.'[9]

Europe after the War was in ruins, facing the anguish of unprecedented human death and suffering. There were no fruits of the Empire to be reaped. There were no roads paved with gold. Instead the cities of Europe had to be rebuilt; and this was the first stage in the process of the demystification of imperial greatness and its humanism, on which the whole colonial apparatus had been built.

The colonial administration used both the stick and the carrot. Schools were set up on Western educational patterns, out of which emerged a middle class which served the Empire. Nevertheless there also appeared a modern consciousness which aspired to change, progress and individual freedom; and this consciousness was fundamental to anticolonial struggles. It was therefore no surprise that many artists in Africa, Asia and the Caribbean who adopted the framework of modernism for their artistic practice were also engaged in the anticolonial struggles of their countries. It was perhaps the anticolonial position held by many artists that helped them 'appropriate' the ideas of rebellion and revolt inherent in the avant-garde. If the attack of the avant-garde in the West was directed at the affluent and dehumanized bourgeois society, the artists in the colonies were concerned with the lack of basic modern progress.

Of course, the situation was not the same everywhere. There were places where there were no schools, and even traditional activities were not allowed. However, when things changed there emerged self-taught artists whose aspirations were no different from those who came from established art schools.

The artists also had the double task of dealing with the prevailing situation: on the one hand with traditional structures (tribal/ feudal) that were re-enforced by colonialism, and on the other, with art institutions that were supposedly modern but were in fact extremely conservative. There were widespread revolts against the status quo, made manifest by the formation of various radical and progressive groups. 43 Group was formed in Ceylon (now

Sri Lanka) in 1943 'to bring together a group of talented painters whose common meeting ground was that their work stood in sharp contradiction to the existing colonial convention, exemplified in the imported and orientalized academicism of the Ceylon Society of Art'.[10]

In India the debate about what is progress and what is progressive, which began over a century ago, is still not resolved. It was never a question of a rejection of traditions, but of how to re-vitalize them in terms of 'modern progress'. This is what Rabindranath Tagore said: 'Fearfully trying to conform to a conventional type is a sign of immaturity . . . I strongly urge our artists vehemently to deny their obligation to produce something that can be labelled as Indian art, according to some old world mannerism . . .'[11]

Throughout history artists have travelled from one country to another in search of patronage, quite often ending up in a dominant centre. The arrival of Picasso, Brancusi, Mondrian, for example, in Paris in the early years of this century, was very much part of this tradition. So when artists from the ex-colonies began to arrive in the metropolis after the War it was not an unusual phenomenon. The independences of their countries removed the constraints, both physical and psychological, from travelling to those places where they could find institutions to support their work. The paradox here is not that of chasing the old colonial masters, but that the lack of modern institutions in their own countries made it impossible for these modern artists to receive all the support they needed. Of course, it would be foolish to ignore other reasons that were to do with the artists' own individual ambitions. It would also be difficult to separate these ambitions from the repressed aspirations, desires, and fantasies of the colonial times.

However, it would be incorrect to conceive the British society as a monolithic power concerned only with its oppressive imperial functions. There also existed a liberal intelligentsia, in the metropolis and in the colonies, whose ambivalence towards the 'natives' was characterized by a good measure of sympathy for their welfare; and in some cases it constituted that progressive section of British people which openly showed sympathy for independence movements.

It should be understood that England has been marginal in terms of twentieth-century modern movements, since all the important movements before the War took place on the Continent. London had never been an international art centre like Paris. It was this consciousness of marginality and the hope that London would develop into an international cultural centre within the independent Commonwealth that created a euphoric spirit among a section of British society that welcomed the arrival in England of artists from abroad.

These artists faced many difficulties in the beginning, no different from those faced by any artist in a new place or country. These problems may have been compounded by the fact that we are here dealing with a society with an imperial past and within which racism has been rampant and overt. One could see in those days notices openly displayed which said 'No Blacks or Coloureds', and there was nothing one could do except to protest individually and collectively. Of course this was the unacceptable face of British society, which was eventually changed. However, it would be a mistake simply to evoke this kind of racist bigotry in order to understand the position of Afro-Asian artists in Britain. This is determined more by the kind of ambivalence about which Homi Bhabha has written.[12] The point here is that this position depends not only on individuals' responses to these artists but also on the attitude of the institutional structures of this society.

However, one is amazed by the kind of support and response which Afro-Asian artists received during their successful period. They began to exhibit their work in the mid-50s, and success followed in many cases. The success of F.N. Souza and Avinash

Chandra had become so phenomenal by the early 60s that there must have been many English artists envious of their success. There was hardly a critic who did not write about them. Souza became so self-conscious of his position that he had to say: 'I make more money by my painting than the Prime Minister by his politics.'[13]

However, despite all their success they remained the Other, in the sense that their Otherness was constantly evoked as part of the discussion of their work. Headlines such as 'Oriental Week', 'Indian Vision' or 'An Indian Painter' were not uncommon, but there were also critics who tried to deal with the problematics of the Otherness, critically and sympathetically, not in order to exclude those artists from the discourse of modern art but to raise the issue of other cultural traditions in relation to modernism. It seems that the most important statement in this respect was made by W.G. Archer: 'Is modern art a closed ring, a private club, a pre-serve for Europe and the United States? Can artists from other countries break in?

'Such questions are posed by the Cuban Wifredo Lam, and the Mexican Rufino Tamayo . . . And they are raised with even greater acuteness by the paintings and drawings of Indian Avinash Chandra . . . [which] with their life-enhancing symbols, brilliant burn-ing colour and gay vitality are nothing if not Indian – Indian to the same degree and [in] the same way as the art of Picasso and Miró is vividly Spanish. Yet just [as] these pioneers of modern painting are part of one world, a world which far transcends national fron-tiers, Chandra, it could be claimed, is more than Indian . . . In his painting, modern art has received an Indian injection and just as Nehru has made an Indian impact on world ideas, we must expect more and more artists from India, South America and the East to [join] the "private club".'[14]

W.G. Archer was not the only person who was aware of the problem, and in spite of the success of some of these artists, many people knew that there was something not quite right. Norbert Lynton had this to say:

'A few years ago there appeared a handsome, internationally published book entitled *Art Since 1945*. It is significant that this book, purporting to present the international art scene of our time, ranged geographically from Poland and Yugoslavia westwards to the United States and simply omitted everything east of Belgrade and West of Seattle. To ignore the oriental contribution to modern art is such an act of ingratitude to a group of civilizations from which many of the concerns and attitudes of modern art derive, that one is justified in interpreting it also as a defensive act against developments that, if seen, would tend to diminish the glory of sections of western artistic achievement.'[15]

Norbert Lynton was not concerned specifically with 'Oriental art', but this quote is the first paragraph of an article he wrote about Iqbal Geoffrey, who was from Pakistan and was a successful artist in Britain at the time.

This concern of Archer and Lynton, amongst many others, was not unfounded. The success of these artists was short-lived – so much so that by the end of the 60s nobody knew or even wanted to talk about them. On the other hand, many of the younger artists of the early 60s, English and White, took over the art scene and became part of the history of the period. What happened to Afro-Asian artists? Why did none of them manage to enter history?[16]

The rise and fall of an artist is not an uncommon phenomenon. Few artists can sustain their position for long. Success is an extremely complex issue, but it can be observed that success in the art market alone is not enough to sustain an artist's career for any length of time, and institutional support is necessary in the consolidation of the artist's position and his/her place in history. Can we conclude from this that Afro-Asian artists did not receive support from the institutions? If so, why not?

Of course, Souza, Chandra, Geoffrey, Bowling and Parvez did

leave London in the second half of the 60s to live in New York, but they left only because they were no longer doing well in England. And they were also lured by the success and glamour of New York. In any case, living abroad should not make any difference to the status of an artist. David Hockney has lived most of his life in California, but is still a favourite of the British establishment. An ex-patriot, Malcolm Morley, who spent little time in Britain during his career as an artist, was given the first Turner Prize a few years ago. The explanation must be that they are *English*.

Why were things so different for Afro-Asian artists? The situation can be better understood in the context of the changes that took place after the War, not only in Britain but worldwide. Since the details are so complicated I have to generalize and simplify the whole thing in order just to explain its relationship with the emergence of a new situation in Britain. If the Commonwealth euphoria of the 50s welcomed Afro-Asian artists as what Denis Bowen called 'a breath of fresh air', the shift of Britain towards America in the 60s became detrimental to the status of these artists.

Given the fact that Britain had lost the Empire and its economic power, its new alliance with an emerging imperial power is understandable. London was not just the focal point of the Commonwealth in the post-war period, it also became an important art centre, which by the early 60s had direct and close connections with New York, the new Mecca of the art world. The opening-up of the New York art market to British artists was a crucial boost to the confidence of the new generation leaving art schools in the early 60s, who soon became part of the international art scene. In fact, without this alliance the emergence of new art in Britain in the 60s is unthinkable. The art schools themselves had an important part to play in preparing those artists who later became successful. From the early 60s it appeared to be common practice for dealers to choose artists from diploma shows. The 'New Generation' exhibitions of the first half of the 60s set the tone and direction of new developments, and were followed by the participation of English artists in exhibitions in New York and elsewhere. At the same time there emerged a new class of art critics, historians and art administrators, whose confidence was formed and enhanced by this change. The Tate Gallery in particular played an important role in the promotion of American interest, in some cases at the expense of British developments.[17]

It is difficult to suggest any direct connection between the situation in Britain and America's use of art (particularly Greenbergian formalism) in Cold War politics, or any collusion between the two in relation to what happened to Afro-Asian artists. But it must be remembered that the objective of post-war American cultural imperialism was not just anti communism but also the assertion of its own cultural hegemony over the world. Freedom of expression in newly independent countries was inevitably affected. It seems that the eventual disappearance of AfroAsian art from the British art scene was not fortuitous, nor can it be explained simply as a result of the emergence of new racism, epitomized by the famous speech of Enoch Powell in 1968 in which he demanded the return of the new Commonwealth peoples to the countries of their origin. It is no coincidence that the British art world became completely white by the end of the 60s – so much so that no major art gallery showed work other than English, American and, to a lesser extent, European. Subsequently no national or international survey of post-war art in Britain has mentioned or included any non-European artist.

But things are changing again, mainly as a result of the anti-racist struggle in Britain, and it is now officially recognized that Britain is a multiracial and multicultural society. Can true pluralism be achieved without recovering what we have lost in the past, for whatever reasons? Can we afford to be complacent any more?

NOTES

1 Edward Said, 'Opponents, Audience, Constituencies and Community', in *The Anti-Aesthetic: Essays on Postmodern Culture*, ed. Hal Foster, Bay Press, 1983, p. 158.

2 Quoted in Partha Mitter, *Much Maligned Monsters: A History of European Reactions to Indian Art*, ch. IV, Clarendon Press, Oxford, 1977.

3 *Ibid*, ch. V.

4 Hugh Honour and John Fleming, *A World History of Art*, Macmillan, London, 1984.

5 E.H. Gombrich, *The Story of Art*, Phaidon, Oxford, 1950.

6 See back cover of *A World History of Art, op. cit.*

7 See catalogue: *Magiciens de la terre*, Centre Georges Pompidou, Paris, 1989; and the special edition of *Third Text*, No. 6, which includes all the articles from *Les Cahiers du Musée National d'Art Moderne*, which was published to coincide with the exhibition, as well as *Third Text*'s critique of the exhibition.

8 Abigail Solomon-Godeau, 'Going Native', *Art in America, The Global Issue*, July 1989.

9 Quoted in Jag Mohen, *Souza in the Forties*, Dhoomi Mal Gallery, New Delhi, 1983, p. 13.

10 Senake Bandaranayake, 'Ivan Peries (Painting 1939–69): The Predicament of the Bourgeois Artist in the Societies of the Third World', *Third Text*, No. 2, Winter 1987–8, p. 90.

11 Quoted in K.G. Subramanyan, *Moving Focus: Essays on Indian Art*, Lalit Kala Akademi, New Delhi, 1978, p. 19.

12 Homi K. Bhabha, 'The Other Question', *Screen*, Vol. 24, No. 6, Nov/Dec 1983.

13 Quoted in Edwin Mullins, *Souza*, Anthony Blond Ltd., London, 1962.

14 W.G. Archer, 'Pictures from a Wider World', *The Sunday Telegraph*, 15 April 1962.

15 Norbert Lynton, catalogue introduction for an exhibition of Iqbal Geoffrey, Alfred Brod Galleries, London, August, 1962.

16 It is interesting to note that Afro-Asian artists were ignored during Norbert Lynton's tenure as the Arts Council's Exhibitions Director in the 70s, and when his book *The Story of Modern Art* came out in 1982 it comprised only white/European artists.

17 The Tate Gallery does not, for example, recognize the independent development of Minimalist sculpture in Britain in the 60s.

41 Amanda Sebestyen, Homi Bhabha and Sutapa Biswas, Reviews of *The Other Story: Afro-Asian Artists in Post-War Britain*, 1989

Rasheed Araeen's exhibition, *The Other Story: Afro-Asian Artists in Post-War Britain*, was staged at the Hayward Gallery in London from 29 November 1989 to 4 February 1990. The exhibition garnered considerable attention from both national newspapers and the art press; it proved controversial and received a mixed response. Critics writing in the mainstream press, such as Brian Sewell in the *Evening Standard* and Richard Dorment in the *Daily Telegraph*, were disparaging of Araeen's attempt to position what they regarded as second-rate artists into narratives of modernist Art History. It was suggested that it was not the race or ethnicity of these artists – or more accurately, white racism – which had led to their exclusion from British art histories, but rather the poor or mediocre 'quality' of their artwork. While critics writing for feminist and politically Left-leaning publications, such as Carole Enahoro in the *Women Artists Slide Library Journal* and John Cunningham in the *Guardian*, were largely supportive of Araeen's aims, he nonetheless faced criticisms regarding the insufficient representation of women artists and the lack of artists working in film and photography. The reviews here by Amanda Sebestyen (published in *City Limits*) and Homi Bhabha and Sutapa Biswas (published in the *New Statesman*) provide an overview of the more nuanced critical responses to *The Other Story.*

*   *   *

Amanda Sebestyen, 'The Other Story', 1989

It's a characteristic of monotone Englishness that Black Art is considered the concern of black people, or of 'anti-racists'. But in this island of sock shops and corporate sponsors, we have a brilliant and passionate art movement, evolving and self-critical, accessible but as deeply layered with thought and history as the Mexican mural movement.

For eleven years, Karachi-born Rasheed Araeen, artist/editor/critic and curator has nursed the idea of a major exhibition of post-war African and Asian artists in Britain. And at last 'The Other Story' is here.

'This is *not* a black art show. This is not an ethnic art show.' Rasheed Araeen speaks in bursts. He's been assailing the English gallery world for years, and as readers of his invigorating journal *Third Text* will know, he has much to say of well-meant council-founded ethnic arts programmes: 'Community artists! These people are the reason I left Pakistan! And now here they are again! Put up by the Establishment!' Buffeted by the high wind of his conversation I edge in a question. What then *is* 'The Other Story'?

'First of all,' he says, 'it's an act of historical justice. A homage to the talented generations who left their home countries and challenged the metropolitan avant-garde. Their successes were often phenomenal, but their names have been erased in their own lifetimes.' (Four artists died in the time the exhibition took to be accepted by the Arts Council).

Araeen's idea of an 'act of historical justice' has meant including in the show a generation of artists excluded from the standard histories of British art.

In 1962 Francis Newton Souza said, quite truthfully, 'I make more money by my painting than the Prime Minister by his politics.' A British passport-holder, Souza now lives in New York. David Hockney lives in California. Question: Which is known for his contribution to British art?

Aubrey Williams' rayed canvases meditate on the original Amerindian inhabitants of the Caribbean. After early success, he lost favour with London critics when he stopped looking 'primitive' and started painting the music of Shostakovitch.

Frank Bowling, whose luminous acrylics strike like light through water, was once a founding member of the Pop Art group along with Hockney, RB Kitaj and Boshier. But Bowling was painting Patrice Lumumba, the assassinated leader of the independent Congo, not Marilyn Monroe: in '64 he was excluded from the Whitechapel's 'New Generation' show, from whence his friends quickly became famous, with the words 'England is not yet ready for a gifted artist of colour.'

Earlier this year Claus Runkel, one of the most interesting younger Bond Street dealers, wrote to the 198 Gallery in Brixton: 'Please take me off your mailing list. I never asked to be put on it in the first place as I have no interest whatever in African or tribal art.'

What has changed since '55 when Chandra was asked to paint elephants and tigers? Or since '75 when Avtarjeet Dhanjal's sculptures were mashed into scrap by the Alcan company which sponsored them? Or, for that matter, since Anwar Jalal Shemza's near-breakdown after hearing art critic E H Gombrich lecture on Islamic art (to which the professor's famous 'The Story of Art' allotted *one whole page*): 'All evening I destroyed paintings, drawings, everything . . . All night I argued . . . All day restlessness sent me from place to place . . .'

'The Other Story' is going to be a landmark. As well as rediscovering 'lost' black artists, an important feature of the show is work by younger, more visible and avant garde artists. And it will be the first ever show of black artists on this scale. But Araeen's choices are already proving controversial.

Rasheed Araeen has chosen to include his own highly conceptual and polemic work in the show. The curator's unabashed praise of himself may well land him in Pseud's Corner, but his catalogue makes a lucid change from the usual High Advertspeak. He argues tensely with each artist in turn, with the critics, the historians, the buyers and, when all else fails, himself.

'There's been an antagonism between the essentialist and the pluralist view of black art,' says writer Paul Gilroy. 'In celebrating diversity and "the dissolution of the unified black subject" (Stuart Hall's phrase), we may be in danger of losing what connects us to each other.'

The most committed 'essentialist' (not always a dirty word) in the show is Eddie Chambers, who works entirely with and for black people. A founder of the Black British Art Movement at the start of the '80s, he's now running the Asian and African Visual Arts Archive in Bristol. Though supportive of 'The Other Story', his approach could hardly be more different from Araeen's.

'If we're expending energies trying to make inroads into white galleries then clearly our energies are being misdirected,' he asserts. Public funding is no better. 'The GLC's contributions to black visual arts were negligible, paltry, hamfisted and fudged. And if your creativity is reliant on state handouts, it's a danger.' As for private patrons, 'if sales of work was what was ensuring our survival, we'd be extinct by now.' Chambers works with 'that massive pool of artists who haven't been deemed knowable', but who he believes are equal to any of the more famous names.

Lubaina Himid has gone even further in the creative quarrel with hierarchies of quality. At the Africa Centre in 1983, she brought together the first black women's art exhibition, and has been working with black women ever since. Her multi-media satires are sharply detailed and funny: Picasso's African nudes sprout Amazon ear-rings, and are chased by art-vultures showering gold; rows of Great Male Genius with brushes pointing from their wooden crotches.

Now she and poet Maud Sulter look like becoming the Gertrude Stein and Alice B Toklas of their generation, evolving a private language of 'Blackwomen's creativity'.

But the rest of the Hayward's 'Story' calls in to question their boldly separatist strategy as a route for all women's advancement. There are only three other women artists in the whole exhibition.

That the historical exclusion which Araeen documents can repeat itself so farcically in another part of the show is incredible. Among contemporary black British artists, female names outnumber male by three or four to one: Sutapa Biswas, Amanda Holiday, Sokari Douglas Camp, Shanti Thomas, Chila Burman, George Melly's favourite Pearl Alcock, Zarina Bhimji, Simone Alexander, Elaine Somerville, Rita Keegan, Nina Edge, Houria Niati. All are shown and known. No tokenism needed.

The only comparable omissions among male artists are Donald Rodney, who uses AIDS and sickle cell anaemia as metaphors for a diseased body politic, and Allan deSouza, whose work also deals with gay sexuality.

But for Rasheed Araeen the issue is not gender but generation: 'This is a historical show,' he says. 'The women artists who came to England in the past have returned to their own countries. There's a new generation still coming out of art schools, and I made my selection several years ago.'

Work by older male artists includes sensual 'Oriental' female nudes. These have been given the benefit of historical doubt. But why were Dhruva Mistry and Anish Kapoor – *today's* two successful purveyors of exotic (and erotic) orientalism to the Raj fans of

England – invited to take part? Surely surprising choices given the curator's expressed hatred of ethnic frills?

'People assume I'm only including work I personally like,' Araeen counters. 'In fact I was intending to comment critically. Perhaps that's why they both refused!'

Two women artists, Veronica Ryan and Kim Lim also declined to show. There is a hint that the 'Black Artist' label may be compromising to those whose careers are already established. Yet painters who believe, with Aubrey Williams, that 'black artists should do their work and let the public find out that they're black afterwards' – like the bold postmodernist Anthony Daley, recruited by the Angela Flowers gallery before he left art school – still encounter the same English resistance to buying their work.

Rasheed Araeen has hit a rock, and not only with the women. Keith Piper, co-founder with Eddie Chambers of the Black British Art movement, says: 'It's obvious that the dominant force over the second half of the decade has been black women.'

A day school at Birkbeck College has already been called on January 27 to discuss these issues. 'It's an exploration, not a confrontation' says organiser Lola Young. It's not a women's meeting, she insists, the all women platform is just a change from '2,000 years of positive discrimination for men.' There's this umbrella title again. 'You wouldn't do this to a whole heap of *white* artists and call it The Story.' Rasheed Araeen and the Hayward's director Andrew Dempsey will be invited to discuss the reappearance of that suspect category The Other, and the show's distinction between categories of high art and community art.

'I have to use my own abilities: and that may include prejudice!' Araeen argues. 'This is also an issue of professionalism. Some women think they can call staying home and knitting, art! There's nothing wrong with knitting – but art is a complex activity! A lot of white artists also think art is just *self-expression*.'

'Self-identification' is exactly how Rita Keegan describes her

Black Women Artists' Slide Index at Fulham Palace. 'It's hard to put yourself in the picture if you're constantly being written out,' she says. 'As an American I had no expectation of my work being included, but I think some of the strongest, most relevant art has been by women of colour, and that has been neglected. I had real problems with the way the show has been selected, and that's why I agreed to give gallery tours. It's important for people to view it in different ways.

'This is one man's choice,' she adds. 'If the show is not viewed as quintessential, it's fine. As long as there are others, and more.'

The last word should go, as it goes in the exhibition, to Sonia Boyce, whose brilliantly coloured and intricately patterned history pictures move from home interiors to empire and from sexual taboos to stock exchange.

'My feeling about the fact that there aren't any Asian women in the show is that Rasheed feels threatened by them,' she says. 'To me its quite glaringly obvious that he is threatened by all of us.

'But it's an important exhibition. Yes, it's the first time the Hayward has put on a show of this kind and it'll probably be the last. It's almost like: the end of the decade, the end of an era, the end of that kind of show.

'I'm still part of a movement; it's difficult now to say where the movement is. It has changed dramatically over this decade, and I'm looking forward to the art that's ahead.'

Homi Bhabha and Sutapa Biswas, 'The Wrong Story', 1989

Homi Bhabha

"The Other Story" contends that the British art establishment has consistently failed to recognise the particular "modernism" of the postwar postcolonial artist. Critics who celebrate the "international" styles of modernist and postmodernist art, and revere the artist as jet-set *flaneur* (the Italian artist Clemente who moves from

Madras to Milan to New York), seem to deny the potential for innovation of those who emerge out of the post colonial cultural migration to the west.

Critics claim that the postcolonial artist is forever the *atelier ingenue* – belated, derivative, second-hand. Unable to handle the mastery of conceptual or abstract forms, the identity of the post-colonial artist must be sought in attenuated "oriental" imagery, an exotic colour tone, a reposeful spiritual calm, an archaic detail.

Now this is not just another theory – it is the story of the reception of this exhibition. Most reviewers have fanned the polemic and the controversy, arguing that the best postcolonial British artists – always the same two solitary figures, Anish Kapoor and Dhruva Mistry – have kept out of the "ghetto" show. None has attempted to ask whether the self-image of metropolitan (post) modernism has to be rethought in relation to this particular, postcolonial hybridity, its cultural migration and its translation of artistic traditions,

Where major questions have to be asked of the show, the critics have failed to do so. For instance, there is an unacknow-ledged problem running through the exhibition in its conflation of modernism and masculinism. The inadequate representation of women artists is dealt with by Sutapa Biswas below.

There remains a serious, unasked question, particularly relevant to one of the most celebrated paintings "in the citadel of modernism" section – Francis Souza's *Black Nude*. Without questioning the expressionist energy of Souza's amazon, there is something unexplored in the use of the woman's body as the erotic object that enables a postcolonial "Indian" iconography to emerge in its modernist form. Despite the obvious reference to the goddess Kali, there is an association of the primitive, the raw and the exotic with women's sexuality, which provides an easy naturalistic reference for his work, making it both access-ible and acceptable.

The general complacency among the critics comes from a value given to the immediate visibility of the image which gives art a spurious autonomy. "What, after all, can the work of artists from such a differing range of backgrounds – Guyana, Pakistan, Sri Lanka, China, India – have in common?" asks Andrew Graham-Dixon (*Independent*, 5 December 1989).

Only the fact, of course, that British imperialism touched them all, imposed a conformity of administrative, educational and cultural practices on the most diverse regions. Only the obvious historical fact that the experience of migration and the formation of minority identities in postwar Britain have been a response to discriminatory strategies of marginality and stereotype that treat you almost equally whether you are Guyanese, Sri Lankan or Indian.

As the essays in the exhibition catalogue testify, these are the other stories – personal, historical, aesthetic – that the artists have attempted to inscribe in their work. But treated as events external to the art-work can only lead Graham-Dixon to give them a more common identity: "*The Other Story* . . . raises important issues, but is not a particularly convincing exhibition, partly for the simple reason that much of the art displayed is *not very good*."

Why should I believe him? Because he tells me that Avinash Chandra's squiggled biomorphs are "uninspired responses" to Klee and Ernst; or that Balraj Khanna's embarrassing figure paintings are on Athena art lines. If a whole *genre* or tradition of artists, who share a postcolonial history, are "tame and derivative", then I want to know more about the power of the precursors, the anxiety of influence, the aesthetic conditions of a "strong" reinterpretation or a creative misreading.

It is, for instance, predictable to suggest that Gavin Jantjes juxtaposes a figure from *Demoiselles d'Avignon* with an African mask: "The point being that Picasso has received too much credit for innovations made considerably earlier by an unknown artist from the Congo." That is *not* to read the balance and disposition of the images.

The line-drawing of the translucent *demoiselle* gazes wide-eyed at the viewer in a familiar figurative pose; the mask, at the other end of the canvas, turns away from the priority of the figurative and the visual to suggest other senses of identity. The two images are linked through umbilical cords that suggest not an unmasking of the Picasso figure, but a challenging tension across the terrain of cultural difference between the visual locus of the aesthetic, and the *sensoria* of other cultural systems. In one sense the two figures are incommensurable; in another, it is this difference that makes possible the negotiation of cultures on equal terms.

The other criteria present themselves in a careful relocation and deconstruction of the values of the "eye". Sonia Boyce's *Big Woman's Talk* provides a feast of sensuous colour and exotic forms that cover the woman's body. But the viewer's eye is elided by the canvas that cuts the woman's head half-way. As you reconstruct her face – outside the frame – her open mouth becomes the displaced eye – a speaking eye through which you hear an "other" story; a story of those whose political and social visibility is often denied, whose testimony is resoundingly silent . . . as in a painting.

No, Mr Graham-Dixon, despite the levels and luminosity of paint, the thickness of description, Frank Bowling's *Great Thames II* shines with a quite different light from Auerbach's *Primrose Hill*. The importance of this exhibition lies in our being able to acknowledge the presence of both artists in a city, and a country, whose vision of itself must change with the emergent, hybrid cultures of its people.

Sutapa Biswas

"The Other Story" is the first time a major exhibition of Afro-Asian artists' work has been shown at the Hayward Gallery. So far, so good. But in common with many "overview" exhibitions it has many problems. *The Other Story* misleadingly implies a collective authority of narrative. It might have been better titled "Rasheed Araeen's Other Story".

A major exhibition, involving contemporary and older generation Afro-Asian artists' work, is long overdue. Given that the bulk of the most exciting work produced in Britain in the past ten years has been the work of younger generation Afro-Asian artists, Araeen jeopardises this by his "hang-ups" about modernism, neglecting what would have been the show's major strengths, particularly the contribution of art works by black women.

In fact, Araeen seems to be misrepresenting the implications of this, by cleverly separating the works of artists Mona Hatoum and Lubaina Himid from the work of Sonia Boyce by the use of isolated categories. Also, he has deliberately missed out the work of artists like Houria Niati, Marlene Smith, Claudette Johnson, Sokari Douglas Camp, Nina Edge, Bhajan Hunjan, Shanti Thomas, Ingrid Pollard, Zarina Bhimji, Amanda Holiday, and so on, whose work would knock the spots off several of the less well-chosen pieces in the show.

It is difficult to follow Araeen's hypothesis. But his argument is with modernism. He is saying that modernism was not exclusive to the west since capitalist development was also taking place in non-western cultures. He asks why it was that, when Afro-Asian artists were involved in modernist debates, they were first framed as "other" in relation to the dominant culture, and second, erased from mainstream history. Araeen rightly places the racist nature of British society as the cause.

However, Araeen's flying the flag for modernism, is a shaky premise for this show. Over the past two decades, there has been strong argument against, for example, the sexist nature of modernism. Ivan Peries's work *The Arrival*, for instance, evokes some of the limitations of modernism. In discussing this work, Araeen reveals his complicity with modernism. "The sensuousness of its main subjects," he writes, "three nymphs [I think here Araeen means three women] in a lotus pond," is an expression of "repressed desires". This does not adequately decode the power of the image or the patriarchal nature of the power structure within which Peries's work and Araeen's comments function.

In the painting, the juxtaposition of three naked black women and phallocencric symbols does not question, but in fact reinforces the power relationship between the male as active creator of the work, and the female as its passive, created subject. The artist places the figure of the women, not only as passive and non-participating, but also as object of the artist's work and spectacle.[1]

That Araeen's selection predominantly comprises painting and sculpture gives rise to other problems. The show omits film, photographic and mixed-media work, which are also common formats in contemporary art practice. The films *Handsworth Song*, by Black Audio Film Collective, *Territories*, by Sankofa, and Isaac Julien's brilliant *Looking For Langston* are excluded.

Noticeably absent, too, are the works of Donald Rodney and Sunil Gupta, whose powerful images explore the body politic: issues that will undoubtedly be central in the 1990s. On the issue of patronage, or the lack of patronage of Afro-Asian artists, this is a valid point, and rightly raised. But it's no less an issue for a generation of younger Afro-Asian artists. For example, the most recent work of Helen Chadwick is fairly well known. Also dealing with the body politic, Chadwick's work has been written about a great deal, but is not as powerful or deeply felt as Rodney's work. Rodney's work is equally worthy of exposure, as is the work of many of the younger generation of Afro-Asian artists who have been excluded from this high-profile exhibition. Their inclusion would surely have made for a richer exhibition.

In the event of Araeen bringing to the public's attention the work of older generation Afro-Asian artists, artists who have been "erased" from history, it is ironic that Araeen himself erases from history the dynamic contributions of younger Afro-Asian artists of today.[2]

NOTES

1. In 2022 Biswas noted that: '*The Other Story*'s marginalisation of the work of Afro-Asian women artists was equally problematic in that it failed to adequately address questions of gender and race in relation to capitalism and to modernism.' Correspondence with the editor, 10 May 2022.

2. In conversation with the editor on 11 May 2022, Sutapa Biswas recalled that in April 2001, Rasheed Araeen told her that the Hayward Gallery had vetoed the inclusion of contemporary artworks made from 1985 onwards. Biswas reflected that had she been aware of this information, her article would have addressed issues of censorship.

Further Reading and Resources

Books

Nick Aikens and Elizabeth Robles (eds.), *The Place is Here: The Work of Black Artists in 1980s Britain*, Berlin: Sternberg Press, 2019.

Rasheed Araeen, *The Other Story: Afro-Asian Artists in Post-War Britain*, London: The South Bank Centre, 1989.

David A. Bailey, Ian Baucom and Sonia Boyce (eds.), *Shades of Black: Assembling Black Arts in 1980s Britain*, London: INIVA, 2005.

David A. Bailey and Allison Thompson, *Liberation Begins in the Imagination: Writings on British Caribbean Art*, London: Tate Publishing, 2021.

Celeste-Marie Bernier, *Stick to the Skin: African American and Black British Art, 1965–2015*, Oakland, CA: University of California Press, 2019.

Eddie Chambers, *Black Artists in Britaish Art: A History since the 1950s*, London: IB Tauris, 2014.

Gen Doy, *Black Visual Culture: Modernity and Postmodernity*, London: IB Tauris, 2000.

Alex Farquharson and David A. Bailey, *Oceans Apart: Art from Britain and the Caribbean*, London: Tate Publishing, 2021.

Amal Ghosh and Juginder Lamba (eds.), *Beyond Frontiers: Contemporary British Art by Artists of South Asian Descent*, London: Saffron Press, 2001.

Kobena Mercer, *Travel and See: Black Diaspora Art Practices Since the 1980s*, Durham: Duke University Press, 2016.

Sophie Orlando, *British Black Art: Debates on the Western Art History*, Paris: Éditions Dis Voir, 2016.

Kwesi Owusu (ed.), *Storms of the Heart: An Anthology of Black Arts and Culture*, London: Camden Press, 1988.

Further Reading and Resources

Rianna Jade Parker, *A Brief History of Black British Art*, London: Tate Publishing, 2021.

Maud Sulter (ed.), *Passion: Discourses on Blackwomen's Creativity*, Hebden Bridge: Urban Fox Publishing, 1990.

Journals

'Black British Art Histories', *Nka: Journal of Contemporary African Art* 45 (November 2019), Special Issue, edited by Eddie Chambers and Maryam Ohadi-Hamadani.

'Rethinking British Art: Black Artists and Modernism', *Art History* 44:3 (June 2021), Special Issue, edited by Sonia Boyce and Dorothy Price.

Archives / Websites

Autograph ABP; autograph.org.uk

Black Artists and Modernism; vimeo.com/blackartistsmodernism

Black British Artists 1980s Archive; bba80.co.uk

Black Cultural Archives; blackculturalarchives.org

Diaspora Artists; new.diaspora-artists.net

Iniva (Institute of International Visual Art); Iniva.org

Making Histories Visible; makinghistoriesvisible.com

Panchayat Collection at Tate Britain; tate.org.uk

Rasheed Araeen Archive at Asia Art Archive; aaa.org.hk

South Asian Diaspora Arts Archive; sadaa.co.uk

The Blk Art Research Group; blkartgroup.info

The Women's Art Library; gold.ac.uk/make

Sources and Permissions

Every effort has been made to contact copyright holders. The editor and publisher would be glad to amend in future editions errors or omissions brought to their attention.

1. *Black Art An' Done: An Exhibition of Work by Young Black Artists*, Wolverhampton: Wolverhampton Art Gallery, June 1981. © Eddie Chambers, Dominic Dawes, Andrew Hazel, Ian Palmer and Keith Piper.

2. Rasheed Araeen, 'Paint it Black', *City Limits*, 13–19 August 1982, pp. 46–7. © Rasheed Araeen.

3. Rasheed Araeen, 'Art & Black Consciousness', paper presented at First National Black Art Convention, Wolverhampton Polytechnic, 28 October 1982; reprinted in Rasheed Araeen (ed.) *The Essential Black Art*, London: Chisenhale Gallery, 1988, pp. 36–41. © Rasheed Araeen.

4. *The Pan-Afrikan Connection*, Nottingham: The Midland Group, January–February 1983. © Eddie Chambers, Claudette Johnson, Keith Piper, and the Estate of Donald Rodney.

5. Bhajan Hunjan and Chila Kumari Burman, 'Mash it Up', *Spare Rib* 128 (March 1983), pp. 52–5. © Bhajan Hunjan and Chila Kumari Burman.

6. John Akomfrah, 'Black Independent Film-making: A statement by the Black Audio Film Collective', *ArtRage: Intercultural Arts Magazine* 3–4 (Summer 1983), p. 29. © John Akomfrah.

7. Imruh Bakari, 'Open Art: The First Open Exhibition of Contemporary Black Art in Britain, organised by Creation for Liberation', *Race Today* 15:3 (October / November 1983), p. 94. © Imruh Bakari.

8. Extracts from Lubaina Himid (ed.), *5 Black Women: Exhibition of Drawings, Paintings and Sculpture*, London: Africa Centre, 1983. © Claudette Johnson and Houria Niati.

9. OBAALA, *Heart in Exile*, London: The Black-Art Gallery, 1983. © Shakka Deddi.

10. Rohan Jayasekera, 'Art Under Attack', *News from the Round-house* (Autumn 1985), p. 5. © Rohan Jayasekera.

11. Colin Prescod, 'Black Artists / White Institutions', keynote address at the *Black Artists / White Institutions* conference, at Riverside Studios, London, 4 November 1985, published in *ArtRage: Intercultural Arts Magazine* 12 (Spring 1986), pp. 32–5. © Colin Prescod.

12. Extracts from Lubaina Himid (ed.), *The Thin Black Line*, London: Institute of Contemporary Arts, 1985. © The Estate of Brenda Agard, Jennifer Comrie, Lubaina Himid and Marlene Smith.

13. Eddie Chambers, 'The Marginalisation of Black Art', *Race Today Review* (February 1986), pp. 32–3. © Eddie Chambers.

14. Gavin Jantjes, 'Art & Cultural Reciprocity', paper presented at the East Midlands Art Conference on 12 April 1986, reprinted in Rasheed Araeen (ed.), *The Essential Black Art*, London: Chisenhale Gallery, 1988, pp. 42–5. © Gavin Jantjes.

15. Sunil Gupta, 'Desire and Black Men', *Ten.8* 22 (1986), pp. 16–23. This edited version from *We Were Here: Sexuality, Photography, and Cultural Difference – Selected Writings by Sunil Gupta*, London: Aperture, 2022. © Sunil Gupta.

16. Errol Lloyd, 'Introduction: An Historical Perspective', in *Caribbean Expressions in Britain*, Leicester: Leicestershire Museums and Art Galleries, August–September 1986, pp. 3–7. © Leicestershire Museums and Art Galleries.

17. Chila Kumari Burman, 'There Have Always Been Great Black Women Artists', paper presented at the Black Visual Arts Forum at the Institute of Contemporary Art, London,

25–6 October 1986, reprinted in *Women Artists Slide Library Journal* 15 (February 1987), pp. 9–12. © Chila Kumari Burman, courtesy The Women's Art Library, Goldsmiths, University of London.

18. Yasmin Kureishi, 'Reworking Myths: An interview with Sutapa Biswas', *Spare Rib* 173 (December 1986), pp. 14–17. ©Sutapa Biswas. This version edited and revised by Supata Biswas, May 2022

19. Sonia Boyce, *Extracts from a conversation with Pitika Ntuli*, in Sara Selwood (ed.), *Sonia Boyce*, London: Air Gallery, 1986. © Sonia Boyce.

20. Salman Rushdie, 'Songs Doesn't Know the Score', *Guardian*, 12 January 1987. © *Guardian*.
Stuart Hall, 'Song of Handsworth Praise', *Guardian*, 15 January 1987. © *Guardian*, courtesy The Stuart Hall Foundation.
Darcus Howe, 'The Language of Black Culture', *Guardian*, 19 January 1987. © *Guardian*, courtesy the Darcus Howe Legacy Collective.

21. Lubaina Himid, 'We Will Be', in Rosemary Betterton (ed.), *Looking On: Images of Femininity in the Visual Arts and Media*, London: Pandora Press, 1987, pp. 259–66. © Lubaina Himid.

22. Keith Piper, 'Black Art: A Statement' (1987), in Rasheed Araeen (ed.), *The Essential Black Art*, London: Chisenhale Gallery, 1988, pp. 46–7. © Keith Piper.

23. Mumtaz Karimjee, 'Black and Asian: Definitions and Redefinitions', *Mukti* 6, Racism and Prejudice Issue (Spring 1987), p. 8. © Mumtaz Karimjee.

24. Samena Rana, 'Disability and Photography', *Polareyes: A Journal by and about Black Women working in Photography* 1 (1987), pp. 14–15. ©The Estate of Samena Rana.

25. Allan deSouza, 'Portrait of the Artist as a Dirty Young Man', *Bazaar: South Asian Arts Magazine* 3 (Winter 1987), pp. 12–13. © Al-An deSouza.

26. Clare Rendell, 'Actual Lives of Women Artists: Rita Keegan 1987', *Women Artists Slide Library Journal* (October–November 1987), pp. 10–11. © Rita Keegan, courtesy The Women's Art Library, Goldsmiths, University of London.

27. Sutapa Biswas and Marlene Smith, 'Black Women Artists', *Spare Rib* 188 (March 1988), pp. 8–12. © Sutapa Biswas and Marlene Smith. This version edited and revised by Sutapa Biswas, May 2022.

28. Ingrid Pollard, 'Reel to Reel: Explorations around Black Women in Film', *FAN-Feminist Art News* 2:8 (Autumn 1988), pp. 12–13. © Ingrid Pollard. This version edited by Ingrid Pollard, May 2022.

29. Maud Sulter, 'Call and Response', *FAN-Feminist Art News* 2:8 (Autumn 1988), pp. 15–17. © The Estate of Maud Sulter. Reproduced by kind permission of the Estate of Maud Sulter.

30. Allan deSouza, 'Interview with Shaheen Merali', *Bazaar: South Asian Arts Magazine* 6 (1988), pp. 2–3. © Al-An deSouza and Shaheen Merali.

31. Gilane Tawadros, 'Other Britains, Other Britons', *Aperture* 113 (Winter 1988), pp. 40–46. © Gilane Tawadros.

32. Rotimi Fani-Kayode, 'Traces Of Ecstasy', *Ten.8* 28 (1988), pp. 36–43. © The Estate of Rotimi Fani-Kayode, courtesy Autograph-ABP.

33. Coco Fusco, 'An Interview with Martina Attille and Isaac Julien of Sankofa', in Coco Fusco, *Young, British and Black: The Work of Sankofa Film and Black Audio Film Collective*, Buffalo, NY: Hallwalls/Contemporary Arts Center, 1988, pp. 23–39. © Coco Fusco.

34. Extracts from Rasheed Araeen and Eddie Chambers, 'Black Art: A Discussion', *Third Text* 2:5 (Winter 1988), pp. 51–77. © Third Text, courtesy Rasheed Araeen and Eddie Chambers.

35. Frank Bowling, 'Formalist Art and the Black Experience', *Third Text* 2:5 (Winter 1988), pp. 78–82. © Third Text.

36. Lesley Sanderson, 'Artist's Statement', in Supata Biswas, Sarah Edge and Claire Slattery (eds.), *Along the Lines of Resistance*, Barnsley: Cooper Gallery, 1988, p. 32. © Lesley Sanderson.

37. Adeola Solanke, 'Donald Rodney', *Art Monthly* 124 (March 1989), pp. 13–14. © Adeola Solanke.

38. Paul Gilroy, 'David A. Bailey: From Britain, Barbados or Both?' (shortened version of the text that accompanied the exhibition *I'm Black, I'm Bajan and I'm British*, Tom Allen Centre, London, 1989), *Creative Camera* 2 (1990), pp. 10–13. © Paul Gilroy.

39. Extract from Gilane Tawadros, 'Beyond the Boundary: The Work of Three Black Women Artists in Britain', *Third Text* 3:8 (1989), pp. 121–50. © Third Text, courtesy Gilane Tawadros.

40. Rasheed Araeen, 'Introduction', in Rasheen Araeen (ed.), *The Other Story: Afro-Asian Artists in Post-War Britain*, exhibition catalogue, Hayward Gallery, London, 1989. © Rasheed Araeen.

41. Amanda Sebestyen, 'The Other Story', *City Limits*, 30 November – 7 December 1989, pp. 16–17. © Amanda Sebestyen.
Homi Bhabha and Sutapa Biswas, 'The Wrong Story', *New Statesman*, 15 December 1989, pp. 40–42. © Homi Bhabha and Sutapa Biswas. Sutapa Biswas's text edited and revised by the artist, May 2022.

Acknowledgements

This book would not have been possible without the good will of the artists, writers and Estates who kindly gave permission to publish their statements, articles and reviews. They all have my sincere gratitude. My appreciation also goes to Sutapa Biswas, Eddie Chambers, Deborah Cherry on behalf of the Estate of Maud Sulter, Shakka Deddi, Al-An deSouza, Sunil Gupta and Brendan Ember, Bhajan Hunjan, Gavin Jantjes, Rohan Jayasekera, Mumtaz Karimjee, David Lawson on behalf of John Akomfrah, Shaheen Merali, Ingrid Pollard, Colin Prescod, and Lesley Sanderson for their assistance in the preparation of their texts and my introductions. Any errors and mistakes are my own. Numerous people and organizations have helped in the development of this book; my thanks to Eddie Chambers, Anjalie Dalal-Clayton, Richard Dyer at Third Text, Gustavo Grandal Montero and Chelsea Collage of Art Special Collections, Althea Greenan and The Women's Art Library, Goldsmiths, University of London, Lubaina Himid and the Making Histories Visible Archive, Derek Horton, Maxine Miller and Tate Special Collections, Hammad Nasar, Lara Perry, Elizabeth Robles, Marlene Smith, and the library staff at The Stuart Hall Library, Iniva, The Ahmed Iqbal Ulla Race Relations Resource Centre at Manchester Central Library, and University of Westminster Harrow Campus. My particular thanks go Josephine Greywoode and Emmy Yoneda at Penguin, and to Sonia Boyce. This book is dedicated to my parents, Luis deAssis Correia and Elizabeth Susan Correia, and to Ian, Theofila and Francisco.

Index of Key Names